Pirate Killers

This book is dedicated to all the men and women of the Royal Navy, past, present and future, who have kept Britain safe from piracy on the high seas and ensured that our economy flourished by keeping the sea lanes open. Some have made the supreme sacrifice to keep this nation secure, and others will do in the future. God Bless you all.

Pirate Killers

The Royal Navy and the African Pirates

Graham A. Thomas

Pen & Sword
MARITIME

First published in Great Britain in 2011 by
Pen & Sword Maritime
an imprint of
Pen & Sword Books Ltd
47 Church Street
Barnsley
South Yorkshire
S70 2AS

ISBN 978-1-84884-240-3

A CIP catalogue record for this book is available from the British Library.

Typeset in 11.5pt Ehrhardt by
Mac Style, Beverley, E. Yorkshire

Printed and bound in the UK by CPI

Pen & Sword Books Ltd incorporates the imprints of Pen & Sword
Aviation, Pen & Sword Maritime, Pen & Sword Military, Wharncliffe Local
History, Pen & Sword Select, Pen & Sword Military Classics, Leo Cooper,
Seaforth Publishing and Frontline Publishing.

For a complete list of Pen & Sword titles please contact
PEN & SWORD BOOKS LIMITED
47 Church Street, Barnsley, South Yorkshire, S70 2AS, England
E-mail: enquiries@pen-and-sword.co.uk
Website: www.pen-and-sword.co.uk

Contents

Preface

The idea for this book began when I ran across references to Riff or Reef pirates operating along the Barbary Coast while researching my book, *Pirate Hunter*, on Captain Woodes Rogers. There didn't appear to be much on the Reef pirates at first until I started digging deeper for this book. In fact, the Reef pirates were part of a much wider picture, the piracy from the Barbary Coast – Algeria, Tunisia, Libya and Morocco. To my surprise I discovered that Barbary pirates had been operating from the seventeenth century right up into the nineteenth century when the incidents with the Reef pirates were documented.

What I found so interesting was that the Great Powers had been unable to put down the piracy that attacked the shipping in the Mediterranean. This body of water was and still is a very busy trade route, as all the countries bordering it trade with each other. For the pirates it was lucrative trade. These were not just pirates they were also religious zealots, determined to attack anyone who didn't believe in the Muslin faith – this meant the great Christian powers of France, Spain, Portugal, Dutch and, of course, England.

As I researched this book I realized that it was not about piracy as much as about the Royal Navy that dealt with piracy along the African coast, from Bartholomew Roberts to the Reef pirates, from Madagascar to Morocco, the Royal Navy engaged pirates wherever they could. *Pirate Killers* is about these men of the Royal Navy who over the centuries have done their duty in attacking and putting down piracy. Many have been wounded or lost their lives in their efforts to make the high seas free from lawlessness.

Today the Royal Navy is engaged with pirates in the Caribbean as it battles the drug trade and with pirates from Somalia and other hot spots around the world. However, unlike the navy of today, the Royal Navy in earlier centuries had no qualms about killing pirates. Diplomacy came first but when that failed military might was used and, yes, pirates were killed. That is why this book is called *Pirate Killers*.

This is the story of the men and women of the Royal Navy who did their duty to the best of their ability to wipe out the scourge of piracy. This is the story of the Royal Navy and the African pirates. In our own day, as piracy from the lawless state of Somalia and other states increases, politicians around the world are going to have to take some difficult decisions. Perhaps they should take a lesson from the Royal Navy.

Graham A Thomas
Warminster, May 2010

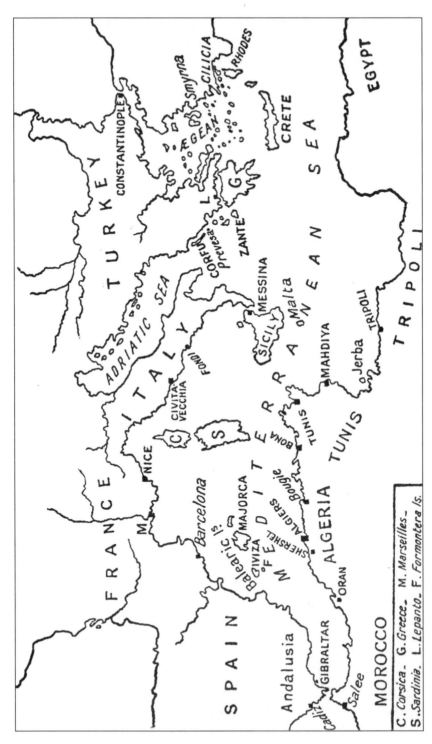

The Mediterranean showing the Barbary Coast of North Africa.

C. Corsica. G. Greece. M. Marseilles.
S. Sardinia. L. Lepanto. F. Formontera Is.

Introduction: Danger in the Mediterranean

He looked out across the sea, the sun blazing and reflecting off the water. There was a ship, apparently with very little sail, off his bow some distance away. Antonio Alloy, Commander of the *Juan Felicca Mary*, paced the deck. His cargo of bale goods and tobacco cleared for Algiers would be lucrative pickings for pirates. He knew there were pirates in this area. He'd heard of the atrocities of the Barbary pirates and wondered now what this unknown ship was up to.

Only two days out from Gibraltar he was near Malaga and only thirty-five miles from shore when this ship had been sighted. He was worried. The unknown vessel looked familiar. He stared through the telescope again and realized that he was looking at a Spanish Guarda Costa and as he went past he saw the Costa raise its sails, turn and give chase. Immediately, Alloy ordered as much sail as possible.

It was 10 October 1834. The wind was blowing them towards the Barbary Coast which was a haven for pirates but he had no choice if he was to get away from the ship chasing them. Hour after hour went by as Commander Alloy did everything he could to keep a distance between the *Mary* and the Guarda Costa. For thirty-four hours he evaded the pursuing vessel then his heart sank as not more than a mile from the Barbary Coast the wind died and the *Mary* was becalmed, in sight of the Costa vessel behind him and in sight of the coast. Ordering the *Mary*'s launch to tow the ship away from the coast he watched his men lower the boat into the sea with ropes and tackle. They rowed hard and Commander Alloy saw the slack tighten. Slowly the *Mary* began to move forward as the men in the launch rowed their hearts out. He heard distant cries from the shore and then saw three Moorish pirate row boats, each apparently containing from forty to forty-five men, rushing from the shore and making towards them. The trap was set.

The Moors shouted and screamed fierce cries as they gained on the *Mary*. Commander Alloy's men rowed for their lives but the three pirate boats gained quickly on the *Mary*. Shots rang out as they came within range. But luck was on the *Mary*'s side – the sails flapped as a breeze sprang up. Immediately, Commander Alloy ordered his crew to steer the *Mary* so the wind filled its sails and they rapidly pulled away from the pirates. To make their escape they had to cut loose their launch, sealing the fate of the men in it.[1]

Commander Alloy was lucky. The wind kept him and most of his crew from being captured and enslaved for life by the pirates of the Barbary Coast.

This action is just one of many recorded incidents where pirates from the Barbary Coast attacked ships in the busy sea lanes of the Mediterranean. The pirates from this area had no qualms about attacking ships from all nations. They began in the sixteenth century and continued into the middle of the nineteenth century.

Throughout this time it was the navy that asserted England's strength and influence in the area, punishing the pirates when British ships and subjects were attacked and captured. The navy used diplomacy as England tried to negotiate with the pirates to win back captured British sailors and when that failed it wrought destruction on the pirates. Operating from Gibraltar, the navy did its best to deal with the pirates operating along the Barbary Coast, engaging with them whenever it was necessary.

One example we'll look at in greater detail is the capture, by Reef pirates from the coast of Morocco, of the British merchant vessel, *The Three Sisters* which was towed into shore. To get the ship back, HMS *Polyphemus*, a steam-powered warship, was dispatched from Gibraltar. Commanded by Captain McCleverty he found the captured ship was defended by some 500 pirates who opened fire on the steamer as it came within range. McCleverty ordered his guns to return fire, pounding the enemy with grapeshot and canister, killing many of the pirates and dispersing them.

Boats from the *Polyphemus* were launched to tow *The Three Sisters* out to sea so she could be taken back to Gibraltar. The remaining pirates regrouped and, hidden behind rocks, opened fire on the small boats as they approached, wounding several men. But the guns from the *Polyphemus* opened up again, allowing the men of the Royal Navy to tow *The Three Sisters* away from the clutches of the pirates back to the *Polyphemus*. They steamed out to sea back to Gibraltar, leaving the pirates with nothing but their dead and wounded.

But who were the Barbary pirates? Peter Earle in his book, *The Pirate Wars*, says: 'The Barbary and Maltese corsairs plundered for the glory of

God as well as their own profit and whose strict rules and organisation provide an intriguing contrast to the more anarchic and individualist pirates of the Caribbean and Atlantic.'[2]

They were different to the swashbuckling pirates made famous by Hollywood. Indeed, if we look at famous mariners of the Elizabethan period such as Drake, Hawkins, Gilbert, Grenville, Raleigh, Frobisher and many others, they are maritime heroes who served their country well but all of them at one point or another were involved in piratical activities or employed and aided piracy.

During the Elizabethan times no real effort was ever made to actually stop piracy because it was seen as an effective way of expanding English commercial interests abroad as well as a way to fight wars without having to commit large numbers of ships, men and materiel. The pirates would attack ships belonging to England's enemies. The men operating from England at this time were more gentlemen pirates, not at all like the pirates of the Golden Age of Piracy at the end of the seventeenth century and the beginning of the eighteenth century. Then pirates such as Blackbeard, Bartholomew Roberts, Charles Vane, Jack Rackham and many others had no allegiance to any nation and attacked whomever they chose.

The pirates of the Elizabethan era were very patriotic and 'motivated by a desire for loot, like pirates of all ages, but also by an intense Protestantism, which manifested itself in religious observance and psalm singing aboard ships as well as in a passionate hatred of the Catholics and especially Spaniards'.[3] The Barbary pirates were similar in that they attacked anyone who they believed threatened their Muslim faith.

In the first decade of the seventeenth century the Mediterranean was a very dangerous place for commercial shipping to operate. The war between Spain and England ended in 1603 and sparked off piratical activity in the area mostly by English privateers no longer needed to wage war against England's enemies. As privateers they would have been attacking and capturing Spanish ships, taking their prizes back to England. Now they simply continued doing what they had done during the war, but as pirates now rather than sanctioned privateers. Peter Earle's definition of privateer shows how slim the difference was between privateers and pirates. 'Those with a taste for maritime violence and robbery could indulge it legitimately in wartime by serving in a privateer that is a private ship commissioned by the government to attack and loot the shipping of enemy countries.'[4]

The main victims of these privateers turned pirates were Venetian ships and their activity caused the Venetian Ambassador in England to complain.

The complaints forced a more rigid interpretation of maritime law in England and some pirate cargos were seized and their crews hung. This crackdown pushed the pirates further into the Mediterranean, to the North African coast, to look for other markets and places to hide.

Morea, a large peninsula in the southern part of Greece known today as Peloponnese, was at the time part of the Venetian empire and became a haven for pirates. It was here that pirates could recruit new crew members, or sell their loot to local merchants, and lie low for awhile and repair their ships without too much interference from the authorities.[5]

In 1608 the Venetian Ambassador to Constantinople complained that, if steps were not taken to rid the peninsula of pirates, then it would become just like Barbary. Indeed, according to Earle many other nations or territories, such as the province of Munster in Ireland, the Bahamas, Madagascar and Bermuda, have been given the label as 'being worse than Barbary'.[6]

So what was so bad about the Barbary Coast? This region of North Africa is made up of Morocco, Algeria, Tunisia and Libya, and at the very beginning of the seventeenth century was utterly frightening to the Christian world. The word 'corsair' comes from corso or corsaro which means privateer. Whether they were in fact privateers or pirates is debatable. Earle suggests that they were on a holy war against the enemies of their faith, while their victims saw them merely as unprincipled, vicious pirates. They were the most feared of all the pirates operating at the time because when they captured prisoners those poor unfortunate people would be enslaved for life. Only those with wealth and power could be ransomed and set free.

But the pirates who operated from Barbary were not just Muslims. They came from all faiths and nations, operating with impunity, attacking vessels of all nationalities. Many of these pirates were English and many gave up their Christian faith and became Muslims. Indeed, the Muslim authorities welcomed English and European pirates with open arms, 'treating them virtually as equals', allowing them to enter high-ranking posts in their governments as well as their military. Some English pirates rose to very high positions without giving up their Christian faith, as can be seen from the story of the notorious pirate Captain Jack Ward.

Ward was born in Faversham and was an illiterate who never spoke except to swear. He was 50 years old, a pauper living rough on the beach in Plymouth, when he was pressed into the Royal Navy but deserted two weeks later with several other men who elected Ward as their captain. Ward and his men grabbed a small ship and sailed away, heading for the

Barbary Coast where he was welcomed. On his way, Ward stole ship after ship, each one bigger than the last. He rose to command a fleet of pirate ships, manned by English and Turkish crews, and his flagship was a large sixty-gun Venetian ship. Unlike pirates like Blackbeard, Ward retired from piracy and lived off his loot as if he were royalty.[7]

But as the atrocities of the Barbary pirates grew over the decades the Royal Navy came to the rescue of the Great Powers and punished the pirates. Let's take a closer look at how they did it.

Chapter 1

First Blood: The Seventeenth Century

The 23rd came in here the Mary of Cork from Nantes, most of her lading salt, for Waterford. The Master reports that the Wednesday before about 10 leagues off Ushant they met an Algerian man-of-war who took them several boxes of wrought silks, ribbons and hats to the value of about 1,000l., although they were hid in the salt for fear of men-of-war. They showed them the Lord Lieutenant's pass, but they said they would not take notice of it. The same day came in to Helford the Elizabeth of Falmouth from St. Martin's with salt, who reports that the same day the same Algerian man-of-war came on board him and searched all though his salt, but finding nothing worth carrying away left him and boarded the said vessel and he saw several packs and cases on the deck, but, the wind blowing fresh, he made the best of his way. The man-of-war he judges to be of 30 guns and she has an orange-tree in her stern. Wind S.W.1

For England, the clashes and wars with the pirates of the Barbary Coast did not really begin in earnest until the seventeenth century. Prior to that there had been some skirmishes but few were recorded.

The Barbary States, as they were known in Christian Europe, were made up of three North African regencies: Algiers, Tunis and Tripoli. According to N A M Rodger, in his book *The Command of the Ocean*, these three states were part of the Ottoman Empire but behaved as semi-independent states at perpetual war with the European states and their Mediterranean neighbours. While many historians have written that their motives for war were religious, Rodger states that there were other factors involved. In the middle of the seventeenth century these factors were similar to the ones faced by Oliver Cromwell.

In 1654 after the establishment of the Protectorate, Cromwell had 160 ships, eighteen foot and twelve horse regiments to maintain. The Civil

War was over and Cromwell faced opposition from Parliament over the question of what to do with the military. He had two problems. The forces that Cromwell had at his disposal needed to be maintained and paid for but they were too weak for him to stay in power by sheer naked force. To make matters worse, the campaigns against Scotland and Ireland were costing more than could be raised by extra taxes.

In August 1654 Parliament demanded that the military be reduced. At the time the navy was subservient to the army and the three key players in the naval forces were the Generals at Sea, Colonel Robert Blake, Cromwell's brother-in-law Major-General John Desborough and the former vice-admiral William Penn. While Desborough concentrated his efforts in administration ashore, the other two men were active commanders at sea.

In October 1654 a petition was sent to Cromwell from the ships' companies of the Channel Squadron commanded by Vice-Admiral John Lawson, complaining about long overdue pay and poor conditions. While Lawson and his captains sympathized with the plight of their men, this act of sending a petition to Cromwell was a political one, a subtle threat that wasn't lost on Cromwell. If he dismissed Lawson, an extremely popular commander, then that threat would explode into full-scale mutiny, so it was even more urgent to find something for the navy to do that was as far away from Whitehall as possible. Disaffected senior officers and unpaid soldiers and sailors could start meddling in politics and this petition was one step towards that action. There was only one answer – a foreign war.

In the Barbary States the situation was similar. A foreign war was the best way to prevent the army from interfering in politics. 'The resulting system of warfare,' Rodger writes, 'was not piracy but public, declared war waged largely by private interests.' Their kind of war consisted principally of raiding other nations, usually Christian cities, towns, villages and ships, for slaves which they would either ransom back or sell but they didn't forget their Christian neighbours in the Mediterranean region. Indeed they made treaties with some while they fought others. They had to have markets for selling the slaves and some diplomatic relations with countries they were not at war with in order to ransom back the people they'd captured.

Rodger tells us that Cromwell had two options for his foreign war, France and Spain. There was an unofficial war with France and so Cromwell sent Blake to the Mediterranean with a full squadron. The presence of the English ships stopped the French from mounting an attack against Naples. Instead of fighting the French, Blake was drawn into a war with Tunis.

In general, the Barbary States adhered to the treaties they made with Christian nations but because these formal agreements were often broken by both sides, they would go to war with their treaty partners. In Blake's case the war was fought over the fact that an English merchant ship had sold Tunisian passengers into slavery in Malta, which infuriated the Tunisian authorities. Their retaliation was Blake's excuse for attacking.

> We hear that a frigate has been sent back express to General Blach with orders to remain off the coast of Barbary and continue to insist boldly upon the pirates of Algiers and Tunis releasing the English slaves and granting the other demands. It is to be hoped that the English will not succeed in this because of the advantage to Christendom if Blach were obliged to punish their temerity.[2]

During Cromwell's time, the Levant Company carried a quarter of all English woollen exports. Other goods traded by the Levant Company included the export of dried cod from the Newfoundland fisheries to Iberia and the Western Mediterranean. One of the main imports from the same area was dried fruit and wine. The company ships were more exposed in the Mediterranean than anywhere else. The threat came from the Barbary pirates operating out of Tunisia, Algiers and Sale (the main port of Morocco).

The Barbarians didn't keep to the Mediterranean; their ships were found in the Atlantic and the Channel. Indeed, in 1687 two small Algerine packets were sent to Holland where they carried off a hundred people for the white slave trade.

Protecting the trade was a haphazard affair with a mixture of convoys, cruisers and direct attacks on Barbary ports. 'The best policy for a Christian trading power was to make itself sufficiently annoying as an enemy, and sufficiently attractive as a friend, to be elected as an ally of the Barbary States – and, equally important, to preserve those alliances by a faithful observance of their terms.'[3] Once alliances had been formed, the pressure on the other Christian states with which the Barbary States were still at war would be a benefit for England. 'This simple realisation was to become one of the essential bases of British commercial and naval operations in the Mediterranean throughout the eighteenth and nineteenth centuries', writes Rodger.

A passenger onboard the merchantman *Merchant Delight*, which was sailing to Barbary to sell large amounts of cotton and other goods, reported that he saw the English fleet near the bay of Porto Farina or El Bahira in

Tunis. The fleet was under the command of General Blake who knew that attacking the well-fortified city of Tunis would have been suicide but attacking the bay was a different proposition altogether. 'Left London with 30 ships, all merchantmen, bound to different parts and we voyaged to Barbary for the disposal of a considerable quantity of cloth and other things. We found the English fleet there, of 25 vessels, with ten others in company.'

As Blake's fleet approached he spied several warships under the cover of the shore batteries. It was 4 April 1655 and Blake manoeuvred his ships into the best firing position. The gun crews from the ships in his squadron scrambled over their decks, making the final adjustments. Blake ordered his ships to open fire and the bay was filled with the roar of English cannon belching smoke and flame.

Captain Crapnell commanding the *Merlin* wrote that 'Many hundred guns were fired on both sides, and from the Turks' castle but few English were killed or wounded.' For hours cannon fire rained down on both sides but while the enemy's guns did little damage to the English ships, English cannon balls ripped into the port, smashing into buildings sending splinters in all directions. 'The Turks seldom or ever heard such a peal before', wrote Captain Crapnell.[4]

Under the cover of the smoke and cannon fire, Blake ordered the enemy's fleet to be burnt. He sent his fireships into their midst and watched as the flames leapt from the fireships onto the enemy vessels. Soon several enemy warships were blazing, flames licking across their decks, men diving overboard to avoid the fire.

General Blach has taken a number of slaves, released many, and captured 14 guns, in addition to the 9 ships burned. It is said that he keeps inflicting serious losses on them and has sailed with the fleet to another port named Suza with the intention of burning ships taking refuge there. Upon this news the merchants of the Levant Company went to the Protector to recommend their interests in the Levant, pointing out that if the Porte took any revenge on the goods of Englishmen at Constantinople it would mean the ruin of a great many families of his most obedient people. The Protector promised them his protection always, but said he could not help supporting the courageous forces of England under General Blach. It is said that his Highness intends to order Blach to sail to the Levant to protect the interests of the nation in case the Turks commit any violence against them.[5]

On the surface this could be seen as a triumph but, as Rodger writes, 'the strategic profit of the victory was less than nothing, as the Dey of Tunis afterwards explained to Blake, with sardonic amusement as the ships belonged to his overlord the Sultan whose local power he was not sorry to diminish'. To make matters worse, the success of the Levant Company's trade in Ottoman ports rested on the goodwill of the Sultan which had now been severely tested by Blake's attack.

This is illustrated in a letter from the Venetian Secretary in England to the Venetian Ambassador in France dated 5 June 1655:

> Last week four merchants representing the Levant Company came to me. After telling me about General Blach's operations against the Tunis pirates, which had prevented them from proceeding to the East to serve the Grand Turk, and had thereby rendered a good turn to the most serene republic, they handed me the enclosed memorial, containing four articles, setting forth the grievances of the Company, for me to forward in order to obtain the redress and justice that they look for from his Serenity. They make this appeal to the supreme authority of Venice before laying their complaints and petition for justice before the Lord Protector who would not deny them his powerful advocacy.[6]

Blake left Tunis having seriously damaged English interests and sailed for another Barbary Coast port in the Mediterranean where he could victual and water – Algiers. Here, instead of sailing in as a conquering hero, he kept the peace. Indeed, he paid well above the market price for ransoming some English captives who had been enslaved by the Barbary States.

Despite the loss of the nine warships, pirates from Tunis and Tripoli continued to attack English merchant shipping for the next three years until Captain John Stoakes was able to negotiate a peace. By a mixture of treaties and attacks, the English were able to extract some concessions from the Barbary States. But their successes were short-lived as the Algerines broke the treaty that had been previously established under the promise of the Grand Turk.

> Uncertain also is the issue of the explanation that will be demanded by this crown of the Algerines for their breach of faith, in violating the last peace ratified by Vice Admiral Alen and the league of friendship which by the previous treaty established under the promise of the Grand Turk they ought to observe inviolate. These corsairs have recently searched

and carried off from an English ship belonging to the Company of the Indies 14,000l. Sterling in hard cash.[7]

To deal with the problem Vice-Admiral Sir Thomas Allin (Alen) was sent to the Mediterranean in 1669 and ended up blockading Algiers and declaring war. In a letter dated 19 April 1669, addressed to the Venetian Senate, the Venetian Ambassador to England stated:

> Admiral Alen has meanwhile arrived in port here, having missed the written instructions to proceed to Algiers. They will give him additional powerful frigates, at least twelve of them, and he will go with resolution to the port of the Algerians to enforce their rights. Yet it will be difficult to recover the money, which passes from hand to hand, or to redeem prisoners, for once they are sold they cannot be ransomed with double the amount. In this connection, in converse with the ministers, I will urge them to generous resolutions and I only hope that just revenge may stir his Majesty and that a bitter war with these corsairs may divert them from helping the Grand Turk.

By August of that year Allin had twenty well armed frigates and some fire ships at his disposal to use against the Algerines.

> He goes to throw himself upon the Algerines and by fire & sword to extort rights from them which those infidels did not observe with his Majesty and which it was impossible to obtain by any means short of violence. The royal instructions to Alen are of the most determined character, being issued by the Council; but I fancy that Alen will think that he has done enough to please the government if he exacts respect and the greater part of the plunder, if he finds himself unable to get the whole. So I am not sure if I can promise myself that these forces will serve to occupy those of the infidels, though I am not without hope that they may divert them. Reports have come that those corsairs are in great alarm about this armament of England, apprehending that it may disturb the quiet with which they pursue their depredations.[8]

The hope was that Allin's forces would subdue the Algerine corsairs and allow trade to continue without hindrance. Allin's instructions were to use whatever means necessary to gain peace and keep trade going. The question was how well he would carry out those instructions, 'it being his duty to bridle the audacity of those corsairs by force'.

This may prevent those corsairs from sending succour to the Turks and that his Majesty may not abate his severity against those infidels. At present they are treating English ships with every respect. With humble flatteries they would like to set on foot a new peace, but before that they will have to render a good account of the robberies committed since the last ratification.[9]

But it was not to be. In a letter dated 11 October 1669 Lord Arlington wrote to the Venetian Ambassador to London that Allin was cruising off the Algerine coast looking for corsairs. He sent Sir Edward Spragge with twelve ships to intercept Algerine cruisers heading for home.

Arlington assured me that the Vice Admiral, fully informed of the opinion of the king and furnished with instructions from the Council, would make it his business to prepare the way for obtaining all due satisfaction by the use of severity. With this opening Arlington said that he hoped this expedition might divert the force of the Turks. He told me that the king had given permission to five English officers to proceed by Toulon to Candia. When the king himself repeated this with his own lips I bowed and told his Majesty that they would be kindly received by the captain general.[10]

A few weeks later, Allin blockaded the port of Algiers, demanding concessions from the Algerines.

Finding them very unwilling to concede this he had made up his mind to declare war on those corsairs and to warn the English merchants in all the ports of the Mediterranean. He had, as a start, taken two barques with wheat and captured seventy Turkish slaves under the very guns of the castle there. It would seem, however that in ten days' time the Algerines may be reinforced by twelve ships of war to enable them to return the compliment to the English nation.[11]

Sadly the winds were against him and he was forced to abandon the blockade. In December 1669 he sailed the fleet to Majorca to refit and prepare to chase the Algerines throughout the winter. In the meantime news continued to come in of the Algerines continuing their attacks on merchant shipping. 'From other quarters have come dubious news of a sudden sally of six Algerine ships, of their giving chase to sundry Dutch merchantmen with the capture of three and of one English one also laden with goods; but it is hoped that this may not be confirmed.'

Dutch trade was suffering heavily at the hands of the corsairs so they armed a squadron of ships and aligned themselves with England in order to defeat the Mediterranean menace. 'The matter is not yet decided, but frequent consultations are being held. It would seem that their policy is to make themselves so strong in the Mediterranean that they will have no reason to fear any mishap to their rich convoys which might be attacked on their voyage to the Levant.'[12]

As Allin's fleet left Algiers reports arrived that six English fishing vessels had been taken by the Algerines. Unlike the pirates such as Blackbeard or Roberts who normally let their captured crews go and just took the cargo, the Algerines took everything, especially the crews of the ships as they would be sold into slavery.

In early January 1670 reports coming from the Mediterranean regarding the activities of the corsairs were confusing and sometimes contradictory. For example, reports of a battle between two English frigates and six Algerine ships suggest that the corsairs won that fight. A letter dated 10 January 1670 from the Venetian Ambassador to the Venetian Senate stated:

> It seems that the good fortune, which at the outset favoured the frigates, turned afterwards to the side of the ships, and the English, by the death of a captain let slip the victory that was in their hands. More definite news is awaited since it is of great consequence that those corsairs should not be encouraged by some success and become strong at sea.

But the *London Gazette* ran a story that suggested this report might be confused with the report where Captain Hubbard was killed in a fight with five to seven Algerine ships in the bay of Cadiz. Rear Admiral Kempthorne, commanding the *Mary Rose*, managed to fight off his attackers and get his convoy into safety.[13]

By April 1670 Allin was given greater powers to deal with the corsairs:

> They are stiffening the orders to Alen, *pari passu* with reinforcements, to seek out opportunities for collisions and wherever possible to beat the Algerines, who have grown more audacious than ever. It is learned here that they have not only refused the exchange of slaves, taken since the last war, but that they have also put out to sea with thirty two pirate ships, the greater part of which are occupying the mouth of the Strait. From the report of certain ships it is learned that other English craft have been chased right into the mouth of the English Channel by three

corsairs, each of which carried an armament of forty guns. They are also cruising in those waters to carry off some ship as a rich prize.

But the corsairs didn't hang around the English Channel for long. The reason for that may have been the reports that Baron van Ghent, commanding the Dutch squadron, was sailing out of Holland to join up with the English fleet in the Mediterranean. This is confirmed in a letter from the Venetian Ambassador in England to the Venetian Senate dated 11 April 1670: 'It is possible that the mere report that van Gent has sailed from Holland may drive them away from these seas and the squadron should not be so numerous provided it was swift, after all the time that they have been talking about sending against the corsairs.'[14]

The stage was now set for a confrontation from which the English supported by the Dutch would not back down. In August 1670 the joint Anglo-Dutch forces met several Algerine ships off Cape Spartel. In that action six Algerine cruisers were driven ashore by Captain Richard Beach and Baron van Ghent. 'I have had no means of writing since 28 July, when I dismissed the *Portland* and *Pearl*, and since then have been cruising about the Straits, looking for 7 Algiers ships reported to be to the westward', Thomas Allin wrote in a letter dated 10 September 1670.

On the 12th, I met Van Ghent to the west of Cape Spartel, with 4 men-of-war on the same design; he with some of his commanders came on board my ship, to consider of the likeliest course to intercept the Turks upon their return home, when it was agreed that he should lie off Cape Spartel, where the *Hampshire*, *Foresight*, and *Portsmouth* were left, and that I should go and keep the mouth of the Straits, between Gibraltar and Ceuta, with the *Bristol*, *Nonsuch*, and *Victory*, and that notice should be given to each other by firing guns. On the 13th, I went to Gibraltar, where I washed and tallowed my ship, and then to Tetuan Bay. I spoke with a Frenchman of St. Malo, going with letters to Cadiz, and as he alleged, with one to the French Consul at Tetuan Bay, which I found to be false; I suppose he went to trade, and he has falsely reported that we took his bread and some goods. We chased the *Gilt Rose* and another upon the coasts of Barbary, but neither I nor Capt. Berry could do any good. We took one of 3 brigantines with 22 men, one of whom had his leg so much spoiled by a shot that it had to be cut off. Her patron, Bondale Alli, had been a captain of an Algiers man-of-war of 24 guns, which was lost in a storm; he told me that some English ships to the westward, a few days since, fought 5 Algerines, three of which were put ashore near Cape Spartel, and there burnt, which has since been confirmed by a Spanish ship from Sariffo. Capt. Beach has orders to join me in the Straits; as the wind has been favourable for him to do so; I presume he must have had some occasion to detain him, so I hope the report is true.[15]

Allin listed the ships destroyed in a letter he wrote dated 26 August 1670 which also went into greater detail about the battle:

After many unsuccessful chases and probabilities lost, I left Capt. Beach in the *Hampshire*, with the *Portsmouth* and *Foresight*, to cruise off Cape Spartel, and went myself to Gibraltar, to keep my station between that and Ceuta. M. Van Ghent, Admiral of the Dutch, cruising out of the Straits with 4 sail, saw 6 Algerines, whom he chased; but night coming on, we gave it up, and Capt. Beach returned to his station. On the 17th we met them again, and after a long and sharp fight, which was ill-managed by the enemy, the whole 6 were put ashore south of Cape Spartel, and in the morning 2 of them were fired by their own hands; but the other 4, being defended from them by the Christians, who remained on board and turned their guns against them, remained unburnt until our boats went and did that service for them.

Allin then talked about the ships that were burnt.

I send a list of the ships burnt, which are those we should have made choice of to destroy, had it been left to us, and limited to the same number. Aug. 26. They are 6 of the 7 that fought with our Newfoundland convoys last year, and that made an attempt on Rear-Admiral Kempthorne, and 4 of them put the *Sapphire* on shore at Sicily, and lately engaged with the *Advice* and *Guernsey*, both of whose commanders they killed. If their force is considered, they were doubtless the Hectors of Algiers, and well able to have fought and beaten all the remaining ships of that place; their loss, when all the sails, rigging, guns, and ammunition are considered, cannot be of smaller consequence than if 12 unrigged hulls had been burned in their Mole.

Many of the enemy died during the ferocious battle. Some were killed as they tried to take up defensive positions around their beached ships. Shards of wood, scraps of metal whizzed through the air as the cannon balls from the English ships pounded the shore line and ripped into the enemy ships. Musket balls tore through flesh as if it was butter.

Sir Thomas Allin continued in his letter that of those men who weren't killed in the fight 'drowned in getting ashore, and the rest are in great danger of perishing before they get to Algiers, which is overland, and through a vast country, some part whereof is inhabited by a people who are very treacherous, covetous, and cruel'.

This action by Captain Beach freed more than 250 Christian slaves and not one English sailor was lost in the five-hour battle. 'If the Turks had not been chased to our ships, they must have come, as they had but 5 days' provisions, on the shortest allowance that man can live on, and so were forced up the Straits, where they had been sufficiently waylaid', Allin wrote. 'I was chasing 2 other men-of-war in the Straits the same hour, and should have taken them but for the wind shifting, and Capt. Beach had stopped a Leghornese bound from Sally (Salee) to Algiers, whose goods I am taking out, and have directed the freight to be paid for them, the commander having confessed that they belong to Turks, Moors, and Jews of Barbary.'

To keep up the pressure against the Turks Allin ordered the *Jersey* and *Foresight* to cruise in the Straits 'till they meet the *Greenwich* and *Assurance*, while I go along the Spanish shore to Alicant, with the *Bristol*, *Nonsuch*, and a fireship'. He then ordered three more ships from his fleet, the *Hampshire*, *Portsmouth*, and *Centurion*, to cruise along the Barbary Coast

> to look out for vessels from Tetuan to Algiers with the remnant of the men of the burnt ships, and to meet me at Algiers, where I intend to carry the news of the disaster myself, so as to try what good effect my appearance there will produce. I hope to receive letters at Alicant, and if I do not meet the *Mary*, *Advice*, *Guernsey*, and *Deptford* ketch on the way, they will find orders there to cruise about the Straits, in place of the *Jersey* and *Foresight*, who are to go eastward with convoys.[16]

The Algerine ships destroyed were the *Flower Pot* of forty-four guns and 400 men, the *Tiger* of forty-four guns and 400 men, the *Leopard* of forty-four guns and 380 men, the *Date Tree* of forty guns and 360 men, the *Shepherdess* of thirty-eight guns and 340 men and the *Golden Rose* of thirty-eight guns and 330 men.[17]

The news of the action off Cape Spartel spread far and wide. The Venetian Secretary to Spain wrote news has reached Cadiz of a considerable victory won by six English frigates against five of the best of the Algerines off Cape D'Espartel. The victors succeeded in burning the whole of them, including the flagship, in releasing 300 slaves and inflicting upon them a loss of over 600 including those who died by fire and by water. This happy success affords universal consolation since it seems likely that this disaster, besides reducing their forces, will be calculated to diminish the audacity of those barbarians who had become exceedingly daring.[18]

The *London Gazette* reported that Allin blockaded the Straits of Gibraltar and gave Van Ghent of the Dutch fleet five English ships under the command of Captain Beach to act alongside the Dutch fleet. These ships (the *Hampshire, Portsmouth, Foresight, Jersey* and *Centurion*) 'took stations off Cape Spartel and on the evening of the 17th sighted a fleet of six Algerine ships. They gave chase and finally drove them all on shore, where they were all burned. 750 Christians including 62 English were rescued.'[19]

Another action took place almost a year later when a small fleet of English ships under the command of Sir Edward Spragge, captain of HMS *Dartmouth III*, destroyed seven Algerine men of war in Bugia Bay. Spragge was initially under the command of Thomas Allin; when Allin went home on leave due to illness, Spragge stepped into his shoes to command the English fleet in the Mediterranean. In his journal he describes the Battle of Bugia Bay.

On the 20th April, when cruising off Algiers the frigates *Mary, Hampshire, Portsmouth* and *Advice* were met, who reported that several Algerine men of war were at Bugia. A council of war was called and it was decided to endeavour to destroy them. The *Hampshire* and *Portsmouth* left to cruise off Algiers. On the 30th the fleet got into Bugia Bay and encountered a gale which seemed likely to carry it and the fireships upon the enemy. But by the time that the fleet got within half a shot of the castles and forts it became dead calm. The winds being uncertain it was decided to make the attempt upon them at night with boats. About 12 on the 2nd May all the boats were sent out with the *Eagle* fireship under Lieutenant Nugent. The attempt failed owing to the miscarriage of the fireships. But for this the enemy ships might have been destroyed without the loss of a man. On the following day the enemy unrigged all their ships and made a boom. On Monday the 8th of May they received several recruits probably from Algiers, who were welcomed by the firing of guns and the flying of colours. About noon the ships were brought broadside on and ordered to anchor in 4 fathoms of water, close under the walls.

At that point Spragge's ships opened fire on the port batteries, fortifications and castle walls. For two hours cannon balls smashed into the wooden and stone structures causing chaos and damage. Musket balls shot through the air, ripping into flesh. Cannon fire from the ships tore into the batteries, smashing them to bits, causing screams of agony from the men manning the guns. Spragge ordered a pinnace to be lowered into the water and it was

> sent in to cut the boom, a task that was very bravely performed. A fireship was then sent in and destroyed all the ships in the port, ten in all, seven of them being the best men of war at Algiers. A Dutchman who escaped from Algiers reports that great execution was done, the castle and town miserably torn and old Treky, the admiral wounded. The ships had been purposely commanded by the Divan to find out the English and fight them wherever they met.[20]

This action led to a treaty between England and Algiers where some trade concessions were made by Algiers but seventeen English sailors were killed and forty-one wounded in the battle.

A few years later, Sir John Narbrough arrived as the commander of the Mediterranean fleet and negotiated a treaty with Tunis by providing them with guns and naval stores in return for trade with the Tunisian state and for English shipping to be left in peace. While the treaty with Algiers still stood, attacks on English shipping were coming largely from Tripoli who had so far refused any attempt at negotiating a treaty.

> Three English frigates of war named *Henrietta*, *Diamond* and *Swallow* have arrived in the port, commanded by Sir John Narbrough, the king's admiral in the Mediterranean, sent against the Tripolitans. He reports that he has eight ships at present under his direction, three of which have already passed this way for the Levant, in pursuit of those barbarians. The other two have gone to careen at Leghorn.[21]

Narbrough then sailed for Malta, which he was using to careen and victual his fleet as well as a rendezvous point, where another six ships were added to his fleet, including two fireships.

During the past months he has twice made a long stay off the mouths of this place when he succeeded in capturing a ship with 120 Moors and burned another ship laden with wheat and three galleons. But he did not succeed in preventing the corsairs from coming out, as on two occasions five ships of war eluded him and went to the Levant. He took a turn towards the Sapienze and Cape Spada after these and is still carrying out his instructions. He has set at liberty here some Greek slaves who swam out while he was off the mouths and sought safety on his ships.

With the royal money he ransomed at Algiers 182 English slaves and ratified the peace with that place as well as with those of Tunis. With the Tripolitans also he entered upon some sort of composition. With respect to the difficulty that the 80,000 reals levied upon the goods of merchants of other nations upon English ships were not in being because the money had already been distributed to the soldiers, it seems that they were ready to agree to his claim that so many Christian slaves should be released, but upon a pact that the Tripolitans should undertake never again to search any English trading ships. This was not accepted as they claim still to search for the goods of merchants of other nations. So he has with him the consul who was at Tripoli, whom he took away because of the continuation of the war.[22]

But the conflict with Tripoli continued and in January 1675 another action took place where more of their ships were destroyed. Narbrough's fleet arrived in the port of Tripoli on Friday 14 January 1675 to find the port filled with Tripolitan ships readying to sail. 'I hoped to have made a lasting peace,' Narbrough wrote. 'But the Dey and government of Tripoli are refusing to make restitution to injuries done to His Majesty and His Subjects. There were ships of war of considerable force in the port of Tripoli, preparing to get out to cruise.' Narbrough ordered that the ships he had carrying fireworks be fitted out as fireships: 'I commanded that all the boats of my Squadron, counting twelve in number should be manned and fitted with fireworks, also I ordered an officer to be a commander in every boat and my Lieutenant Cloudesley Shovell to be Commander-in-Chief of them all.'

He then ordered the ships to 'attack the enemy in their port'. At midnight the English ships moved into the port and

seized the guard boat, boarded the ships and fired them and utterly destroyed them all, some Turks and Moores slain, the rest fleeing to save themselves. This action was performed in less than an hour's time without sustaining great damage on our part, other than the expense of some ammunition, fireworks and fireboats. Such was the mercy of Almighty God towards us that not one man of ours was killed, wounded or touched nor a boat in any way disabled but all returned in safety.

Four ships managed to break free but were chased by Cloudesley Shovell and ultimately burnt, the colours of each of them brought 'in triumph along to my ship. Our men employed in the boats, in this particular action were one hundred fifty and seven all behaved themselves as becometh Englishmen.'[23]

In this case, Cloudesley Shovell attacked the enemy's ships in their own harbour, burning four of their best men of war without losing a man. A few days later, Narbrough engaged several ships from Tripoli and sank four of them in an exchange of cannon fire.

Sir John being to the eastward of Tripoli met with 4 Tripolines with whom he and only another ship so warmly engaged that he killed 600 men and pursued them into Tripoli where the government sent out to him to treat, and that he had concluded an honourable peace with them, they having delivered all the English slaves. This we give credit to, because Sir John had dispatched convoys for Smyrna and Scanderoon in February and according to our advices from Malta, he left himself only two men-of-war.[24]

These two actions persuaded the Dey of Tripoli to sue for peace, which according to Roger was 'more satisfactory not only than was expected now but what was ever yet obtained by any prince from that nation'.[25]

However, the treaty between England and Algeria that came out of the attack by Spragge's forces had been regularly broken by vessels of many nations claiming to be English merchant ships. Under the terms of the agreement between the two states the Algerines were allowed to stop merchant shipping but would send English ships away unharmed. But ships of many other nations claimed this benefit, posing as English merchant ships, which infuriated the Algerines who declared war in 1677, blaming the English for having broken the treaty.

The Algerines made the first move by sending out small squadrons of fast cruisers designed to attack the convoys running from the Mediterranean up the Spanish and French coasts to England. For two years the Algerines attacked these convoys, causing havoc. Their ships were faster than anything in the English navy at the time. By 1669 Narbrough had thirty-four ships, roughly the same as the Algerines.

Narbrough's campaign against them was temporarily crippled when they captured his supply ships. Narbrough had no base near the enemy from which he could mount an attack, although in Tangier they should have had a base that supplied them with everything they needed. But Tangier had some major shortcomings. It was under almost constant threat from a determined enemy, despite the garrison of 3,000 men stationed there. The fortifications were too short to protect the town and too long for the garrison to hold properly.

> It is necessary to use another kind of force against the Moors. On two occasions they have appeared before the walls of Tangier and now they are getting ready everything required for a general assault. The last letters of the 24th July bring similar news from that place. The governor writes that the Moors have come down in great numbers from the neighbouring mountain of Moxfen. They had taken up their quarters between the forts outside the lines; but he succeeded in driving them away by heavy salvoes of musketry and by a prompt sortie of a part of the garrison. Here they would much prefer that the Ambassador Arundel should prevent a conflict by negotiation.[26]

The harbour was also unsafe. It was situated right in the Straits of Gibraltar and was an exposed anchorage. To protect the harbour from the mighty force of the Atlantic, a mole was built and after twenty years' work in 1683 it was 479 yards long, contained some 170,000 tons of stone and was still half finished. Evidence suggested that the harbour was silting even as the English worked feverishly to build it.

Tangier was also a poor base because of the expense of bringing everything from England. A naval base should be a place where trade flourishes, where merchants and contractors can provide skills, commodities and stores. Tangier had none of this.

> I am extremely troubled to see on what a fatal rock Sir John Narbrough's squadron are in danger to be ruin[ed] by the failure of victuals at Tangier. But I am in hopes the Governor will have found means to furnish those five or six ships, that want most, six weeks' or two months' victuals, as you find by our scheme or calculate of victuals, which we send you from the Board of Tangier to-night.[27]

So while the English had a colony at Tangier the commanders in the Mediterranean used other ports. Spragge used Port Mahon while Narbrough used Leghorn and Malta for his operations against Tripoli, and for his attacks on Algiers he used Cadiz and Port Mahon as well as Leghorn. All of these ports could provide supplies that were not available at Tangier.

English naval tactics were still being formed for dealing with the Barbary pirates. For example, direct attacks on the large and well-fortified cities were rarely successful. Blockades also proved to be a fruitless exercise as there were hundreds of miles of coast to be blockaded and there were few anchorages close by that could be used for victualling so the supply chains were long and hazardous. By contrast the fast Algerine cruisers were able to slip in and out of ports and small harbours under the cover of darkness almost at will and harry English trade routes.

The best defensive tactic turned out to be strong convoys coming directly from England into the Mediterranean and back again. Squadrons of warships were available to reinforce the convoys at strategic points. However, the Straits of Gibraltar were the critical point for the convoys. Here they could be easily attacked by Algerine cruisers and other Barbary Coast pirates. Conversely the Straits were also a good place for the English to attack Barbary Coast pirates coming into the Mediterranean from their Atlantic raids.

Narbrough's instructions from Whitehall were clear:

Warrant to the Lord Chancellor to cause the Great Seal to be applied to three instruments of even date therewith, empowering Sir John Narbrough, commander-in-chief in the Mediterranean, to treat and conclude with the governments of Algiers, Tunis and Tripoli what shall be found necessary for strengthening or renewing the treaties with them and for making such alterations therein or additions thereto as shall be found necessary.[28]

Before he could even contemplate negotiating peace the Barbary pirates had to be subdued and force would have to be used. By September 1677 Narbrough had his fleet patrolling in the Straits of Gibraltar where they could lie in wait for returning Algerine ships and their prizes. The war with Algiers still raged and their ships were faster than the ships Narbrough had in his fleet. 'I want extremely clean frigates that sail well, and provisions and stores to be lodged at Tangier', he wrote in a letter to Samuel Pepys dated

2 September 1677. Narbrough noted that he had two Algerine ships of war in his possession, the *Date Tree* of eighteen guns and about 100 men and the *Orange Tree* of twenty-two guns and about 110 men:

> The latter was in the English Channel lately and there took two small English vessels. One we have retaken; I have sent Capt. Canning to chase after the other, who, I hope, will recover her. Sir Robert Robinson in the *Assurance* seized the *Date Tree* and retook the small English vessel near Cape Spartel; Capt. Harman in the *Sapphire* seized the *Orange Tree* in the channel of the Straits. I hope we shall get hold of more of them. I keep cruising in the channel of the Straits' mouth, so that no ships can pass but we see them. It's the only place to annoy the Algerines. I wish the *Kingfisher* with me and some frigates that sail well large. We took those by out sailing them. These Turks tell me there are five or six men-of-war in the great sea. I am laying wait for them in the mouth of the Straits.[29]

Not all the battles the English had with the Algerine ships were as one-sided as the ones described here. In one battle more than forty ships were involved in the destruction of just one Algerine man of war, as Captain Thomas Leighton, commanding the *Portsmouth*, wrote:

> At daybreak this morning, as we lay cruising in the Straits' mouth a little eastward of Tarifa, we made the *Rose* of Algiers, formerly commanded by Canary but now by a Lübeck renegado, of about 40 guns and 350 men, most Levantine Turks and the rest renegadoes, plying to windward an easy gale.
>
> On our commanding him to send his boat on board, he immediately ran out his lower tier of guns and put himself in order to fight, on which we fired six or seven shot through him, which he only answered with a like number and a volley of small shot and clapped his helm a weather and bore away. We continued the chase and fired guns to give notice to Sir J. Narbrough and the rest of our fleet then at Tangier, who all weighed or cut and spread themselves in a line from Cape Spartel almost to Cape Trafalgar, in all near 40 sail, some merchantmen, the rest frigates, fireships and shallops. The Turk haled to the northward, thinking to run out ahead of them all, but, finding Sir John Ernley to reach upon him, after several shot received from and returned him, tacked and stood away to the southward, receiving each ship's broadside and himself continually firing great and small shot, and had certainly

escaped, had not Capt. Canning, who was the southernmost and leewardest ship, poured a broadside into him and shot away his maintopmast, after which he continued fighting and bore away under the *James*' stern, who presently stood with him, and laid him on board on the luff on the larboard side, and soon after the *Charles* on the starboard quarter and lay board and board above an hour and a half, continually firing broadsides into each other, and, having entered a considerable number of men, both steered off, the Turks still keeping the lower gun deck and firing small shot out of their ports at our boats sent to enter more men, their great guns being all dismounted. Capt. Canning was killed in laying her on board by a small shot in his breast and David Floyd's brother was killed in entering and cut to pieces by the Turks. I can give no account of what number we have lost, but I am sure they are a great many by what I saw killed on board the prize. The galleys were both very much disabled and are ordered to be towed into Tangier, we being sent to convoy the Malaga fleet.[30]

Organizing convoys was at first a complex affair but over the years it became routine for the navy. They were set up in London in consultation with ship-owners and merchants. Orders were passed from the senior officer to the crews of the escort ships that, once at sea, positioned themselves on the windward side of the convoy. At night escorts moved so they were ahead and astern of the ships they were escorting.

It was reported there that Sir John Narbrough had fought the admiral of the Algerines and forced him to put up a white flag, that thereupon Sir John sent a boat of men to receive their submission, but the Turks slew them, that Sir John, renewing the fight, took the ship and drowned the Turks. I very much doubt the story and wonder it should get into Holland, before it reached England.[31]

Admiral Arthur Herbert who took over as commander-in-chief of the Mediterranean from Narbrough was much more successful than his predecessor. In 1683 he managed to end the hostilities with Algiers and negotiated a treaty that lasted for 135 years.

Chapter 2

Madagascar: Pirate Haven

While most of this book concentrates on Barbary Coast piracy and how the Royal Navy dealt with it, piracy also flourished from many other parts of Africa. Up and down the West Coast of Africa, for example, piracy was rife and much of it centred on the convoys that carried out the slave trade between Jamaica and the United States.

In the late seventeenth century, during King William's War, news that pirates were operating in the Red Sea set alarm bells ringing in England. In 1693 a letter from the Governor of Jamaica said that several privateers from that island had navigated their way to the Red Sea and were committing atrocities. Reports of their activities began to reach England and soon the government had a large file on the pirates operating in the Red Sea. They were known as the Red Sea Men and they were using Madagascar as their base.[1]

Peter Earle states in his book *The Pirate Wars*, that the *Jacob*, a privateer, set sail from New York in November 1690 with a commission to hunt down French shipping. Instead of following the commission, the crew turned pirate and sailed her via the Cape Verde Islands to Madagascar. From here the pirates began cruising for booty in the Indian Ocean and in June 1692 they moved into the Red Sea and captured four ships. Each sailor netted more than £400 – a massive sum. They then set sail for St Marie's Island on the northeast coast of Madagascar, which was a growing pirate haven.

On this island was a trading post run by Adam Baldrige, who was financed by one of the wealthiest New York merchants, Frederick Phillipse, a slave trader for the American market. Hearing of the enormous wealth that was brought in by the men of the *Jacob* through correspondence with his agent, Baldrige, Phillipse decided to combine his slaving activities with pirate trade.

He instructed Baldrige to sell supplies to the pirates from the *Jacob*, along with food and drink for some of their booty and six guns from the ship that he mounted onto his fort. The crew of the *Jacob* split up, with some staying on the island where there was 'a growing white community of pirates and beachcombers and delights in the form of drink and native women'. The rest sailed back to New York and bribed the governor with Arabian gold to allow them to go ashore. They also gave him their ship.

News of the wealth that pirates could gain in the Red Sea soon spread and ships of all sorts began to head for Madagascar so they too could cruise in the Red Sea and capture Arabian gold. Financial backing for these voyages came largely from American merchants who also fitted out the ships and made a handsome profit on their investment. The returning pirates with their loot were left unscathed as colonial officials would take their bribes and look the other way. 'Those American slave traders who were accustomed to seek their human cargo in East Africa and Madagascar took the pirate business in their stride', writes Earle.

Acting for other merchants as well as Phillipse, Baldrige ensured the goods they sent would be useful to the pirates. Rum and beer, food, clothing, guns and gunpowder were sent, along with the supplies they'd need for the slaves. Baldridge in his turn would then fill the ships for the return journey with slaves. Usually, these slave traders would return not only with their human cargo but also with some pirates as passengers who wanted to return to civilization to spend their ill-gotten gains in style.

Some pirates sailed under the protection of a privateering commission to give them at least an impression of legality but some didn't bother. In May 1694 Henry Avery, second mate of the private warship *Charles*, led a mutiny, took command of the ship and sailed for Madagascar. The *Charles* along with another private English warship the *James* was anchored in the Spanish port of La Coruna where they had been waiting for over a year without pay to mount a raid against the French. Discontented, most of the men threw their lot in with Avery – it wasn't hard for him to take the ship and to have the crew on his side. Twenty-five men from the *James* joined him. He allowed the captain and twenty men loyal to the captain to row ashore. Avery renamed his captured ship the *Fancy* and set sail.

Madagascar was used as a base by many pirates who intended to intercept heavily laden merchant ships travelling into the Arabian Sea towards the strait of Babs-al-Mandab (the Babs) into the Red Sea. Most of these merchant ships would sail between the continent and Madagascar as they headed up the African coast, past Zanzibar towards the Babs. Madagascar was a perfect place for pirates to operate and disrupt trade throughout the Arabian Sea and the India Ocean. Virtually every well-known pirate at one time or another used Madagascar or St Marie's Island as their base.

Captain Charles Johnson wrote about Avery in his book *A General History of the Most Notorious Pirates* and his account of one of the most well-known pirates forms the basis of many modern histories of the man. While some of his crew were eventually captured by the Royal Navy, Avery wasn't and he represents one of the few pirates who got away.

Avery, like most pirates, had a career that was short and in his case successful. According to Johnson, Avery was born in Plymouth in 1653 and went to sea early in his life with the Royal Navy. He served for sometime as midshipman on HMS *Kent* and HMS *Rupert*. However, by 1694 Johnson tells us he was aboard the *Charles*, which had been hired to plunder and raid French shipping. Johnson wrote of Avery:

> Being a fellow of more cunning than courage, he insinuated himself into the good will of several of the boldest Fellows on board the other Ship as well as that which he was on board of: having sounded their Inclinations before he opened himself, and find them ripe for his design he, at length, proposed to them, to run away with the ship, telling them of what great wealth was to be had upon the coast of India.

For months they'd been in the port of Coruna without seeing any action and then on the evening of 7 May 1694, at 2200hrs while Captain Gibson, drunk as usual, was in his cabin Avery and the men quietly went about securing the ship, weighed anchor and put to sea, 'without any disorder or confusion'. Gibson was still sleeping it off in his cabin while Avery, now in command, slowly sailed out of the bay towards the open sea.

When Gibson woke up to the motion of the ship and the sounds of the tackles being worked he realized something was wrong. According to Johnson's account Avery told Gibson he could join the pirates and Avery, now in command, would make Gibson one of his lieutenants but if he didn't want to join him then Gibson would be put into one of the boats and sent ashore to safety. Gibson chose the latter option and was rowed away from his former ship. Avery continued sailing for Madagascar. Along the way he and his crew plundered three English ships in the Cape Verde Islands and captured two Danish ships near the island of Principe, on the west coast of Africa. He continued round the Cape of Good Hope heading for Madagascar. Finally, after several months at sea, they dropped anchor at the northeast corner of the island and went ashore for provisions, water and wood.

The pilgrim fleet of Muslim ships that every year sailed from the Indian port of Surat across to the mouth of the Red Sea at Mocha, then on up to

Mecca, was a ripe target for pirates. These ships were loaded with treasure and wealthy passengers and merchants. Usually, the merchants sailing with the pilgrims would trade their wares, cloth and spices for gold and coffee. The Great Mogul, emperor of the Mogul Empire in India, often sent his own ships with the fleet. Avery's plan was a simple one – to intercept the fleet and plunder what he could.

It was September 1695 and the *Fancy* (the *Charles* renamed) with Avery commanding was cruising off Mocha near the mouth of the Red Sea. Avery had fitted the ship with more cannon so she now boasted forty-six guns with a crew of more than 150 men. While Avery cruised the area, more pirate ships joined him as they waited for the fleet to arrive.

The first of the pilgrim fleet of ships to be plundered was the *Fath Mahmamadi* which the pirate fleet stripped of gold and silver. A few days after this ship was plundered, the lookout on the *Fancy* far above the deck sighted a white sail on the horizon and Avery ordered the men to put on as much sail as they could to catch it. The ship they were chasing belonged to the Great Mogul himself. The *Ganj-i-Sawai* was a massive vessel of forty guns.

As the small fleet of pirate ships approached, Avery ordered his guns to open fire on the *Ganj-i-Sawai*. The first broadside smashed into the Muslim ship's mainmast, sending it crashing down onto the deck. One of the cannon exploded, sending shrapnel and splinters in all directions, mowing down men and causing carnage. The crew of the Muslim vessel had no chance against the determined attack by Avery. The fight lasted two hours and was very one-sided. When the pirates boarded the vessel they met with little resistance.

Onboard the vessel was one of the Great Mogul's daughters and her various attendants, several slave girls and many wealthy merchants. When one of Avery's crew was captured later by the Royal Navy he confessed at his trial that they embarked on an orgy of plunder, torture and rape while the two vessels lay tied together becalmed on the Arabian Sea.

Avery now having made his fortune with this one act of piracy decided to retire, so he left the other pirate ships and headed for the West Indies and from here slipped into obscurity, with legend saying he lived out his life in luxury on a tropical paradise. Others say he died in obscurity, poverty-stricken in the village of Bideford in Devon. Avery was never captured. Six of his crew were caught and put on trial in the Old Bailey where they were sentenced to death.

We can see from a letter written by Captain William Burrough to Samuel Herron of the Royal African House just how effective Avery was:

Chapter 3

West Africa

By the mid-seventeenth century piracy along the West African coast was becoming more and more of a nightmare for merchants and traders. Sierra Leone was a main port for pirates who were using it to attack slave ships up and down the coast. One such was the *Trompeuse*, a thirty-two-gun warship commanded by a French pirate, Jean Hamlin. He sailed from the Caribbean across the ocean to Sierra Leone. Once there, he went on a rampage, capturing many slave ships and seizing their cargo. Some of these slave ships had gold and other riches in addition to their human cargo.

Once he'd finished his successful plundering Hamlin set sail for Dominica and then into St Thomas in July 1683 where the pirates were able to easily sell their goods to eager merchants. Captain Carlyle of HMS *Francis* got wind of Hamlin's arrival and setting out from the Leeward Islands station he boldly sailed into the harbour at St Thomas on 27 July 1683 and set fire to Hamlin's ship then sailed away again, leaving behind a wake of diplomatic problems. The Danes owned the island and objected to Carlyle's actions and the French objected to the burning of the *Trompeuse* which had been a royal ship before she turned pirate.

Piracy dwindled during the nine years of King William's War. 'Former pirate now fought former pirate as privateers in the service of England, France, Holland and Spain.'[1] According to Peter Earle this war, which brought William III to the English throne, also brought a fundamental change in the attitude of the government towards piracy. Earle describes a mutual understanding between government and merchants who realized that not only could they make themselves very wealthy but they could also make the nation rich. This meant that trade had to be protected. From this point forward English governments were committed to ensuring that 'trade, shipping and the empire itself would be promoted, protected and controlled for the benefit of the merchants and government alike'. So pirates could not be countenanced in this brave new world. Maritime violence would be employed through the Royal Navy or through legally commissioned privateers, not through pirates. This was a complete change from Elizabeth I's reign when piracy had been condoned as promoting trade.

Under the new government rules pirates were to be tracked down and exterminated as enemies of the state and all of mankind, as well as of 'capitalism and commercial expansion'.[2] The tool the English government would use to expand trade and enable capitalism to flourish was the Royal Navy. They would do this by ensuring that proper well-armed ships were used against the pirates – with crews well-trained and ready for battle.

Another key stronghold of pirates was a group of islands off the coast of West Africa known as the Cape Verde Islands. A Portuguese colony, pirates based there attacked shipping plying the coast as well as the rich slave ships that came from America and the West Indies laden with goods to pick up slaves and then head back across the ocean with their holds full of chained human cargo. For pirates these were easy prey and they caused severe mayhem to trade in this part of the world. The pirates were not interested in the slaves carried by these large vessels but in what they carried to West Africa before picking up their human cargo and the various rich passengers and cargo sailing back to America or the West Indies.

But as the seventeenth century came to a close two actions were fought which would act as a deterrent to pirates. The first took place on 26 May 1698 when HMS *Bedford Galley*, commanded by Captain Hollyman, sailed into the harbour of the Isle of Maio, an island of the cluster of the Cape Verde Islands. Hollyman was acting on a tip that a pirate ship was anchored in the harbour. When he arrived he found two large ships tied up, both flying the French colours. One was a pirate ship of fourteen guns and the other was the French prize they'd captured. The pirate crew were made up of a wide variety of nationalities.

Hollyman sent a search party over to the pirate ship. The wily pirate captain had put most of his men below decks and claimed that the two French vessels were just trading ships. But he was unable to convince Hollyman's men and so, while the search party from the *Bedford Galley* were still onboard, the pirate cut his cables, raised his anchor and set sail. Immediately, Hollyman ordered the sails to be raised and with the canvas catching the wind he gave chase to the pirates. For hours he chased the other ship, plastering it with cannon fire every time he was able to bring the *Bedford Galley* within broadside firing range. Shot after shot poured into the pirate vessel, tearing it to pieces, splinters and wooden shards flying in all directions. Using scrap bits of metal stuffed into canisters fired out of the cannon the hot shrapnel cut men down mercilessly and most of the pirates in command were killed, leaving the decks littered with corpses, but the few survivors were determined not to be caught by the Royal Navy warship and so threw everything overboard they could to lighten their vessel.

Finally night came. The French pirate ship was shattered by Hollyman's relentless fire. It sank during the night and the following morning when Hollyman surveyed the scene he found the sea littered with wreckage and several corpses had been washed ashore on the nearby island.

Word got round about this entanglement with the Royal Navy and for a short while the islands were clear of pirates, but by 1700 they were back again as there was an encounter between French pirate Emanuel Wynn and the warship HMS *Poole*, under the command of Captain John Cranby. In early July Cranby chased Wynn for several days. According to Earle, Wynn was the better sailor but Cranby's accurate guess on Wynn's intended route brought them together on 6 July 1700 when Wynn sailed into a cove on Brava Island.

This cove was the perfect hiding place as the entrance was extremely narrow and protected by rock on all sides. Outside the entrance the water was too deep for Cranby to anchor and he couldn't sail into the cove because the pirates had placed themselves in defensive firing positions and would be able to fire at will causing great casualties. He sailed up and down outside the cove, firing his cannon at the rocky shore, which killed and maimed several pirates.

In the end, he sailed to Fogo Island nearby to ask the Portuguese for help. He sailed back again with 100 Portuguese soldiers whom he landed on the other side of the island. With the soldiers making their way across land to attack the pirates and take the ship Cranby then sailed round to the entrance of the cove and waited. However, he didn't wait long enough. When the soldiers didn't appear as he had expected he sailed back to where he'd landed them to see what was happening. This was Wynn's chance. As the sun set he raised his anchor, unfurled his sails and slipped out of Cranby's grasp. But he left behind some of his crew who were slaughtered by the Portuguese soldiers who finally came storming out of the mountains.[3]

Though Cranby didn't catch Wynn this action and Hollyman's had the effect of ridding the Cape Verde Islands of pirates. By 1702 there were no reported accounts of piracy in the Islands or along the West African coast. The same was true for India and America. It was also the year of the start of the War of Spanish Succession so many pirates joined up to fight instead. Others, however, headed for Madagascar.

In late 1719 the Royal Navy dispatched two forty-gun warships to escort the slaving ships sailing for the West African coast via the Cape Verde Islands. Their job, once they'd delivered their convoy of slave merchant ships to the various slave stations along the West African coast, was to hunt for pirates. They remained in touch with the slaving stations ashore and with each other, and were to return home when their provisions ran out.[4]

Two more ships were sent out less than a year later in 1720 with very similar orders. But by 1722 the tactics changed and a ship was sent out every six months, partly to conduct a diligent search for pirates along the long West African coastline but also to pick up the convoys of slave ships heading for the West Indies. Once they were there, they joined the Jamaican squadron for a few months then cruised along the North American coast helping to search for pirates in that area as well.

The problem of piracy was tackled in several ways by the English government. One was by issuing pardons to pirates so they would give up their piracy and turn to more honest work. One such individual was Benjamin Hornigold who was the King of The Pirates on New Providence before the arrival of Governor Woodes Rogers. Blackbeard was mentored by Hornigold. When Rogers arrived, Hornigold took the pardon and began hunting pirates on behalf of the governor.[5]

Another policy was to increase naval patrols in the areas heavily used by the pirates. Then there was reward money offered for the capture of pirates along with commissioning privateers to go out and capture pirates, and finally the trial and execution of as many pirates as possible. David Cordingly writes in his book, *Under the Black Flag*, that 'some of these measures were more effective than others, but the combined effect of all of them was to eliminate piracy as a serious threat to trade'.[6]

In 1700 new and more effective legislation came into being with the Act for the More Effectual Suppression of Piracy, which ended the need for pirates who had been captured to be taken to London for trial and execution by the Court of the Admiralty. It meant that overseas Vice-Admiralty Courts could be held in the colonies and that the death sentence could be used. Once the pirates were found guilty the Act stipulated that, if they were sentenced to death, they must be executed on or near the sea.[7]

A pardon, issued by King George I on 5 September 1717, had some effect. Several pirates in the West Indies accepted it but 'the test of this particular measure was whether the pardoned pirates abandoned piracy for good, and whether the number of pirate attacks was significantly reduced', according to Cordingly. Though it was effective in the Bahamas it was ineffective in most other areas. In Africa it had no effect whatsoever, nor did the Royal Proclamation issued in 1717 granting substantial rewards for the capture of pirates. The only real deterrent for piracy here was more warships.

By 1718 the Royal Navy was the most effective tool that Britain had in fighting pirates. It boasted 13,000 seamen, sixty-seven ships of the line, fifty fifth-rate and sixth-rate warships and seven sloops. The smallest of the ships of the line would normally have had more than fifty guns, far more firepower than even the largest of the pirate ships. 'Most pirate ships were sloops of ten to twenty guns, and in an encounter with a third-rate ship of seventy guns they would have been blown out of the water.'[8]

The most famous and successful of battles between the Royal Navy and pirates along the West African coast was the one that resulted in the death of Bartholomew Roberts in February 1722. This battle between Roberts and Captain Challoner Ogle commanding HMS *Swallow* saw more than 285 pirates killed or captured and fifty-two of the captured men hanged at Cape Coast Castle (in modern Ghana).

By the year 1723 there were only a handful of pirates left. Almost a thousand pirates had been killed or captured in the Royal Navy's anti-piracy campaign. They hunted and attacked pirates in the West Indies, Atlantic America and Africa and throughout this campaign the Royal Navy lost more than a thousand men, mostly to disease. With all the big pirates – Blackbeard, Kidd, Roberts, Avery and others – all either dead or no longer active, there remained only small gangs of pirates led mostly by Edward Lowe, or former crewmates of his. These criminals of the high seas were hunted down relentlessly by the Royal Navy but some proved very difficult to capture and slipped through the net on several occasions.

A real escape artist Lowe managed to elude the Royal Navy only to be captured by the French after his crew mutinied and set him adrift in a small boat. He was later hanged in Martinique.

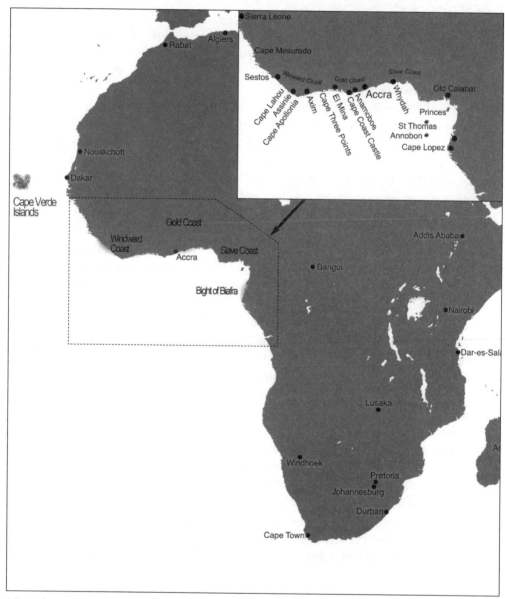

Map of West Africa During Roberts' Time.

Chapter 4

Black Bart is Dead

In the last chapter we touched on the death of Bartholomew Roberts (Black Bart) at the hands of the Royal Navy. This action took place along the coast of West Africa and was one of the most successful anti-piracy operations in the Royal Navy's history. It had the same significance as the death of Blackbeard as it was a chief factor in the demise of piracy along this stretch of coast.

Roberts and his crew were essentially English or of European origin and his death, the capture of his crew, plus the trial and execution of many of them, sent a very clear message to what remained of the European pirates operating in these waters and around the world. Roberts was a man full of drive and energy and one of the most successful of all pirates, taking more than 400 ships during his career. He was certainly a thief and possibly a killer but not the ruthless brutal one of popular legend.[1] Roberts was an officer aboard the slave ship *Princess* when it was captured by pirates. A sober and solitary man, Roberts abhorred gratuitous violence and had no stomach for alcohol; instead he constantly drank tea, which set him apart from his fellow pirates. He was a skilled officer and a highly intelligent and disciplined man. When he was dragged from the *Princess* by pirates onto their ship it changed his life forever.

He was born in the village of Little Newcastle, Pembrokeshire, around 1682 and, though his family were middle class, in that region they still faced grinding poverty. Roberts was tall, large with a swarthy Welsh complexion – Captain Charles Johnson referred to him as a 'black man'.[2] Much of the information in this chapter comes from Johnson's book, *A General History of the Most Notorious Pirates*, which was originally published in 1724, just two years after Roberts died. Johnson's account of Roberts's actions, the pirate's death and the trial and execution of the men captured is highly detailed.

Roberts's downfall began on 6 February 1721 when Ogle's HMS *Swallow*, in company with HMS *Weymouth* commanded by Captain Mungo Herdman, raised their anchors and set sail as escorts for six merchantmen heading for West Africa. As they left Spithead, the *Swallow* and the *Weymouth* sailed with their charges, the *Wheydah*, the *Martha*, the *Cape Coast* and three smaller sloops. The *Swallow* itself was a mighty warship of fifty guns and two decks that had been launched two years before from Chatham Dockyards.

Captain Ogle was an experienced commander and came from an ancient family. He was almost exactly the same age as Roberts at 40 but their paths were entirely different. Ogle was a rising star in the navy. He entered the service in July 1697 under a scheme that would today be called a fast-track officer training programme. In 1661 King Charles II introduced this scheme where the trainees were known as 'king's letter-boys', in order to encourage the more high-class or better families to enlist their sons into the navy. Ogle was a lieutenant by the time he was 21 and the following year received his first command in the Mediterranean where he served with distinction and honour during the War of the Spanish Succession.[3]

The ships left Spithead and headed for the open sea. Two months later on 9 April the convoy arrived at the mouth of the Sierra Leone River and continued sailing until 18 June, when they anchored off Cape Coast Castle to a fifteen-gun salute from the shore batteries.

All along the coast fever and disease raged. The two warships left their charges at Cape Coast Castle and headed south to the Isle of Princes, some two hundred miles away. Here the ships had a good harbour and there was a small fort at St Antonio on the southwestern side of the bay. They immediately began to career and clean their ships. This meant hauling everything that wasn't bolted down off the ships onto the shore and then using ropes, pulleys and muscle power to pull each ship onto its side so its belly could be cleaned and repaired. While this was being done the men stayed ashore, sleeping in tents. The surgeon onboard HMS *Swallow*, John Atkins, wrote in his memoirs that the men were left to their own devices while the ships were being cleaned and enjoyed themselves with the wives and girls of the local natives, from whom they also stole. 'They drank vast quantities of palm wine, many pawning their own clothes and possessions to buy it and often slept in the open air, exposed to the elements.'[4]

St Antonio was ringed with densely forested mountains and, as was the custom with European sailors at the time, Ogle had the little tent settlement built in a sheltered, leeward area. The advantage of this was that it provided protection against hurricanes and typhoons. The disadvantage was that the settlement was muggy, stifling and oppressive, without any wind or breeze to relieve the heat. In the rainy season it would be worse.

Ogle had hoped to beat the rains while they were careening their ships but the rainy season came early. By mid-August the rains had come and the air was heavy and thick. Atkins wrote that the sun was uncommonly hot during the day but the evenings were cold and damp, with the dew being so heavy it soaked the men's beds right through. By 26 August Ogle noted that most of the men were sick.

By this time the *Swallow* was back on the water, the crew having finished careening her. As everything was being loaded back onto the *Swallow*, the *Weymouth* was then careened. The men worked in the oppressive heat, and as the days went by fewer and fewer reported for duty. Ogle was worried. As he wandered the beach watching his men slowly succumb to illness he knew he had to do something. Mosquitoes buzzed all around them as they worked. Sweat poured from the men, some almost fainting in the humidity.

Captain Ogle decided to rent the houses of the natives to get the sick men into some form of shelter, away from the insects and the oppressive humidity. He sent Atkins to rent the houses and supervise the transfer of the men into these temporary hospitals. But there was little Atkins could do. He wrote that the sick men's temperatures were very high and that they all suffered from raging thirst, 'frenzies, convulsions and sweats'. The healthy men were moved back onboard the *Swallow* and this helped to stem the tide of the disease. Atkins tried everything he could to cure the sick men but he only managed to compound their suffering. What he didn't know was that the men had malaria and that they needed quinine.[5]

Johnson tells us they buried a hundred men in just three weeks. 'This misfortune', Johnson wrote, 'was probably the ruin of Roberts, for it prevented the men-of-war's going back to Sierra Leone.'[6]

While Ogle was prepared to move everyone into the town and wait for reinforcements to arrive from England, Atkins knew that the only thing that would save the men was to leave the Princes as soon as possible. Ogle agreed but their departure was delayed when, on 5 September 1721, they discovered a crack in the keel of HMS *Weymouth* which had been caused when she'd run aground on a sandbar near Gambia. On inspection, the damage to the keel was far worse than they'd first thought and it would need to be repaired before they could get the *Weymouth* under way again.

After the repairs had been carried out they were ready to leave. On 20 September the two warships managed to lower their sails, haul up their anchors and head out to sea. However, the sickness had taken its toll, with

100 men dead and 200 sick. Indeed, the *Weymouth* was so badly stricken they needed to use twenty slaves from another ship in the harbour just to haul up her anchor.[7]

In this dreadful state they headed back up the coast to Cape Coast Castle. The *Weymouth* arrived first on 22 October and by this time there were only sixty men able to man the ship which had left England with a complement of 240. The death toll had risen to 160. On the *Swallow* things were slightly better. They could muster eighty healthy men out of a full crew of 274.[8]

The depleted state of the two warships meant that the coast of West Africa was vulnerable and General Phipps, governor of Cape Coast Castle, knew it. Though they hadn't been seen since mid-September there were rumours of the pirates' activities coming from company agents, local natives and merchants to Phipps and the Royal Navy men at Cape Coast Castle.

Phipps had survived for almost twenty years in the job and was now the senior company official in the region. He remained healthy when everyone else around him died. He had absolute control over the colony and spent most of his time within the walls of the castle. He lived like a king. Nearby the castle Phipps had his own private orchard that was more than ten miles in circumference and provided him with all manner of fruit and vegetables.[9]

Built of bleached white stone the grand castle boasted twenty-eight guns that pointed out to sea, not to defend the fort from natives but from other Europeans who might try to invade. Below ground level, carved directly out of the stone, were dank, dark, dungeons that housed the slaves waiting to be shipped to the New World. Sometimes more than a thousand slaves would be kept in those terrible places where the only light was through small iron grates in the ceiling and walls.

Above ground level it was a different story. Phipps's rooms in the castle were comfortable and spacious and his living area looked directly down on the main hall and the chapel so he could keep an eye on his employees. Phipps had his own private walkway along the battlements so he could see what ships were coming into the harbour.

The reports about the pirates were disturbing. Phipps was also worried that, instead of having two warships each with a full healthy complement of men, Ogle could barely scrape together one ship's crew out of the two. But they had to know if the rumours were true. On 10 November 1721, Ogle set sail from Cape Coast Castle, leaving the *Weymouth* behind so its crew could recuperate, and headed west along the Windward and Gold

Coasts. The plan was to press men from merchant ships operating in this area into service aboard the *Swallow*. Johnson tells us that Ogle met with a Portuguese ship whose captain told him that he'd seen an English ship chased into the port of Junk, but a few days after this he met with Captain Plummer commanding the *Jason* out of Bristol who hadn't heard or seen anything. So where was the pirate?

Roberts was holed up at Old Calabar which is today in southeast Nigeria. Old Calabar River was a perfect place for the pirates to hide, with its many inlets and creeks. The thick dense foliage on either side of the river banks steamed with heat and humidity and this area was known to have a very high mortality rate. Entrance to the river was restricted by a sandbar across its mouth which meant that ships had to use a narrow channel to gain the river. Only a skilled pilot could be used to negotiate this difficult access.

Roberts found his pilot in Captain Loan, commanding a brigantine the *Joceline*, when they arrived at Old Calabar at the end of September 1721. Though pressed into service Johnson tells us he was well paid. 'Here therefore they sat easy, and divided the fruits of their dishonest industry, and drank and drove care away', Johnson wrote of Captain Loan, 'who for this, and other services, was extremely well paid according to the journal of their own accounts'.[10]

While at Old Calabar, the pirates took at least three ships, two from Bristol and one large ship, the *Hannibal*, belonging to the Royal Africa Company. The *Hannibal* was a 90-ton brigantine and was taken on 1 October. The captain and company man were used appallingly by the pirates who beat them, mistreated them and stole all their clothes.

In his book, *If A Pirate I Must Be*, Richard Sanders suggests the reason Roberts and his men abused the captain and company man of the *Hannibal* so brutally was that 'the pirates immediately recognised in both men the type of officers who had made their lives a misery as sailors on the slavers'. So the pirates showed no quarter to these two men and repeatedly struck them with the flat parts of their cutlasses as well as beating them whenever the fancy took them. They threw the cargo overboard, stripping the ship down to a hulk to use it as a storage ship while the rest of their fleet was being careened. Within a few days of this capture the captain was dead from fever and by the time the *Hannibal* was able to make the Gold Coast only six men of its original crew remained alive.[11]

All was not smooth sailing for Roberts. There were rumblings and plots throughout the pirate crew. Many of the men had been taken when their ships had been captured and forced into piracy. They were forever plotting their escape; at the same time more hardened pirates were dissatisfied with Roberts's authoritarian rule. Usually, on pirate ships, captains were elected by the crew and most key decisions were put to a vote but Roberts was becoming more and more like a captain of the Royal Navy, imposing discipline rather than keeping the democratic approach that drew so many to the pirate way of life. The lure of freedom and liberty that most pirates enjoyed was beginning to suffer as Roberts imposed his will.

Roberts knew somewhere along the coast were the two Royal Navy warships. Their crews were disciplined, trained and ready for combat. For his men to have a fighting chance against them he knew they must be trained and ready. It was a daunting task when most of the crew were almost always drunk. Training them and imposing his will was breeding discontent and was threatening his power. This was Roberts's dilemma.

However, the plots within his own crews were not the only thing he had to contend with. The natives at Old Calabar were causing him problems as well. 'They refused to have any commerce or trade with them, when they understood they were pirates.'[12] Though Johnson doesn't go into detail about the natives at Old Calabar, Sanders does. He says the natives were known as the 'Efik' and were 'an aggressive, entrepreneurial people'. These natives had been visited by pirates before. Indeed, Johnson tells us that Edward England landed in roughly the same place and so badly used the natives there, killing some and raping the women, that when Roberts arrived and the natives realized they were pirates they shunned them completely. Roberts sent men ashore to trade with the Efik but when the men came back empty-handed he was furious.

An example had to be made. Roberts ordered forty men to be fully armed and sent across to the main Efik town. By this time both his ships, *Royal Fortune* and the *Ranger*, had been careened and were both back in the water. The men gathered onto the deck of the *Royal Fortune* with pistols and cutlasses. Climbing into the boats they were lowered into the water and rowed ashore.

From bow to stern the gunports on the *Royal Fortune* opened and the cannon were run out, their crews ready to fire. As the boats drew nearer the shore, the guns fired, sending shot smashing into the wooden huts of the town. Reaching the shore, the men jumped out of their boats and shouting ran forward. The Efik, realizing what was happening, sent a force of 2,000 men to meet the advancing pirates. 'The pirates advanced within pistol shot; but finding the loss of two or three made no impression on the rest, the Negroes thought fit to retreat, which they did', Johnson wrote. Suffering heavy casualties the Efik retreated out of the town as the pirates swarmed through it, setting fire to as many buildings and structures as they could. 'This terrified the natives, and put an entire stop to all the intercourse between them; so that they could get no supplies.'[13] With the village burning, the natives hostile and his own crews hostile Roberts had no choice but to leave as soon as he could. They set sail for Cape Lopez.

On 7 January 1722, the *Swallow*'s anchor splashed into the water, the crew scurried over the deck, hauling the sails down, the ship's pinnace was lowered into the water. Ogle climbed down from the *Swallow* into the pinnace and was rowed ashore to talk with General Phipps. By this time the illness that had swept through the *Weymouth* had dissipated and those that had survived were in better shape, so much so that the *Weymouth*, along with some soldiers from the fort, had sailed to the Dutch port at Des Minas to demand restitution of some goods and men that were being illegally detained by the Dutch. While they were away, 'an express came to General Phipps, from Axim, the 9th and followed by another from Dixcove (an English factory)'.[14]

Both messages indicated that three ships had taken a galley near Axim Castle and also taken a trading ship that belonged to the Royal Africa Company. According to Johnson, Ogle decided to head for Whydah because it was more than likely that the crews of the prizes the pirates had taken would tell them that the *Swallow* was nearby and in good health. Knowing this the pirates wouldn't want to hang around so they would head for the best port in the area where they could lie low and secure their prizes. Whydah was the most likely place.

Ogle weighed anchor, leaving Cape Coast Castle and headed out to sea. But he was delayed at Accra waiting for a company ship and again at Apong, where he lost a whole day waiting on another company ship according to Johnson. Finally, the *Swallow* left Apong on 13 January and arrived at Whydah on the 17th.

Whydah was a centre for the slave trade as well as being a trading post but as the *Swallow* arrived in the harbour Ogle and his crew could see the port was still in state of chaos from an attack by Roberts only three days before. The French ships still at Whydah were now so jittery that they began to make haste to leave at the sight of the *Swallow* sending signals to each other. However, they soon discovered the Royal Navy ship was not there to attack them. The same was also true of the English and Portuguese ships still there. 'Those at anchor', Johnson wrote 'were all honest traders, who had been ransacked and ransomed.'

The governor of Whydah was Mr Baldwin, who received a letter stating that the pirates were at Jaquin further down the coast. Ogle lost no time and at 0200hrs weighed anchor and arrived at daylight on 16 January where he discovered that the pirates had been and gone. That same evening the *Swallow* arrived back at Whydah.[15]

Prior to this Roberts had been in the West Indies, successfully plundering ships and settlements there, in command of the forty-two-gun French warship he had captured two years previously. After adapting the French ship to his own tastes he launched her as the *Royal Fortune*. His consort was a captured brigantine renamed the *Good Fortune*.

Commanded by Captain Anstis the crew of the *Good Fortune* voted one night to break with Roberts's command and go plundering on their own. They had had an extremely successful season of piracy and there was no reason why that wouldn't continue with or without Roberts so they simply slipped away from the *Royal Fortune*.

Roberts shrugged this off and continued heading for West Africa. The first place he reached was the Senegal River, which was a French colony. The French had two warships on station to protect the colony and patrol the nearby coast. They decided to challenge the pirates and headed for Roberts.

Roberts watched the French vessels close on the *Royal Fortune* and then ordered his guns to be run out. One by one, along both sides of the ship, the gun doors were opened, the cannon pushed out ready to fire. He then ordered the black flag to be hoisted. By this time the French vessels were too close to break away without having to fight. Seeing the massive ship with its guns out must have sent terror into the hearts of the French, for they immediately surrendered without firing a shot.

Roberts took both French ships as his own. Transferring some of his most trusted men onto the two new prizes, he sailed with his little fleet down the coast to Sierra Leone in June 1721 where he adapted the two French prizes to serve his own purposes. The larger of the two ships, had sixteen guns and Roberts renamed it the *Ranger*, while the smaller vessel with only ten guns he called the *Little Ranger* and turned it into a store ship for the rest of his fleet.[16]

In June 1721, the *Royal Fortune*'s anchor splashed into the waters of the Sierra Leone River as Roberts ordered the sails lowered and stowed. He had the ships careened and refitted and traded with the trading post on the banks of the river. He learnt that HMS *Swallow* and HMS *Weymouth* had been there the month before but had set sail on their patrol of the coast and wouldn't be due back until the end of the year.

This gave him the perfect opportunity for continuing his plundering unmolested by the Royal Navy ships who were many miles away in the south. With his ships ready for sail, Roberts weighed anchor, unfurled his sails and slipped his moorings, heading out to sea. The little pirate fleet then headed down the coast plundering everything in their path. When they arrived at Sestos Roberts saw a frigate sitting in the harbour, its captain and most of the crew ashore, and he captured it. This ship was the *Onslow* and was the property of the Royal Africa Company. It was much better than his own *Royal Fortune* so he took it as his own and renamed it the *Royal Fortune*.

They continued their cruise down the coast and on 12 January 1722 Roberts sailed into the harbour at Whydah. From this point onwards he would be known as one of the most vicious pirates that ever sailed the seas. As they approached the harbour Roberts ordered his gunports opened, the guns run out and his gun crews ready to fire. The black flag was raised. More than eleven ships rode their anchors in the harbour. You could imagine him grinning from ear to ear at the sight of such a haul. The ships were English, French and Portuguese. Each of the French ships had thirty guns and more than 100 men – had they been ready to fight they should have been more than a match for Roberts. However, they didn't fight, instead they surrendered. Johnson states that this quick surrender was because most of the commanders and men were ashore, 'according to the custom of the place, to receive the cargoes, and return the slaves, they being obliged to watch the seasons for it, which otherwise, in so dangerous a sea as here, would be impracticable'.

Roberts lowered his boats into the water and watched them row ashore, sending the first of many messages demanding the ransom of each of the ships. With most of the commanders onshore there was nothing they could do to fight the pirates. The boats from Roberts's ship rowed back and forth with offers and counter-offers. Each time the men had to run the gauntlet of the waves crashing on the shore, rowing like mad to beat the surf and the heavy currents. They must have been exhausted. In the end the ransom for each ship was eight pounds of gold dust per ship, which Sanders tells us was worth around £5,600.[17] Some of the captains asked Roberts for a receipt which he was happy to provide. Johnson actually copied the contents of the receipt in his account of the pirate.

This is to certify whom it may or doth concern, that we GENTLEMEN OF FORTUNE, have received eight Pounds of Gold Dust, for the Ransom of the Hardey, Captain Dittwitt Commander, so that we Discharge the said Ship. Witness our Hands, this 13th of Jan 1722 – Batt. Roberts, Harry Glasby.

Every ship provided the requested ransom except for one.

The commander who didn't was Captain Fletcher, commanding the *Porcupine*, an English slave ship. Why he didn't decide to follow suit with all the others and ransom his ship is anyone's guess but Johnson states that, when he was sent for while he was ashore and given the demand, Fletcher 'excused it as having no orders from the owners'. While this may be the official line Johnson himself felt that Fletcher refused because he just didn't want to deal with thieves, and that he thought Fletcher felt the ship wasn't worth the ransom being demanded. Either way, Fletcher refused Roberts's demands.

Furious, the pirate decided to set an example and burn the *Porcupine*. But he was in a hurry. During the lengthy ransom negotiations a letter had been intercepted which was sent by General Phipps of Cape Coast Castle to the local agent of the Royal Africa Company (Mr Baldwin). The letter had two messages, one was to alert Baldwin to the pirates' presence on the coast, saying that they had been seen windward of Cape Three Points, and the other was that the *Swallow* was pursuing them to Whydah.

In light of this news Roberts decided to gather his crew together and persuaded them that they had to move quickly 'for, says he, such brave fellows cannot be supposed to be frightened at this news'. Most of the men were drunk and after hearing Roberts read out the letter some wanted to stand and fight while others postured and complained, but when the vote was taken the majority of the crew were for leaving as soon as possible. Once again, the boat pushed away from the *Royal Fortune*, not with messages this time but loaded with men, barrels of tar and all the materials they would need to set fire to the *Porcupine*. Johnson states that Roberts intention was to transport 'the Negroes, in order to set her on fire; but being in haste, and finding that unshackling them cost much time and labour they actually set her on fire with eighty of the poor wretches on board, chained two and two together'.[18] The man in charge of this expedition was John Walden, a cruel and quick-tempered man who had been forcibly taken from a merchant ship on which he was serving off Newfoundland in the summer of 1721. Roberts had given him orders to take off the remaining crew and the slaves.

In the steaming heat of the West African coast, Walden and his team rowed as quickly as they could across to the *Porcupine* and boarded it, sweat pouring from each man from the humidity. Hatchets smashed into the tops of the wooden barrels and the men kicked them over onto the deck, the tar pouring out. As the men spread the tar over the deck, Walden sent the mate of the *Porcupine* below decks with the keys to unlock the slaves. But Sanders tells us the man was nervous. 'The pirates became impatient and beat him, but this only slowed him further.'

Time dragged on while the mate fumbled with the lock. He received a cuff across the head for being so slow. His fingers shook from fright and nerves. Walden knew that Roberts was desperate to get away. He shouted at the mate, threatening to kill him if he didn't unlock the chains. But the mate couldn't get the key into the lock or make it work. Another cuff and the mate dropped the keys. He was kicked and told to pick them up.

Walden shouted at the man again but it was no use. Every minute they wasted the *Swallow* was getting closer. Walden knew it. He could wait no longer. Walden ordered everyone on deck. The tar was lit and the pirates all climbed over the side into the boat with Walden coming last. They quickly rowed away as flames licked over the tar, setting the wooden deck on fire, and the *Porcupine* began to burn.[19] Below decks the eighty slaves were still chained together, shouting, screaming and crying as they heard the crackling of the flames above them grow stronger. Captain Ogle later wrote to the Admiralty about the incident that the slaves had the choice of 'perishing by fire or water: those who jumped over-board were seized by sharks, a voracious fish in plenty in the Road, and in their sight, torn limb from limb alive'.[20]

The screams and cries of the slaves echoed across the water as the *Porcupine* burnt. The pirates rowing away from the doomed ship must have been haunted by the screams of those unfortunate people caught in the inferno. Some could be seen jumping into the water, still chained together, only to be torn apart by the sharks. There was nothing any of the people watching from the shore or from the other ships in the harbour could do. We can only imagine the horror that the people witnessing this atrocity must have felt. Even in those days when slaves were looked upon as commodities and not as people this atrocity must have melted the coldest heart.

What did Roberts think of it? Sanders states that 'it was in his bones to view Africans first and foremost as commodities rather than human beings. The atrocity was against his orders. But there is no record of Walden or anyone else being disciplined for their actions.'[21] This makes sense, as Roberts had spent many years serving aboard slave ships. Every one of the slaves died. Men, women and children perished by fire or sharks. Perhaps Roberts instilled the need for haste into his men when he ordered the

Porcupine burnt – to show everyone that he was in control. The fact that he read out the intercepted note before he sent his men to burn the ship explains their haste.

While the *Porcupine* burnt some of the men from the *Ranger* were plundering one of the French vessels, a ship of twenty guns. Bigger than the *Ranger* it was a sleeker ship and the pirates ransacking it decided to take it for themselves – despite the fact that Roberts had already received a ransom for the ship from its captain.

Under the cover of darkness, on 13 January 1722, just two days after arriving, the order to leave rippled quickly through the little pirate fleet. The *Royal Fortune*'s anchor was hauled out of the water, its sails unfurled and she caught the wind, moving out of the harbour in company with the *Ranger* and the French twenty-gun prize. Behind them the *Porcupine* continued to burn.[22]

Twenty-four hours later, Captain Ogle arrived in the *Swallow*, sailing into a scene of chaos and desolation. Ogle and his men were appalled by Roberts's actions and more than ever they were determined to get him. The question was: where would he go? 'I judged they must go to some place in the Bight to clean and fit the French ship before they would think of cruising again, which occasioned me to steer away into the Bight and look into those places which I knew had depth of water sufficient.'[23]

The Bight of Benin was south and so Ogle ordered a southward heading with as much sail as they could muster so they could grab every bit of wind. The pirates could have been anywhere. Johnson suggests that there were some obvious places they could have gone: Calabar, Princes, the River Gabone, Cape Lopez and Annabona. The navy warships touched at each of these places until, three weeks later on 5 February 1722, Ogle spotted three pirate ships anchored in the lee of Cape Lopez. One ship, the largest of the three, was flying the king's colours and pendant and Johnson states that the crew of the *Swallow* thought it was Roberts.

Ogle ordered the helmsman to steer a course for the anchorage. But the course was slow in the face of an easterly gale that was steadily getting worse. The lowering skies signalled an approaching storm. The wind was picking up, the currents getting stronger and to make matters worse there was a sandbar between the *Swallow* and the pirates. Ogle was forced to bear away to the northeast as they were 'unexpectedly deep in the bay, and was obliged to steer off, for avoiding a sand called the French Man's Bank'.[24]

The approach of the ship caught the attention of the pirates who judged the *Swallow* to be a merchantman obviously alarmed by the presence of the pirates, which was why it tacked away. Ogle had arrived at just the right time. Roberts and his men were refitting the French prize which was renamed the *Ranger*. The old *Ranger* still lay riding its anchor alongside the *Royal Fortune* while the newly named *Ranger*, or *French Ranger* as Johnson calls it, was being careened. The *Royal Fortune* had already been careened so Roberts now waited for the new ship to be ready to sail.

When it was ready, shortly after the *Swallow* arrived, Roberts ordered 'the *French Ranger*, which was then on the heel to chase out in all haste, bending several of their sails in the pursuit'.[25] The combined firepower Roberts now had at his disposal would have caused severe problems for Ogle if the two ships attacked him together. The new *Ranger* had been loaded with thirty-two guns, bringing the total number of cannon to seventy for Roberts. He also had more than 252 men between the two crews. Against this impressive total were the fifty guns and 250 men on the *Swallow*. 'He was facing the most powerful, experienced pirate crew in the Atlantic and the outcome was by no means certain.'[26]

According to Johnson, the pirates believed the *Swallow* to be a Portuguese merchantman loaded with sugar. He suggests that sugar was needed for the punch which the pirates were running out of and this ship would provide them with the opportunity to replenish their stocks. Indeed, Sanders states this is the reason why Roberts gave this prospective prize to the crew of the *French Ranger*.

Before this, while the ship was being careened, he sent twenty of his best and most loyal men across to it, including John Walden and William Main his boatswain. Roberts wanted to be sure that, once the new *Ranger* had taken the prize, they didn't just desert him.

The *French Ranger*, now righted in the water, under command of Captain James Skyrm with the additional men onboard, headed quickly out to sea to pursue the *Swallow*. Black clouds filled the sky, blotting out the sun as the storm approached. High winds filled their sails and in the distance they could hear peels of thunder getting louder and louder. Excitement shot through the pirates as they gained on the *Swallow*, many brandishing their cutlasses on deck and 'swearing every minute at the wind or the sails to expedite so sweet a chase'.

The canny Captain Ogle realized that the pirates had not recognized his ship for what it was and decided to keep the ruse going, so he ordered his men to slow the *Swallow* down, allowing the pirates time to catch up. 'He maintained the same course but spilled the wind from his sails by bracing the yards, leading the mainsheets aft and bringing the tacks of the mainsail and foresail on board.'[27]

The pirates gained quickly. The *Swallow* 'humoured the deceit and kept off to sea, as if she had been really afraid', Johnson writes. 'Under the direction of Lieutenant Sun, an experienced officer, as to let the Ranger come up with her, when they thought they had got so far as not to have their guns heard by her consort at the Cape.'

By 1000hrs the pirate ship was close and Skyrm ordered the forward chase guns to open fire. Ogle could see that the *Ranger* was flying an English ensign, a Dutch pennant and the black pirate flag. Within an hour the *Ranger* had cut the distance between the two ships. As the *Ranger* drew closer, Ogle watched his prey and waited. Finally at 1100hrs Ogle swung the *Swallow* right into the path of the pirate ship. As Lieutenant Sun barked out orders the lower gunports were quickly opened, the guns pushed out and the gun crews made ready as the powder monkeys ran the gun deck, providing ammunition and charges for the cannon.

'Fire!', yelled Lieutenant Sun just as the *Swallow* cut across the *Ranger*'s bow. The cannons roared one after the other, raking the *Ranger*'s decks. Shards of metal screamed through the air, ripping into men's flesh. Limbs were blown off by the shot while flying splinters of wood cut the men down where they stood. Above the roar of the cannon came a sudden clap of the thunder and flash of lightning. Captain Skyrm ordered a new course that would get his ship alongside the *Swallow*. But the steering of the pirates was very erratic. Like a well-oiled machine the crew of the *Swallow* moved quickly over the deck preparing for the next broadside, while Ogle ordered several course corrections to get his warship in range of the pirates. He ordered full sail and several minutes later the *Swallow*'s gun crews were able to fire again.

Cannon after cannon roared as the *Swallow* swept past the *Ranger* plastering it with cannon fire and musket shot. Splinters of wood, shards of hot shrapnel from canisters filled with bits of metal, tore through the air ripping into the men on the open deck of the pirate ship. A cannon ball smashed into the topmast, sending it crashing down to the deck. The deck was awash with blood and the men slipped and slid as they tried to fight back. Confusion reigned. Skyrm screamed as a shot tore his leg off and sent him crashing to the deck. Undaunted, he managed to get up and continued to shout at his men to fight while hopping around on his good leg. Another cannon ball tore the leg off John Walden.

The battle lasted for only an hour but it was no real contest and by 1500hrs that afternoon the pirates struck their colours and surrendered. They had had ten men killed outright, and twenty wounded, 'without the loss or hurt of one of the King's men', Johnson wrote. The swell of the sea had increased and the wind was getting up. Ogle now needed to secure the *French Ranger* as quickly as he could before the sea was too rough to take the prize, so he ordered the *Swallow*'s pinnace to be sent across to secure the pirate ship and crew. John Atkins, the surgeon onboard the *Swallow*, was in the boat as it was rowed across to the *French Ranger*.

Half a dozen of the most desperate and hardened pirates on the *French Ranger* decided to blow up the ship rather than be captured. Johnson states that the men gathered round the 'last of the powder they had left in steerage, and fired a pistol into it, but it was too small a quantity to effect any thing more than burning them in a frightful manner'.

As Atkins climbed aboard he saw a scene of carnage. Debris from the topmast lay strewn across the deck, mixed with the blood of the dead and wounded, powder, splinters of wood, rigging, sails and spent shot. The topmast had brought some of the rigging down with it, adding to the confusion and destruction.

With the storm almost upon them the men of the *Swallow* quickly set about securing the pirates and starting repairs to the pirate ship while Atkins tried to dress the wounded. Skyrm, though his leg was shot off, 'would not suffer himself to be dressed or carried off the deck'.[28]

William Main and Robert Ball had been horribly disfigured by the blast of powder. As Atkins looked at the two men he spied a silver boatswain's whistle hanging from Main's belt so he turned to him and said, 'I presume you are the Boatswain of this ship?' 'Then you presume wrong,' Main answered. 'I am the Boatswain of the *Royal Fortune*, Captain Roberts commander.' 'Then Mr Boatswain,' Atkins replied. 'You will be hanged I believe.' 'That is as your Honour pleases,' said Main. He then told Atkins that there were 120 men on the *Royal Fortune* like him, 'as clever fellows as ever trod shoe leather: would I were with them!'

Turning away from Main, Atkins approached Roger Ball who he could tell from his horrific burns had been close to the explosion. Ball was sitting in a corner, conscious, 'with a look as sullen as winter, bearing his pain without the least complaint'. Atkins asked him what happened, how he managed to be so badly burnt. Ball replied that another one of the hardened pirates, John Morris, had fired his pistol into the powder, 'and if he had not done it I would'. 'I'm a surgeon,' Atkins said. 'I can dress your wounds if you desire it.' 'If anything is applied to me I'll tear it off,' Ball swore. However, after some time Atkins did manage to dress Ball's wounds. During the night he fell into delirium and started raving about how brave Roberts was, 'saying he should shortly be released, as soon as they should meet him'. As his delirium worsened Ogle's men strapped him to the forecastle, with Ball resisting with all his strength, despite his injuries. He died the next day.[29] On board were more than a hundred men, according to Sanders, including twenty-three slaves and sixteen Frenchmen who had been taken when their ship had been seized at Whydah and who had been held prisoner ever since.

Though Ogle had taken the *French Ranger* his biggest prize was still back at Cape Lopez. The weather was getting worse and a decision on what to do with the *Ranger* had to be made quickly. 'They once thought of setting her on fire, but this would have given them the trouble of taking the pirates wounded men on board themselves.' Johnson tells us that Ogle was sure that the *Royal Fortune* wouldn't leave without the *French Ranger* so 'they lay by her two days, repaired her rigging and other damage, and sent her into Princes, with the French men and four of their own hand'. Sanders tells us that Ogle decided to keep the wounded men and the Frenchmen on the *French Ranger*, along with a handful of his own men, while shackling the remaining pirates below decks on the *Swallow*.

The tropical storm hit in the early hours of 7 February 1722 the ink-black sky pierced with flashes of lightning followed by peels of deafening thunder. The two ships rode the heavy seas as the wind sent needles of rain slashing across their decks. On the *French Ranger*, the men worked feverishly to finish the repairs until Ogle was satisfied she was ready to leave the *Swallow* and head for the shelter of Princes Island.[30]

As Ogle watched the *French Ranger* go he turned back to his officers and ordered a new heading, back to Cape Lopez to get Roberts. On the evening of 9 February the *Swallow* arrived just outside the approach to the harbour and the crew of the navy warship could see ships at anchor. Throughout the ship the crew made ready for the final fight with the pirates but again the weather was closing in on them and the dusk was fast approaching. Torrential rain swept across the decks while the sky cracked with thunder and lightning, so Ogle decided to wait until dawn to attack. He bore away to windward, fighting the gales and driving rain. Fortunately, the pirates hadn't seen his approach.

The following morning the weather eased and Ogle brought the *Swallow* back to Cape Lopez and this time they could see three ships riding their anchors, Roberts's *Royal Fortune*, the abandoned old *Ranger* and a third ship, a small merchantman called the *Neptune*[31] commanded by Captain Hill and said by Ogle to be owned by the Royal Africa Company.[32] Ogle was pleased because he rightly thought that this ship meant the pirates had captured another prize and so would be celebrating 'for they did not doubt but the temptation of liquor and plunder they might find in their new prize, would make the pirates so confused'.[33]

Sanders suggests that Hill's presence was not as a prize but as a friend or business partner. The *Neptune* was the ship onto which Roberts had loaded the crew of the *Wheydah* sloop when they were leaving the port of Whydah. Roberts and his men had not robbed the *Neptune* there so 'it's likely they may have reached an arrangement. Hill may have been bringing them supplies.'[34] Indeed, according to David Cordingly, Captain Hill played no part in the battle but he and his men 'took the opportunity to plunder the cargo of the *Little Ranger* while the *Royal Fortune* was at sea'.[35]

So, although this wasn't a prize, the pirates had still been celebrating, according to Johnson. Roberts himself paid no attention to the reports from the crew of the arrival of this ship. 'Roberts' crew discerning their masts over the land went down into the cabin to acquaint him of it, he being then at breakfast with his new guest, Captain Hill.' Roberts took no notice of this report and most of his men didn't either, while some suggested the approaching vessel might be a Portuguese ship or a French slave ship. But, as Johnson tells us, 'the major part swore it was the *French Ranger* returning, and were merrily debating for some time on the manner of reception, whether they should salute or not'.

To increase their confusion, Ogle had ordered the French ensign to be hoisted as he approached the anchorage. But on the *Royal Fortune* one seaman, David Armstrong, a deserter from the *Swallow*, wasn't confused. He knew exactly what the ship was that was approaching them. Six months previously he'd been picked up by the pirates at Axim and though he tried to warn his fellow pirates they still had their doubts, 'but as the *Swallow* approached nearer, things appeared plainer, and though they were stigmatised with the name of cowards, who showed any apprehension of danger, yet some of them, now undeceived declared it to Roberts'.

Filled with fear, Armstrong went below decks, barging in on Roberts who was still at breakfast and garbled out the news. Instead of immediately ordering all sail to try and get away, Roberts's reaction was to brand him and all the rest of the pirates who were 'undeceived' as cowards, saying they were afraid to fight.

Cursing, Roberts left Hill at breakfast and went up on deck to have a look. Through the telescope he could see the ship and the French colours. But suddenly he saw the gun ports raised, the cannon run out and the King's colours hoisted. Now his reaction was entirely different. 'Being perfectly convinced, he slipped his cable, got under sail, and ordered his men to arms, without any show of timidity, dropping a first rate oath that it was a bite, but, at the same time, resolved like a gallant rogue, to get clear or die.'

Perhaps at this moment, Roberts knew his luck had run out and that he was going to die or in order to rally his frightened and drunken men he decided to make a stand, a show of resistance. He went back below decks and 'put on a crimson waistcoat and breeches, a hat with a red feather, slung a pair of pistols on a silk sling over this shoulder and issued orders with a bold unconcern'.[36]

Anxiously watching the *Swallow*, Armstrong told Roberts that the naval ship sailed 'best upon a wind and therefore, if they designed to leave her, they should go before it'. This meant that the *Swallow* sailed best with the wind coming in from the side. If Roberts could get the wind directly behind him he might be able to outrun the warship. But time was running out and his options were limited. He settled on a bold move, to head directly towards the *Swallow*. At the moment, the wind was from the south and the *Swallow* was sailing in the face of it. If Roberts headed directly for the *Swallow* he would have the wind behind him. He could then exchange broadsides and if not too badly damaged head quickly out to sea and outrun Ogle. If, however, the exchange of broadsides caused massive damage he would ground the *Royal Fortune* and 'everyone to shift for himself among the Negroes'. If he couldn't do that then his last desperate gamble would be to come alongside the *Swallow* and blow up both ships.

The skies were heavy with dark clouds and rain continued to pour down, lashing the decks. By 1030hrs that morning, the *Royal Fortune* had slipped her anchor, raised her sails and was heading directly for the *Swallow*. Roberts was desperate, most of his men were drunk, 'passively courageous, unfit for service', according to Johnson. He knew they would not be able to match the skill of the naval gunners but he hoped they could get past the first broadside.

As the ships drew near each other, buffeted by the force of the gale, Ogle made ready, barking out his orders. The gun crews worked quickly and effortlessly. As the *Royal Fortune* came along side and opened fire, Ogle ordered his own gunners to fire. The naval gunnery was accurate, devastating and shot off the mizzen topmast of the *Royal Fortune*, that came crashing down onto the deck, tearing and snagging the rigging and sails.

Rain hammered the decks of the ships and over the crash of the cannon thunder roared 'like the rattling of 10,000 small arms three within three yards of our heads'. As the wind shifted and changed direction with the storm's growing intensity, a bolt of lightning split the top of the *Swallow*'s main mast. Though the *Royal Fortune* was faster than the *Swallow*, Roberts was unable to get away. 'Had he taken Armstrong's advice to have gone before the wind, he had probably escaped; but keeping his tracks down, either by the wind shifting or ill steerage or both, he was taken aback by his sails.'

The *Royal Fortune*, now in front of the *Swallow*, headed out to sea, but onboard the night of revelry was taking its toll and their steering was erratic. The sea boiled and frothed around them as the storm grew stronger. Ogle's crew had training and discipline on their side and it wasn't long before the *Swallow* was gaining: 'The pirate sailing better than us, shot ahead above half gun shot, while we continued firing (without intermission) such guns as we could bring to bear.'[37]

Catching the wind, the *Swallow* came up again to the *Royal Fortune*, delivering another devastating broadside. On the deck of the *Royal Fortune*, splinters, shards of hot metal and shot flew all around them, tearing into the sails and rigging and ripping into the men. The wooden hull crashed and splintered as cannon balls smashed into her. On the decks the pirates had to contend with driving rain under the accurate fire from the *Swallow*'s guns, the soaked and slippery deck splashed with blood.

Roberts, resplendent in his crimson waistcoat, boldly barked out orders to his men, showing no fear as he moved among them, desperately trying to keep their morale up. But suddenly the orders stopped coming. Roberts spun around, hit by grapeshot, clutching his throat which had been ripped away and fell across the blocks and tackle of one of his guns. 'One Stephenson, from the helm, observing ran to his assistance and not perceiving him wounded, swore at him, and bid him stand up, and fight like a man.' But when Stephenson discovered his mistake and that his revered leader was dead, 'he gushed into tears, and wished the next shot would be his lot'.[38]

Cannon balls from the *Swallow* plastered the deck of the *Royal Fortune*, tearing into the rigging, sails and masts, until around 1330 hrs the main mast came down, smashing across the deck. For another half an hour the pirates tried to fight on but their leader was dead and the men had no stomach for more bloodshed so at 1400hrs they surrendered.

Johnson states that the *Royal Fortune* had forty guns and 175 men, forty-five of whom were black, and that despite the ferocity of the battle only three men were killed and several wounded, but the *Swallow* came away from the fight without a single casualty. The great pirate Roberts was dead. One of the greatest menaces the high seas had ever seen was gone. Between July 1719 and his death in February 1722 Roberts had taken more than 400 prizes, more than any other pirate. He'd travelled an astounding 35,000 miles and commanded one of the largest pirate crews far longer than any other pirate captain ever did, including Blackbeard.[39] 'When Roberts was gone, as though he had been the life and soul of the gang, their spirits sunk; many deserted their quarters, and all stupidly neglected any means for defence, or escape; and their main mast soon after being shot by the board, they had no way left, but to surrender and call for quarters.'[40]

Remembering the explosion that took place on the *Ranger*, Ogle decided to keep the *Swallow* some distance from the damaged *Royal Fortune* in case any of the more hardened pirates decided to try to blow her up. In fact, on the pirate ship James Phillips went down to the powder room with a lighted match to do just that. He confronted a sentry, Stephen Thomas, put there by Henry Glasby, the sailing master and a man who had been forcibly taken from his ship into piracy. A fight broke out between Thomas and Phillips as they struggled for the match until Glasby arrived and subdued Phillips.[41] 'Some of the desperados showed a willingness that way, matches being lighted, and scuffles happening between those who would, and those who opposed it', Johnson wrote.

In the bow of the *Swallow*'s boat Lieutenant Isaac Sun looked at the *Royal Fortune* as the men rowed towards the stricken ship. He too remembered the incident with the *Ranger* and must have wondered how long it would be before another explosion rippled across the water. He had no idea how close it had been but as he climbed aboard the *Royal Fortune* he was met by Glasby, who helped him quickly secure the pirate vessel.

Sun and his men found more than £2,000 of gold dust stashed away in the *Royal Fortune*. One of the key things that would prove Ogle had indeed beaten the famous pirate, Roberts, would be to have his flag. 'The flag could not be got easily from under the fallen mast, and was therefore recovered by the *Swallow*.' The flag had a figure of a skeleton on it with a man brandishing a flaming sword, which, Johnson states, was to illustrate the defiance of death itself.

By 1900hrs the prisoners from the *Royal Fortune* were chained and shackled below decks on the *Swallow*, alongside their colleagues from the *Ranger*. Ogle then ordered all sail be made back to Cape Lopez where the abandoned *Little Ranger* still rode her anchor. Perhaps he also wanted to have a word with Captain Hill. However, when they arrived the *Neptune* had gone and so had just about everything on the *Little Ranger*. She had been plundered of '2,000 pounds of gold dust (the shares of those pirates who belonged to her) and Captain Hill in the *Neptune*, not unjustly suspected, for he would not wait the man-of-war's returning into the Bay once again, but sailed away immediately, making no scruples afterwards to own the seizure of other goods out of her'.

While a series of thunderstorms, tropical storms, and tornadoes ripped through the island over the next few days, Ogle and his crew repaired and careened the *Swallow*, collected wood, water and food and carried out extensive repairs on the *Royal Fortune*. Finally, on 18 February, the weather eased enough for the *Swallow* to set sail in company with the *Royal Fortune* and the *Little Ranger*. The first port of call was the Isle of Princes where the French *Ranger* was anchored. Then all four ships headed back up the coast to Cape Coast Castle.

On 16 March 1722 the lookout on the castle wall spotted sails on the horizon. Arriving in the bay below the castle the *Swallow*'s anchor splashed into the water and the castle batteries fired off a twenty-one-gun salute. The following day the pirates were transferred from the various ships of the little fleet to the castle where they were locked up in the dungeons to stand trial.[42] Indeed, Johnson tells us the pirate prisoners, once they were locked up in the castle, were ready to take any opportunity to escape, 'for they were very uneasy under restraint, having been lately all commanders themselves; nor could they brook the diet, or quarters, without cursing and swearing, and upbraiding each other, with the folly that had brought them to it'. The authorities, according to Johnson, were so concerned about the pirates escaping that they were manacled and shackled together, and the prison strongly barricaded, while a heavily armed officer stood guard night and day.

The determined action by Ogle earned him a knighthood but sadly the *Royal Fortune* and the *Little Ranger* were destroyed when they were smashed to pieces on the rocks under Saltpan Hill in Jamaica. Ogle had taken both ships with him to the West Indies and was caught in a hurricane just as they arrived. They couldn't save the two prizes as they only just managed to keep the *Swallow* afloat by cutting away the mast to prevent her from heeling over and by laying as many additional anchors as they could.

The numbers of pirates captured differs depending on the source. Sanders tells us that Ogle captured 166 white pirates, with 147 standing trial.[43] Cordingly states that the Ogle's operations meant that 268 men were rounded up altogether. Of these 77 were 'black Africans, and 187 were white men, which included a number of seamen and passengers recently captured by Roberts during his raids along the African coast'. Ogle, Cordingly tells us, took all these men to Cape Coast Castle where all the white men were put on trial. Of these fifty-two were hanged and another seventeen sent to England to serve prison sentences in the Admiralty's Marshalsea prison. All but five of the white men were British.

Chapter 5

Trial and Execution

Roberts was dead and his men from the *Royal Fortune* and the *Ranger* were now captives held at the fortress at Cape Coast Castle. All that remained was for them to be tried and sentenced. No matter where they were in the world, courts would be convened which had their authority under the Seal of the Admiralty. This was how the Royal Navy dealt with pirates: through direct operational engagement and through an Admiralty Court set up to mete out justice, to try, convict, sentence and execute the pirates who had been taken prisoner by the navy.

In the case of the Roberts pirates a court was convened. We know this because of the detail that Captain Charles Johnson records in his account of Roberts. Johnson stated that most of the pirates would say that they were forced into committing the acts of piracy for which they were tried. 'It may be concluded that the pretended constraint of Roberts on them was very often a complotment between parties equally willing; and this Roberts several times openly declared, particularly to the *Onslow*'s people, who he called aft, and asked of them who was willing to go, for he would force nobody.'

The date of the trial of these pirates was 28 March 1722 and it was probably the largest trial of pirates set up by any Admiralty Court anywhere. In all, Ogle had captured 166 pirates and some had died on the long voyage back to Cape Coast Castle in the sweltering, festering crowded hold of HMS *Swallow* where most of the pirates had been chained up. In the end, 147 pirates were tried by the court.

There was no jury at this court. That privilege had been taken away from captured pirates when the Act for the Most Successful Suppression of Piracy was passed in 1700. The reason for this Act was because juries in the far-flung colonies and settlements were often reluctant to convict pirates. In place of the jury was a panel of seven men, officers and officials who would try the pirates. In this case, the panel was made up of

Lt Barnsley and Lt Fanshaw from HMS *Weymouth*, the secretary for the Royal African Company at Cape Coast Castle Mr Edward Hyde, the merchants Francis Boye and Hendry Dodson and finally General Phipps Governor of Cape Coast Castle. Captain Herdman commanding HMS *Weymouth* was appointed President of the court while Captain Ogle, the hero of the hour, was the prosecutor.[1]

Because they were so far away from the types of courts that would have been in operation in London, Johnson tells us that the circumstances under which the pirates were tried was 'exempted from lawyers and law books, so that the office of register, of necessity, fell on one not versed in those affairs, which might justify the court in want of form supplied with integrity and impartiality'.

However, the lack of lawyers and law books made the proceedings difficult. Since most of the acts of piracy had been committed on or against Royal African Company ships the pirates couldn't be tried for those acts alone by the panel because, with the exception of the officers, the panel were made up of company men who were 'interested parties'. It was then decided to try them all for their actions against HMS *Swallow* but that would have meant that almost all of them would have been guilty. According to Johnson the way the court got around this was by bottoming everything out on the *Swallow*'s depositions, 'which were clear and plain and had the circumstance of time when, place where, manner how and the like', and then by looking at the career of the pirates. This way they could see if the men had been forced into piracy or had done the acts voluntarily.

They decided to base their criteria of piracy on three things: 'first being a volunteer amongst them at the beginning, secondly, being a volunteer at the taking or robbing of any ship; or lastly, voluntarily accepting a share in the booty of those that did'.[2]

The proceedings for the trial were taken down in meticulous detail by John Atkins who had been appointed as court reporter. Atkins's detail is impressive and his notes on the trial fill 180 pages. Among other things, this record shows the day to day life of Roberts and his men. It also shows just how prolific this pirate crew really was, taking more than 400 ships and having to fight for only two of them.[3]

Atkins's record provides brief biographies of the pirates, how the crew was organized, what the rank structure was, which pirates took their turns aboard the prizes they'd captured, how the plunder was divided up, what the process of decision-making was, how the chain of command worked regarding meting out punishment and rewards, and what the pirates did in their spare time. When it came to killing people, other than the casualties of battle, they did not wantonly kill people that they had captured as more ruthless pirates did: the one exception was the slaughter of the slaves at Whydah where they set fire to the ship with the slaves still chained together in the hold. But the court wasn't interested in this act. For the men of the court that slaughter was just another attack on property, it was not murder. The charges against the pirates were 'treason, robbery and being the common enemies of mankind', and not murder. It is highly likely that Johnson used Atkins's notes to write his account of Roberts and the detailed trial proceedings.[4]

The morning of the trial a breeze blew in off the sea but despite this the stifling oppressive heat in the main hall left everyone drenched in sweat as the court convened. Through the high open windows the waves could be heard crashing against the rocks below as the charge was read out against the first batch of prisoners. The trial would take weeks to go through all the men and they began first with the most obviously guilty and the most obviously innocent.

According to Johnson the trial began with the prisoners divided by the ship on which they were taken, either from the *Ranger* or from the *Royal Fortune*. So on 28 March the prisoners from the *Ranger* appeared before the court: some seventy men. They all pleaded not guilty to the charges of sinking, burning and robbing of company ships and for attacking the *Swallow*.

Three officers of the *Swallow* were then called by the court to give evidence, Lt Isaac Sun, Ralph Baldrick boatswain and Daniel McLaughlin the mate, who gave a brief account of how the pirates 'attacked and fought the King's ship'. The court then asked the prisoners how they came to be onboard the *Ranger*, 'and their reason for so audacious a resistance as has been made against the King's ship'.

The response was that they had all been taken out of the *Ranger*, that they had all signed the pirate articles and that most of them had shared in the plunder except for those who had only been there a short time. However, they declared that 'that neither the signing, nor sharing, nor in the resistance had been made against His Majesty's ship, had they been volunteers'.

As the court went from man to man the answer was the same, they were all forced into piracy and had acted on terror of death, 'which law amongst them was to be the portion of those who refused'. 'Who made these laws?' the President asked. 'How did the guns come to be fired?' came another question from the court. 'Why didn't you desert your station and mutiny when so fair a prospect of redemption offered?' The men replied as they had before that they had been forced into acting as they had.

There was no doubt that the men had put up a fight against the *Swallow*: that was already proven from the evidence of the ship's officers. This left the crucial question of whether the men had taken part in the plundering of ships voluntarily if they were to be indicted and convicted. Johnson tells us the court decided that, because many of the men had been forced, 'they would hear further evidence for, or against, each person singly, in relation to those parts of the indictment, which declared them volunteers, or charged them with aiding and assisting, at the burning, sinking, or robbing of other ships; for if they acted, or assisted, in any robberies or devastations, it would be a conviction they were volunteers'.

In the afternoon, the court brought the men from the *Royal Fortune* before them. The charges were similar to the charges read to the prisoners in the morning and, as with the morning group, they pleaded not guilty. Again, the same officers from the *Swallow* gave evidence of the resistance of the pirates to His Majesty's ship with each officer providing a brief account of the battle that took place.

'What have you to say in your defence?' the court asked the prisoners. The replies that came back were similar to the answers the court had from the prisoners in the morning, In this case, many of the men said that, had they not assisted in the resistance against the *Swallow*, Roberts would have shot them. The court decided again 'that further evidence should be heard against each man singly, to the two points, of being a volunteer at first; and to their particular acts of piracy and robbery'. With the bulk sessions out of the way, the long procedure of hearing the men in small groups or singly began.

On 31 March, there were bright flashes of lightning and thunder claps tore the air around Cape Coast Castle. The wind brought slashing rain and, when the thunderstorm had passed, the humidity in the air had cleared, making the proceedings of the court that day more bearable. That day the first batch of men was tried, the hardliners and the ring leaders.

The morning saw William Magnes, Thomas Oughterlauney, William Main, William Mackintosh, Valentine Ashplant, Joseph Walden, Israel Hind, Marcus Johnson, William Petty, William Fernon, Abraham Harper, William Wood, Thomas How, John Stephenson, Charles Bunce and John Griffen brought before the court. The evidence against them was given by two members of the crew of the *King Solomon*, Captain Joseph Trahern and his mate George Fenn. Between them both men gave their versions of how their ship had been taken. They were riding at anchor near Cape Appollonia in Africa and saw a boat rowing towards them filled with pirates. They thought the boat was coming from a ship that lay three miles to the leeward of them. As the boat drew near, they prepared for the attack, but the crew of the *King Solomon*, instead of preparing to repel the pirates, laid down their weapons and the pirates boarded the ship and robbed her.

'Can you charge your Memory with any Particulars in the Seizure and Robbery?' the President asked. 'Yes,' Trahern replied. 'We know that Magnes, Quarter-Master for the pirate ship, commanded the men in the boat that took us, and assumed the Authority of ordering her Provisions and Stores out.' He continued his deposition saying that Main took charge of taking the cables and rope and beat some of the crew of the *King Solomon* for not moving fast enough. Trahern stated that Petty supervised the plundering of the sails and canvas, while Harper, who was the cooper on the pirate ship, looked after the cask and tools, Griffin went after the Carpenter's stores and Oughterlauney, 'as pilot, having shifted himself with a Suit of my Clothes, a new tye Wig, and called for a bottle of wine, ordered the ship, very arrogantly to be steered under Commodore Roberts' Stern'.

More evidence was given against the pirates and in their defence each of the prisoners in their own way stated that Roberts forced them to take the ship and upbraided them for cowardice if they refused. 'So that Roberts forced ye upon this Attack?' the President said. 'Roberts commanded us into the boat, and the Quarter-Master to rob the Ship, neither of whose commands we dared refuse.' Knowing that the pirates had elected Roberts as their leader and captain and Magnes as their quarter-master the court asked the prisoners why they would vote for men who everyday forced them to do such distasteful things. There was no reply from each of the pirates and the court found them guilty.

Fifteen Englishmen and eighteen Frenchmen were then brought before the court. Most of the Englishmen had either been musicians on board the pirate ships and been held as prisoners while the others had been onboard only a few days and hadn't taken part in any capture or robbery. They, along with the French, were acquitted.

In the afternoon, Thomas Sutton, David Sympson, Christopher Moody, Phillip Bill, Richard Hardy, Henry Dennis, David Rice, William Williams, Robert Harris, George Smith, Ed Watts, Joseph Mitchell and James Barrow came before the court. Giving evidence against them was Geret de Haen, master of the *Flushingham* taken near Axim, along with Benjamin Kreft master and James Groet mate of the Dutch vessel *Gertruycht*. They said that the pirates had plundered their ships and behaved in a vile outrageous manner, 'putting them in bodily fears, sometimes for the ship, and sometimes for themselves'. The court found them all guilty.

The day ended with the first death sentences being pronounced when the court ordered that David Sympson, William Magnes, Richard Hardy, Thomas Sutton, Christopher Moody and Valentine Ashplant be brought before them again. The President looked at the six men standing in front of the panel. He and the rest of the judges had heard the evidence and had deliberated. Now all that remained in that far-flung settlement was to pronounce sentence. He looked at them for some time. Silence hung over the court. Then he said: 'The crime of piracy, of which all of ye have been justly convicted, is of all other Robberies the most aggravating and inhumane, in that being removed from the Fears of Surprize in remote and distant parts, ye do in Wantonness of Power often add Cruelty to Theft.'

After a few minutes the President ended his speech by passing sentence on the men.

Each of you, are adjudged and sentenced to be carried back to the Place from whence you came, from thence to the Place of Execution, without the Gates of the Castle, and there within the Flood-Marks, to be hanged by the neck till ye are dead. After this, ye, and each of you shall be taken down and your bodies hanged in Chains.

Three days later the six men were hung.

Over the next few days men would be tried singly and there would emerge one or two key witnesses for the prosecution in damning the pirates. One of these men was Captain Joseph Trahern, master of the *King Solomon*, and the other was Harry Glasby, sailing master aboard the *Royal Fortune* and one of the more senior of the men aboard that ship.

According to Johnson, William Phillips was brought to the court before Glasby and, in this case, Trahern was the prosecution's chief witness along with George Fenn the mate onboard the *King Solomon*. Phillips had been boatswain of the *King Solomon* so Trahern knew him well. Recounting the taking of his vessel Trahern testified that as the pirate boat drew near the men aboard the *King Solomon* could see from the number of men in the boat, the cutlasses they were brandishing, the muskets in plain sight and their shouting curses that they were pirates, 'and being hailed, answered, Defiance, at which I snatched a musket from one of the men, and fired'. Trahern turned to his men and asked if they would stand by him to defend the ship.

'What was the reaction from the pirates?' asked the court. 'They returned a volley and cried out they would give no quarter if any resistance was made.' Trahern continued by saying that Phillips 'took upon himself to call out for quarters, without my consent, and misled the rest to laying down their arms, and giving up the ship, to half the number of men, and in an open boat'.[5]

Moreover, according to Trahern, Phillips was quick to volunteer his services to the pirates and, as Johnson writes, was 'very forward and brisk in robbing the *King Solomon* of her provisions and stores'. He also was instrumental in having his captain, Trahern, badly treated by the pirates and even signed the articles of the pirates, though he claimed he did so at gunpoint. 'The whole appeared to be an untruth from other evidence, who also asserted his being armed in the action against the *Swallow*.' Shuffling their papers, Phipps and the rest of the panel consulted each other, took into account his testimony that he had been forced from honest trade and the testimony from Trahern. After some time they pronounced Phillips guilty.

Harry Glasby was next up before the court as a prisoner, before he became a witness for the prosecution. Unlike Phillips there was a string of witnesses, from fellow prisoners, who swore that Glasby was coerced and forced into doing Roberts's bidding.

All the prisoners were held in the dungeons below the castle and on 2 April, Glasby was brought up to face the court. It was Trahern who said that, although he was in a senior position, the pirates took no notice of him. Indeed, Trahern testified that Glasby told him, 'How hard a condition it was to be a chief among brutes.' Trahern also testified that Glasby showed no inclination for the pirate way of life at all.

Several witnesses testified that Glasby was a prisoner and that he had tried on many occasions to stop the actions of the pirates becoming too excessive. Joseph Wingfield, another prisoner with Glasby, said the sailing master was 'civil beyond any of them', and believed that when the brigantine that he had been serving on was voted to be burnt Glasby 'was the instrument of preventing it, expressing himself with a great deal of sorrow, for this and the like malicious rogueries of the company he was in'. 'How did the prisoner act?' asked the court. 'I believe he acted with reluctancy, as one who could not avoid what he did.'

Elizabeth Trengrove who had been a passenger on the *Onslow* with her husband and taken prisoner when Roberts took that ship, testified that when the pirates came onboard she'd heard of Glasby's good character and 'I enquired of the quartermaster, who was then on board a-robbing, whether or not I could see him? And he told me, no, they never ventured him from the ship, for he had once endeavoured his escape, and they had ever since continued jealous of him.'

More witnesses, men who had been taken from a variety of ships by Roberts's men, such as Edward Crisp, Captain Trengrove and Captain Sharp, all testified to Glasby's good character, saying the good treatment they received when they fell into the pirates' hands was largely due to Glasby. James White, a musician, testified that during the action against the *Swallow* he did not see Glasby manning the guns, or giving orders, 'either to the loading or firing of them; but that he wholly attended to the setting, or trimming of the sails, as Roberts commanded'. He believed that Glasby was the man who prevented the hard core pirates from blowing up the *Royal Fortune* when it was captured, 'by setting trusty sentinels below, and opposing himself against such hot-headed fellows as had procured lighted matches, and were going down for that purpose'.

This was corroborated by Lieutenant Isaac Sun who testified that when he came onboard the *Royal Fortune* to take possession of it after the defeat by the *Swallow*, he was told that Glasby had seized a lit torch from James Phillips who was going below to light the fuses that would blow the ships to bits. 'He had heard also, that after Roberts was killed, the prisoner ordered the colours to be struck; and had since shown, how opposite his practice and principles had been by discovering who were the greatest rogues among them.'[6]

It was then time for Glasby to stand up and talk in his own defence. He began by saying he had been taken by the pirates when he was the chief mate of the *Samuel*, commanded by Captain Cary. To get away from the pirates he hid himself on the ship but they found him 'and beat him and threw him overboard'.

Johnson's account of the trial does not note that the pirates must have fished Glasby out of the water and imprisoned him but he does state that seven days later the pirates demanded Glasby sign their articles. He refused and 'was cut and abused again'. After this he decided that a more humble behaviour might make life easier for him.

Glasby testified that the shares the pirates gave him, after he became more humble, he 'returned to such prisoners as fell in his way', Johnson wrote in his account. 'Indeed, he had made a small reservation and had desired Captain Loan to take two or three moidores from him to carry to his wife.'

He then told the court he once tried to escape from the pirates in the West Indies along with two others. 'But I was sentenced to be shot for it, by a drunken jury; the latter actually suffered and I was preserved only by one of the chief pirates taking a sudden liking to me and bullying the others.'

At Hispaniola, Glasby told the court he tried to escape again and all he had was a compass to help him find his way. The part of the island he was on was so desolate and remote that he couldn't get his bearings and was forced to return to the ship after two or three days wandering. He finished his defence by saying that Captain Cary and other prisoners of the pirates had signed affidavits that he had been forced from his employment, 'and though I cannot produce them, I humbly hope the court would think highly probable from the circumstances offered'.

After conferring with his colleagues, the President said that they had found

> many parts of the prisoner's own defence had been confirmed by the evidence, who had asserted he acted with reluctance, and had expressed a concern and trouble for the little hopes remained to him of extricating himself. That he had used all prisoners well at the hazard of ill usage to himself. That he had not in any military capacity assisted their robberies. That he had endeavoured his escape with the utmost danger.[7]

The court found Glasby not guilty and acquitted him of the charges against him. From that point on he was one of the key voices for the prosecution that sealed the fate of many pirates. 'Again and again he was called, and again and again it was his voice, above all, that decided whether a man lived or died.'[8]

Captain James Skyrm, commander of the *Ranger*, was brought before the court after Glasby. Several of the men who had been acquitted testified that during the battle with the *Swallow*, Skyrm had ordered the men to fight, 'and the guns to be loaded and fired', Johnson wrote in his account of the trial. He stated that Skyrm held a sword and threatened any man that wouldn't man his station and fight. 'Although he had lost a leg in the action, his temper was so warm as to refuse going off the deck, till he found all was lost.'[9]

According to Johnson, Skyrm said in his defence that he had been forced into piracy when the ship he was mate on, the *Greyhound*, from St Christopher had been taken by the pirates in October 1720 and that the pirates 'drubbed him and broke his head'. Skyrm went on to testify that over the months since he was captured his sense of shame had been blunted and that for many months he'd been sick and that he had been forced to go after the *Swallow* by Roberts against his will. Johnson also wrote that Skyrm testified that, although he was captain, he had no authority, 'and could not be obeyed, though he had often called to them, to leave off their fire, when he perceived it to be the King's ship'.

The court dismissed Skrym's defence outright because the evidence against him showed that in the circumstance of losing his leg, he remained on the deck until he was sure all was lost and 'was more alert on such occasion than was now willing to be thought'. The court also dismissed his claim that, even though he was captain of the *Ranger*, he was never obeyed. Instead, they believed he had the authority and will to direct the men during the engagement with the *Swallow* and the evidence from the witnesses about how he stood on deck with a sword, threatening to beat any man who refused to fight showed he was more than a captain in name only. He was found guilty by the court.[10]

As a chief prosecution witness Glasby gave favourable testimony for twenty-four of the pirates: men like Isaac Russell and George Ogle who had been forced into piracy as Glasby had. Both Russell and Ogle escaped the noose and so did many of the others that Glasby identified who had conspired to escape with him. But he pointed the finger of guilt at forty-six men in total.

One of those men was John Walden, who had lost his leg on the *Ranger* during the battle with the *Swallow*. Glasby testified that Walden was a 'brisk hand', which meant that he was a staunch pirate. Walden was one of the pirates who was willing to believe the *Swallow* was a Portuguese ship carrying sugar, 'because sugar was very much in demand'. It was Roberts who called to the *Ranger* crew and told them to right the ship and get under sail because 'there was sugar in the offing'.

The court asked Glasby if Walden and the rest of the men went on board the *Ranger* voluntarily. Glasby replied that the men 'who went from the *Fortune* on Board the *Ranger*, to assist in this Expedition, were volunteers and the trustiest men among us'. Walden was found guilty.

On 5 April, Peter Scudamore was called before the court. He had been the surgeon on board Roberts's ship the *Royal Fortune* and claimed he was a forced man. But a battery of witnesses testified differently. Both Captain Trahern and Captain Sharp testified that he'd stolen medicines and medical instruments from their ships and had argued with Roberts for some of the surgeons on the captured ships to be brought aboard the *Royal Fortune*. Glasby testified that Scudamore had signed the pirate's articles 'with a great deal of alacrity, and glorified in having been the first surgeon that had done so'. He stated that the surgeon wanted to sign the articles for the others that were to follow him and that 'he was now, he hoped, as great a rogue as any of them'.

Other witnesses from the *Royal Fortune* also on trial for their lives testified that they had seen Scudamore talking for long periods to the slaves, trying to get them to riot and seize the *Swallow* as it sailed from Cape Lopez to Cape Coast Castle. Mr Child, another fellow prisoner, later acquitted, said Scudamore spoke several times to the black slaves sometimes in their Angolan language about killing all the white people on board the *Swallow*, taking the ship and forming an entirely new company of Negroes at Angola. Child was also one of the pirates that Scudamore tried to recruit for his plan of overthrowing the crew of the *Swallow* and taking the ship. Child told the officers in charge of Scudamore's duplicity. Isaac Burnet backed up this evidence by stating that he heard Scudamore ask another pirate, James Harris, if he wanted to come into the project. Burnet then told the authorities.

In his defence, Scudamore said it was merely a hypothetical argument for passing the time. He said he was a forced man and that his conversations with the Negroes were 'just a few foolish words but only by way of supposition, that if the Negroes should take it into their heads, it would have been an easy matter in his opinion for them to have done it'. The court was not impressed with his defence and found him guilty.

Glasby again testified against another prisoner, Robert Johnson, who had been one of the twenty men on the boat that had robbed the *King Solomon*. 'All the pirates on this, and the like service, were volunteers, and he, in particular, had contested his going on board a second time, though out of this turn.'[11] He was found guilty.

One man's case dragged on for days. This was George Wilson, the only pirate who demanded the right to cross-examine witnesses for some considerable time. John Sharp, master of the *Elizabeth* where Wilson had been a passenger, testified against Wilson. He stated that he had paid the Negroes on Sestos a ransom to bring Wilson on board. 'I thought I had done a charitable act in this until meeting with one Captain Canning, who asked me why I would release such a rogue as Wilson was.' He also added that Wilson had volunteered to be with the pirates and had not been forced as far as he could tell.

More damning evidence came from the surgeon of the *Elizabeth*, Adam Comry, who stated that while Wilson was a passenger on the ship, he had been very civil and polite before the pirates arrived. 'Yet I understand 'twas through the prisoner's and Scudamore's means that I had been compelled among the pirates.' Sweat rolled down his face from the oppressive heat in the castle as Comry continued his testimony. 'The prisoner was very alert and cheerful, my lord, at meeting with Roberts; hailed him, told him he was glad to see him and would come onboard presently.' Wilson even went so far as to borrow a clean shirt and pair of trousers from Comry, 'for his better appearance and reception'. 'He willingly signed their articles and used arguments against me to do the same', Comry continued. 'He said they should make their voyage in eight months to Brazil, share 600 or 700 pounds a man, and then break up.'[12]

Comry went on to say that Wilson hoped he would be voted by the crew as chief surgeon because he would then be set up with a larger share than the other pirates. However, the men from the *Ranger* voted for Scudamore as chief surgeon, 'to get rid of him, the chief surgeon being always to remain with the commodore'.

Next, Trahern was called to testify for the prosecution against Wilson. In the hot humid court he was asked if he had any opportunities for observing the prisoner's conduct. 'Yes, I did,' Trahern replied. 'He seemed thoroughly satisfied with that way of life, and seemed particularly intimate with Roberts; they often scoffing at the mention of a man-of-war and saying, if they should meet with any of the turnip-man's ships, they would blow up and go to Hell together.'

'What else of the accused conduct did you observe?' 'That his laziness had got him many enemies, even Roberts to him, on the complete of a wounded man the prisoner refused to dress, that he was a double rogue, to be there a second time and he threatened to cut his ears off.'

In his defence Wilson stated he had been surgeon with John Tarlton from Liverpool who was the master of their ship. He went on to say that he met Roberts for the first time on the coast of Guinea who ordered him to 'fetch his chest', which meant he was to come aboard with Roberts. Wilson stated under oath that in the act of gathering his personal belongings he took that as an opportunity to escape, 'for the boat's crew happening to consist of five French and one English man, all as willing as myself and we agreed to pus the boat on shore and trust ourselves with the Negroes of Montzerado'.

This, said Wilson to the court, was a dangerous thing to do not only because of the treacherous seas in the area but also because the natives often 'took a liking to human carcasses'. Wilson and the others remained there for five months until a ship, under the command of Thomas Tarlton, brother of John Tarlton, put in to trade with the natives. Wilson pleaded with Tarlton to come aboard but he was refused 'a release of this captivity, or as much as a small supply of biscuit and salt meat'. According to Wilson Tarlton refused him because he'd been with the pirates.

The significance of this incident can be seen when shortly afterwards he was picked up by a French ship that paid the ransom for him from the natives and he was taken away but as he had contracted an illness was deposited at Sestos where Captain Sharp eventually found him and brought him away. The ship that Sharp commanded was the *Elizabeth*, which was soon taken by Roberts and where Wilson met Thomas Tarlton again, 'and thoughtlessly used some reproaches of him, for his severe treatment at Montzerado; but protests without design his words should have had so bad a consequence, for Roberts took upon him, as a dispenser of justice, the correction of Mr Tarlton, beating him unmercifully'.

Wilson went on to testify that he felt that Roberts's actions in beating Tarlton must have had other motives rather than his own words about how badly Tarlton had treated him. Regarding Comry's testimony about how he had been so friendly with Roberts, Wilson said this was down to his immaturity and also that he was pretending to be a great friend to Roberts, that his actions of ingratiating himself 'as every prisoner did, for a more civil treatment and in particular to procure his discharge', Johnson wrote in his account of the trial.

Wilson's case dragged on until 17 April when it was adjourned. This allowed the court to continue trying the other pirates and when Wilson was brought back he was found guilty. But he was not sentenced to execution then and there because of his part in betraying a plot by the hard-core pirates to overthrow the *Swallow* and take charge of the ship. Instead, Wilson was given the right to return to England and argue for a pardon.[13]

Benjamin Jeffreys, John Mansfield and William Davis were found guilty after testimonies from Glasby and Trahern amongst others were heard by the court.

Phipps, Herdman, Ogle and the rest of the court had heard hours and hours of testimony from the pirates. Most of it saying they had been forced into piracy and that they had been mistreated as prisoners of the pirates. The court heard that when men were truly reluctant to join all they received was a beating and none of the so-called forced men had been executed for not joining Roberts, regardless of the testimony they'd heard. They concluded that a large proportion of the pirates had been lying.

However, the court had no doubt about the level of destruction the pirates had committed on their captured ships and the belongings of individuals. In particular, ships belonging to the Royal African Company were more severely ravaged than others. But many ships that Roberts plundered went on to complete successful voyages. The *King Solomon*, for example, in June 1722 sailed for Jamaica with more than 300 slaves. In some cases, it appears as if Roberts wasn't interested in plundering the cargos of the ships he captured but demanding that they pay a kind of tax for letting them go. 'At Whydah he took just eight pounds of gold from each ship, although some were carrying far larger amounts.'[14]

After more than three weeks of testimony the trial ended on the 20 April and seventy-two pirates had been sentenced to hang. However, twenty of those men had their executions commuted to seven years servitude in the mines at Cape Coast Castle which, considering the appalling conditions there, was a much slower death than being hanged by the neck. That left fifty-two pirates who were executed. Of the rest, seventy-four were acquitted, twenty were sentenced to servitude in the mines, and only two were given a respite, while another seventeen were sent back to England to serve prison sentences at the Admiralty prison at Marshalsea. This mass execution was the single largest execution of pirates in the Admiralty's history, which makes the Royal Navy truly an organization of pirate killers.

Chapter 6

The Battle of Algiers: The Road to Destruction

Any account on the actions of the Royal Navy against pirates in African waters whether it be along the west coast or against the Barbary Corsairs must mention the Battle of Algiers. Yet few today know this battle even existed. It took place on 27 August 1816 and is unique in a number of ways. It was one of the last actions by Royal Navy ships that moved solely under the power of sail. It was a massive ship to shore artillery barrage that included rocket-launched missiles.

The bombardment lasted almost ten hours and was one of the most intensive sea-borne artillery barrages ever, resulting in the deaths of several thousand men. Admiral Lord Exmouth, also known as Sir Edward Pellew, commanded the fleet that carried out this audacious and massive attack. Though victorious, the casualties suffered by the Royal Navy that day were more than Nelson suffered at Trafalgar.

We have seen in earlier chapters how difficult it was for England to suppress the white slave trade carried out by the Barbary corsairs. The elements that lead up to this battle started back in the sixteenth century. It is a story, 'which contains a strange mixture of elements: religious bigotry, commercial greed, racial prejudice, economic exploitation and military incompetence'.[1] Before we go into the details of the battle itself it is worth taking a look at this background.

For centuries the Barbary corsairs were lumped together under a single name 'The Turks', which was used by the Christian European powers to describe these raiders. Truth and myth mingled together to the point where the Turks became the bogeymen of Europe. 'He was a Satan in human form. The Turk was an alien, a murderous dark-skinned foreigner.'

Legend had it that the Turks raped and ravished women, captured children and enslaved their Christian hostages for their depraved indulgences. They were essentially kidnappers. The life they led and their culture revolved around this action of kidnapping and ransoming off their hostages or enslaving them to do the menial tasks of their society. We know the three cities that these activities were centred around were Tripoli, Algiers and Tunis.

The Barbary Coast stretches some 1,500 miles along the coast of North Africa, from the Straits of Gibraltar to the Gulf of Sirte. The people of this stretch of fertile land were part of the Carthaginian Empire and when Carthage was sacked by the Romans, they became part of the Roman Empire and enjoyed peace and prosperity for 500 years under Roman occupation. They became Christians until the eighth century when Islamic forces invaded and the people accepted Islam as their faith.

In the fifteenth century the Turkish or Ottoman Empire was on the rise and began sweeping through the Mediterranean, north into the Balkans, down into Egypt and of course into Barbary. They either conquered the areas they took or, in the case of Barbary, which was already ruled by Arabs, they made alliances. The centre of this empire was Constantinople. In Europe they attacked as far north as Vienna where they were finally stopped.

By the sixteenth century the Ottomans were at their peak, especially during the reign of Sultan Suleiman the Magnificent who consolidated and developed the empire. Helping him was Kheir-ed Din Barbarossa, the man who reorganized the Ottoman Navy into an effective and potent fighting force and in 1529 fortified the port of Algiers, turning it into an impressive naval base, and the fleet dominated the Mediterranean.

But the empire was too large for it to be ruled by Constantinople and gradually the power of the Sultan faded as the distant provinces gained more freedom. To govern the far-flung territories governors (pashas) were appointed. But many of these pashas were ineffective because they didn't understand the local problems and so could not solve them. So local leaders were elected in these far-flung provinces, known as deys, and their appointments would be approved by the Sultan.

The Barbary Coast was one of these areas and both Algiers and Tunis enjoyed increasing autonomy from Constantinople as the years went by. Indeed, by 1750 the Sultan's control had almost entirely disappeared, though certain obligations remained such as sending troops to support Turkish forces should they be involved in war, or having the Sultan act as an adjudicator in high-level disputes. But essentially the Barbary States were left to their own devices.

The economy of Algiers was in decline by the late sixteenth century as most of the fertile land had been completely exhausted, with the old

Roman irrigation systems having fallen into decay and disrepair. Worse still there was no deep tradition of putting everything right through hard work so the states would take what they didn't have from others. This was how the culture of robbery, kidnapping and ransom began – a reign of terror that lasted nearly three hundred years.[2]

The governments of the Barbary States granted licences to their best sea captains in much the same way that European governments provided letters of marque for seafarers to plunder and capture the ships of the nation's enemies. Initially, the corsairs combined with the Sultan's forces to attack the Christian states in the Mediterranean such as Venice and Genoa but they soon separated and went sea-raiding throughout the summer seasons and carried out small hit-and-run attacks on Christian towns and villages that were poorly defended and fortified. As far as the frightened Christians were concerned, these raiders were all Turks.

To make matters worse, renegade English sailors found their way to the Barbary States and joined them. These men, such as Jack Ward, taught the Barbary captains about navigation in the waters around France, England and Ireland, 'and provided the impetus to the expansion of Corsair activities by introducing the square-rigged round ship'.[3]

Men like Ward and Dutch adventurer Captain Simon Danser set the example others followed. Both men made fortunes working with the corsairs and helped to push the boundaries of their activities further north. These men also provided the knowledge to the corsair captains (*rais*) for building square-rigged vessels that would allow them to extend their activities into rougher seas beyond the Mediterranean. Raids along the coasts of nations such as England, France, Spain, Denmark, Madeira and Portugal were commonplace and in 1627 the corsairs raided the Irish coast.

What made the corsairs so successful were their quick and nimble ships. They had to be small but large enough for open sea cruising, be unobtrusive but also have a hold that was large enough to carry a force of fully equipped warriors for fighting, be shallow enough for coastal work and have the ability to carry large numbers of prisoners. The merchantmen these corsairs attacked were much larger, slower and more heavily armed. The corsair ships sacrificed armament for speed and manoeuvrability, which meant that when they were trading broadsides, the corsairs usually got the worst of it.

Their tactics were effective and simple. Corsairs would hide in the lee of an island used as a navigation point and when their victims came close to the island to get their bearings the corsairs would come tearing out and be alongside in a matter of moments. They might come out of the evening sun as it set on the horizon, making it hard for their victims to identify them until it was too late. Like most privateers the world round they would use the ruse of flying different colours, usually those of their victims until they were within hailing distance. For their activities in the Mediterranean corsair ships usually had crew members onboard from a wide variety of places who spoke different languages so there was always someone who could converse with the victim while the *rais* (captain) prepared to attack.

Sometimes the corsairs would use ships they'd captured as bait to lure their prey into their clutches. In addition to sails the corsair ships often had a row of oars for attacking other ships that were becalmed. This gave them greater flexibility but also meant that on leaving port they would have to carry enough provisions to feed the crew, the slaves manning the oars and any prisoners.

People were the treasure they were interested in. Unlike the pirates operating elsewhere, such as Blackbeard, Roberts or Avery, the corsairs were only interested in certain types of cargo: people meant profit because they could be ransomed. While the ransom negotiations were taking place those same people could be put to work as slaves.

There are stories of prisoners being treated with appalling harshness by the corsairs. Eyewitness reports state that the corsairs would rampage through a captive ship, stripping everyone naked, torturing officers to find out who the wealthiest passengers were and all the while completely stripping the ship bare. If it was a good ship and could be converted for part of the corsair fleet it would be sailed back into port as a prize but more often than not it was either sold or sunk.

The captives would be chained up in the holds of the corsair ships in sweltering heat and appalling sanitary conditions. Once arriving back at port their fate would be worse. They would go into quarantine barracks to ensure any diseases they carried didn't infect the local population. From there, the men would be taken to the public auction. In these slave markets they would be physically inspected in the open to see if they were fit for years of hard labour while their ransoms were negotiated. They were commodities like animals, checked and examined to ensure that the people bidding for them were making a sound investment that would produce a quick return through ransom or a longer term investment through slave labour. In another building the women were also physically examined to see if they were worth the money bidders would pay for them.

All the prisoners were held in large buildings known as *bagnios* where conditions were squalid and miserable. The European nations had consulates in the three main ports of Algiers, Tunis and Tripoli and a large part of their jobs was to act on behalf of those prisoners who were wealthy or influential. For the less important prisoners the consulates were there to make block payments for their release, while also paying a regular fee to the corsair governments. Ransom payments from public charities throughout Europe were paid by groups of monks from Rome known as the Redemptionist Fathers.[4]

The whole thing was highly organized. Both sides trusted the Jewish business communities who often acted as brokers and bankers, advancing money in Barbary which they could get back in Europe through subsidiary banks. Because they had networks throughout the Mediterranean the Jews were able to provide large transactions through letters of credit which meant that their deals were usually much faster, which helped free those prisoners who could take advantage of the Jewish services. The Jews were also able to provide life insurance, so that the owner of a slave could insure that man's life in case he died of disease before his ransom was paid.

For the women things were slightly better. There were three basic ways their captivity could go. Depending on their connections they could be ransomed quickly and freed or if they were attractive or intelligent they could be sold as wives to local men who could afford them. If neither of these criteria fitted then they could become part of the harem 'where as concubines they would suffer more than anything else from boredom and overeating'.

However, atrocities were committed. Reports from people who had been ransomed and freed told of rape, murder, torture, mutilation, depravity and bestiality. These reports may have been exaggerated, not least for commercial reasons, so former captives could sell more copies of their accounts of what had happened to them. These reports also helped to propagate the myth of the 'Terrible Turks'.

Algiers was by no means a major power yet it took three centuries for the corsair activities to be finally stopped. Indeed, between 1541 and 1829, the Christian European powers and the United States made no less than eighteen expeditions but none achieved the desired outcome – the end to Christian slavery. The Algerines were bombarded from the sea several times, their port and docks wrecked, their fleets virtually wiped out, but they sprang back and continued their nefarious activities.

The reason for this is partly due to cynicism by the major powers of the day, incompetence and that ever-present bogey – the lack of political will. Roger Perkins and Captain K J Douglas-Morris say in *Gunfire in Barbary* that one reason why the corsairs weren't crushed was because of the terrain. 'The North African coast is rocky and dangerous swept by powerful currents and exposed to sudden, violent storms. The ships of that period could not safely navigate the Mediterranean between November and March.' In addition, throughout the three centuries of Barbary corsair activity the European powers were busy fighting each other and lacked the resources to send against a fortified, well-defended port like Algiers. 'The Christians lacked adequate tools for the job.'

As we have seen in earlier chapters, England negotiated treaties with the Barbary States where, to ensure the corsairs stopped attacking English ships and taking English slaves, the English paid a tribute which was part currency and part military supplies such as cannon, firearms, powder, goods and ship-building materials. Of course, these treaties never really held up but they were preferable to an all-out war. Also, during the Napoleonic Wars many Mediterranean ports were closed to the British so putting into the corsair havens for repairs and supplies was necessary for them and on a political level some form of friendship with the Deys made sense.

So what led to the attack by Lord Exmouth on Algiers in 1816? Towards the end of the eighteenth century the humanitarian movement had become enshrined in European philosophy. The idea that 'all men are created equal' took hold and created the climate that led to the French and American Revolutions. In Britain, the Abolitionist movement was building. 'The traffic in human lives from Africa to the Americas, was a dominating issue as the nineteenth century opened.'[5]

While the Abolitionists directed their energies against the black slave trade they did not recognize the Christian slaves being taken by the Barbary corsairs. Even though it had been going on for centuries there is very little documentation of the Abolitionists ever uttering a word regarding these Christian slaves. Some senior officers within the Royal Navy were appalled at the lack of recognition of the Christian slave problem. Nelson himself felt that allowing the corsairs to go unpunished tarnished the reputation of Great Britain.[6] But he was so heavily involved in the war with France that there was little he could do to stop them.

However, there was one man who played an active role in mobilizing opinion against the Barbary corsairs, specifically against Algiers. He was retired naval officer, Admiral Sir William Sidney Smith. Smith joined the Royal Navy at the age of 12 in 1777 as a midshipman on HMS *Tortoise*. From there he had many adventures, including a courageous bid to burn the French fleet as it lay anchored in Toulon harbour, serving with the Swedes in their conflict with the Russians, a daring escape from a prison in Paris and, perhaps most notable, his defence of Acre during the war with

Napoleon that thwarted the French emperor's attempts to conquer India. As a naval officer he served in Morocco, Egypt and the Levant. He also gained diplomatic experience at the Court of the Ottomans in Constantinople as Joint Minister Plenipotentiary, which gave him a unique perspective on how the Turks thought and acted. While he spent several years fighting Napoleon's France he loved the country and ended his career in Paris. 'As a consequence Smith was uniquely situated: he had the reputation, the experience, the detail awareness and the international connections required to mobilise European opinion.'[7]

Smith had seen firsthand the suffering that had been caused by the enslavement of Christians at the hands of the Turks and decided to do something about it. In 1814 he set up the Knights Liberator of the Slaves in Africa and appointed himself president. He began a public relations campaign almost entirely financed from his own fortune. He wrote letters to every head of state across Europe, to all the important and influential men he could think of. These were political men of high influence, men of letters, philosophers and those people who had influence and power in the European courts and governments. Thousands of replies came flooding back, all pledging support, and one amongst them was perhaps the most important.

It was a letter from Lord Exmouth who accepted Smith's invitation to become a Knight Liberator in a warm and supportive reply. Exmouth stated he would give all the support he could to Smith's cause. This is ironic, considering that in Smith's last command he had been Exmouth's second-in-command and both men had entirely different temperaments to the point where 'Exmouth expressed a considerable dislike for his subordinate.'[8] But now we have Exmouth fully and completely on side and committed to the ending of Christian slavery.

The first meeting of the Knights took place in Vienna in 1814 but their progress was stunted by the sudden return of Napoleon from exile in 1815. Smith hired several hospital wagons and attached his party to Wellington's Army. When the Battle of Waterloo was over Smith spent three days rescuing the wounded who still lay on the battlefield, left for dead after the armies had gone.

The battle over, Smith returned to Paris and continued his crusade against Christian slavery. No expedition to Barbary could be mounted until the New Year because of the bad weather so the first time Exmouth visited Algiers, Tunis and Tripoli was in March 1816. The bombardment of Algiers was to take place only six months later.

But before we get to the detail of the battle there is one other piece of the puzzle that needs to fall into place: the involvement of the United States Navy with the Barbary corsairs. During the American War of Independence the Royal Navy was thinly stretched, fighting the French, the Spanish and the Dutch, so they were unable to press home any advantage with the small fledging American navy. The Treaty of Paris in 1783 formally ended hostilities and recognized the new republic of the United States of America.

With peace restored the young nation began to expand its trade. American ships began to sail into the Mediterranean and became, like everyone else before them, victims of the corsairs. Many Americans were taken as slaves and the USA opened negotiations with the Deys for their release. The Deys' response was that they would have to pay a tribute like all the European nations did in order for the corsairs to leave the US merchant shipping alone.

The USA had emerged triumphant over one of the most powerful nations on earth and they had no desire to accept any compromise. They declared all-out war in 1803. By 1805 they'd managed a release of American slaves from Tripoli but in Tunis and Algiers they continued to pay tribute. The War of 1812 however, changed that. The Royal Navy came out of that war bruised and battered while the Americans, now having the upper hand against the most powerful naval force in the world, decided enough was enough and dispatched a squadron of warships to the Barbary Coast in 1815.

The Americans delivered an ultimatum to the three Deys that stated that no more tribute would be paid by the USA to the Barbary States, that all its citizens held by the corsairs were to be immediately released, along with all the ships and cargo and part of the money paid to the Deys in tribute was also to be returned. All three Deys capitulated and signed peace treaties, the last being signed in Algiers in June 1815 without a single shot being fired. The American commanders went home as heroes, having achieved everything they'd set out to achieve.

In England the effect was one of deep resentment. This upstart nation had managed to achieve what the English had failed to do over decades, even centuries. The Barbary States stuck to their agreements with the USA, which meant the corsairs didn't molest their ships after 1815. The Royal Navy had suffered defeats in the War of 1812 to a nation that had no sea-faring tradition. They'd been continually frustrated by the activities of the corsairs and now with the American coup resentment and jealousy reared their heads. For Lord Exmouth, he'd lost his younger brother in the fighting in Saratoga and he had declared his loyalty and support to Smith's cause. For him, it was personal.

In Algiers the Dey, Omar Bashaw, was a tough opponent in total command of his people. By the time Exmouth first visited Bashaw the Dey had been in power less than twelve months. The man was uneducated and ruthless. 'Forty-two years of age, of medium build, olive-skinned and with keen flashing eyes, he impressed his visitors as an alert and intelligent leader.'[9]

Rather than intellectual ability Bashaw's rise to power was put down to his ruthlessness and understanding of his people and culture. On 7 April 1815 he was elected dey. The man before him had ruled for only sixteen days before being strangled slowly by his own soldiers in the public marketplace. In Lord Exmouth we have a different leader, altogether one with far more experience, intelligent and daring. We know far more about Exmouth than we do about Bashaw. Born Edward Pellew on 19 April 1757 in Dover, he came from a comfortable home and was one of six children. His father was a captain with the Dover Packet Service.

In December 1770 Pellew joined the Royal Navy after being educated at Truro Grammar School. Pellew became midshipman on the thirty-two-gun frigate HMS *Alarm* under Captain Stott and served for three years in the Mediterranean Fleet. During this time, *Alarm* visited Algiers when Captain Stott delivered a formal complaint about how the British Consul to Algiers had been badly treated. This complaint was rejected and Stott was forced to leave with the Consul onboard. One wonders how much influence this episode had on young Pellew.

However, his tenure with Stott ended abruptly when the captain was so irritated by a prank that he left the boy at Marseilles. Pellew managed to secure a position as able seaman when he returned to England on the thirty-six-gun frigate HMS *Blonde*. The ship, in company with HMS *Juno* and twenty transports, was sent to Canada to take part in the American War of Independence.

With the Americans defeated at Quebec, the action moved south onto Lake Champlain and Pellew had his first taste of command. The British had no warships operating on the lake or the subsequent waterways, while the Americans did. The importance of the lake was as the waterway from Quebec to the Hudson River which led to New York.

Pellew was promoted to midshipman and sent south to help in the construction of a small fleet of warships on the lakeshore. He became third in command on the newly built schooner *Carleton* and in their first engagement both his captain and the master were lost, which meant he was in command at the age of 19. He acquitted himself so well that his actions were brought to the attention of his superiors and he was given official command of the *Carleton*.

Over the next few years he commanded small sloops and saw action against the French, mostly around the south coast of England, and in May 1782 he was promoted to the post of captain at the age of 25. However the American war was just coming to an end; for three years the Royal Navy was laid up and the young Pellew found himself ashore with no work.

By 1786 he was commanding a thirty-two-gun frigate HMS *Whichelsea* in the North Atlantic on routine peacetime work. Here he honed his skills as an excellent seaman and hard taskmaster. His reputation was increasing and so at the outbreak of war with France in 1793 he was given command of the forty-gun frigate HMS *Nymphe*. In June of that year he engaged a French frigate of equal firepower in what would prove to be an important step in his career. After a long and hard battle with heavy casualties on both sides Pellew secured the French surrender and brought the ship, *Le Cleopatre*, into Portsmouth as a prize. This action gave a huge boost to English morale and Pellew was given a knighthood, with several other rewards and honours being bestowed on the other officers. So important was this victory that King George III announced it from his box at the opera house in Covent Garden.

He was then given the command of a bigger and more heavily armed frigate HMS *Arethusa*, with his base now at Falmouth, forming part of the squadron of frigates under the command of Admiral Sir John Warren. Pellew distinguished himself even further in two major actions while serving as part of the Falmouth Squadron. He took a French frigate *La Pomone* during an action off Guernsey, which was brought back as a prize and put into the service of the Royal Navy. A few months later he captured an even bigger French frigate, the *Revolutionnaire* which was also brought into Royal Navy service. Again the Admiralty recognized his actions and put him in command of the Falmouth Squadron.

On 25 January 1794 Pellew became involved in a daring and courageous rescue. A massive storm hit the West Country and several ships found themselves sheltering in Plymouth Sound. One such was the *Dutton* a transport ship that the War Office had hired to move supplies and troops to the West Indies. The ship was full of soldiers and passengers, many sick with fever. To try to get to more shelter the master decided to move the *Dutton* to a little inlet known as the Cattewater that offered more protection against the mounting storm. But before he cleared the Sound the ship struck a reef and was swept onto the rocks under the Citadel where it was pounded mercilessly by the ferocious waves.

Hearing the news of the wreck Pellew arrived on the scene and managed to get out to the ship using a line, climbed aboard and began to direct rescue operations while the sea slowly tore the *Dutton* apart. Small boats followed his example and battled their way out to the stricken ship while Pellew supervised the unloading of passengers, the sick, the women and children and the sailors. Shortly after the last person had been taken off, the *Dutton* disintegrated under the pounding waves and disappeared.

For his actions Pellew received a baronetcy and, not yet 40, became Sir Edward Pellew, Bart of Treverry. He was involved in more actions against the French and by 1799, after nearly thirty years in frigates, was given command of a ship of the line, the seventy-four-gun HMS *Impetuous*. For two years Pellew spent his time blockading the French and putting down mutinies in his own ship.

In 1802 the Treaty of Amiens was signed, bringing peace between France and England. The peace treaty didn't last and in May 1802 Pellew was back at sea commanding the eighty-gun HMS *Tonnant* which had been a French ship taken at the Battle of the Nile. At the end of 1804 Pellew was given command of the East Indies squadron and promoted to Rear Admiral of the White. He sailed for India to try to counter the powerful French forces operating there that were taking a huge toll on English merchant shipping. For two years his ships harassed the French and had minor successes until 1806 when Pellew launched a massive attack against the Dutch naval base at Batavia. Dutch resistance quickly crumbled and the British casualties were very light.

In 1809 Pellew returned to England, now a vice-admiral and was appointed as Commander-in-Chief of the North Sea fleet that saw his ships involved in a year of long blockades of French ports and settlements. After this he was made Commander-in-Chief of the Mediterranean fleet, which he held from 1811 to 1814 when the war with France finally ended and Napoleon was sent into exile. With the arrival of peace many honours and rewards were given out and Pellew was made a peer of the realm, his title of Lord Exmouth given to him as it was the name of the closest seaport to him that wasn't being used by another peer.

When Napoleon escaped from Elba in 1815 all of Europe was in an uproar. Pellew who had been enjoying peacetime with his family was reappointed as Commander-in-Chief of the Mediterranean fleet with his flagship the ninety-eight-gun HMS *Boyne*. His fleet sailed to Marseilles where they landed 4,000 troops to support the loyalists. Pellew himself, now in his fifties, went ashore and personally led the troops. Clearing the surrounding areas he marched on Toulon and captured it.

With Bonaparte's defeat at Waterloo Pellew was instructed to turn his attention to the Barbary States and negotiate lasting treaties with the Barbary corsairs, which is how Bashaw and Exmouth came to square off against each other. The opening moves began in September 1815 when Exmouth received secret orders to proceed to Tripoli, Tunis and Algiers to negotiate peace treaties with each state. As winter set in Exmouth knew that attacking immediately would be out of the question because of the winter gales. He moved the fleet to Livorno and waited. During this period Exmouth dispatched one frigate, the HMS *Banterer* on a secret intelligence and reconnaissance mission of the port of Algiers. The ship was to have minimum contact with the shore and only its commander, Captain Warde, understood the purpose of the mission.

His orders were given to him by Exmouth at the end of January 1816 and by February Warde was back with a highly detailed report that included 'an assessment of Algerine morale and soundings of the sea-bed. Particularly astonishing is the fact that he identified the calibre and exact location of nearly six hundred Algerine cannon.'[10]

Using Warde's report Exmouth made his plans and sailed from Livorno on 4 March 1816, stopping along the way in Genoa and Port Mahon, and arrived at the Bay of Algiers on 1 April. The fleet consisted of five ships of the line including Exmouth's flagship HMS *Boyne* along with seven frigates and sloops.

Now in Algiers Exmouth was met by the British Consul Mr McDonell who gave him the most up to date information about the city. Exmouth went ashore and met with Bashaw and his officials. Initially, Exmouth's goal was to ensure that the people on the Ionian Islands would have the same rights and protection as British subjects enjoyed who were in Barbary, to negotiate treaties on behalf of the Kingdom of the Two Sicilies and of Sardinia.

He managed to get an agreement from Bashaw that he would immediately release 357 out of 1,000 Sicilian slaves, with Exmouth paying 1,000 dollars per head for each person released. He also managed to get forty Sardinian slaves released at a cost of 500 dollars. Bashaw and Exmouth signed a treaty that brought the people of the Ionian Islands under the representation of the British Consul. However, no British slaves were released during these negotiates nor did Bashaw agree to end slavery.

In Tripoli and Tunis Exmouth negotiated similar deals for much less cash outlay but there was no deal struck for releasing British slaves. After sending his account of his meeting with the Day, Exmouth received communication from London. The government was unhappy, because Exmouth had failed to negotiate a treaty and had paid inflated prices for the release of people who were not British subjects.

Compared to the American success a year earlier Exmouth's achievements must have been seen as completely ineffective. Instead of returning to England, Exmouth went back to Algiers and dropped anchor for a second time in the bay on 14 May. Again he met with Omar Bashaw for several hours and he told him that economic prosperity for Algiers lay in a future of sound international trade rather than the corsairs' illegal activities of trafficking in human cargo. Exmouth said that 'rejection of this principle could lead only to armed conflict with a united Europe'. He left feeling hopeful.

However, the following morning the Dey refused to sign the treaty and the discussion turned to a heated argument that ended with Exmouth storming out furious. As he left he told the also angry Bashaw that he would withdraw the British Consul. Bashaw countered saying that McDonell couldn't leave until he paid his debts. McDonell was arrested before Exmouth and his officers managed to get back to their ship.

Infuriated, the Dey was virtually unintelligible as he ordered that all British subjects and anyone protected by Britain be rounded up and arrested. Messengers were sent out in all directions to carry out the Dey's instructions but as they had been shouted in a rage these orders were open to interpretation and were to have far-reaching consequences for Bashaw and Exmouth. As cooler heads prevailed, the Dey must have realized that picking a fight with Great Britain was not a good idea and so sent out orders cancelling the original orders to have every British subject arrested. But he forgot about one rider who headed for Bone on horseback, some 250 miles away from Algiers.

While this rider was heading for Bone, Exmouth and Bashaw patched up their differences and the Dey agreed to send an ambassador to Britain to negotiate a treaty on Christian slavery. Exmouth and the Dey met again on 19 May, parted on good terms and the fleet left Algiers that day. When he returned to England a flood of criticism was levelled against Exmouth for his actions with the Barbary States. Most of the criticism was that he hadn't gone nearly as far as he should have to punish the Deys and force them to sign treaties.

Much of this criticism stemmed from the events that had taken place in Bone. Britain had exclusive trading rights with Bone which had been granted to them by the Algerine government ten years earlier. There was valuable coral-fishing on the nearby coast which Britain didn't take advantage of but instead rented the concession to local Christians who were from the Kingdom of the Two Sicilies. The day the messenger arrived with the Dey's orders was a holiday and hundreds of local Sicilians were on the beach celebrating. Perhaps the messenger interpreted the Dey's orders for arresting British subjects and those who enjoyed British protection to mean killing them. The local militia heard what the messenger said and attacked the Sicilians on the beach killing hundreds.

As the reports came in about the massacre British public opinion demanded action. On the continent Britain was a laughing stock, having been completely unable to do anything about slavery and piracy in Barbary. Scarcely had Exmouth arrived back in England when he was summoned to the Admiralty and 1 July 1816 was given command of an expedition to Algiers. This time he could use force.

Chapter 7

The Battle of Algiers: The Fleet Sails

We drank to his Lordships health and then everyone went to sleep, almost like dead men.[1]

July was a busy month for Exmouth as his fleet prepared to sail. Ships from both Portsmouth and Plymouth made up the fleet. The expedition was to be a reasonably short one and as a result the amount of food and water needed would not be as much as for longer cruises. That meant the holds of his ships could be crammed with munitions, which in addition to the usual powder and shot also included large numbers of Congreve rockets.

These had not been tried in large quantities before. Along with the rockets there were other innovations loaded onto the ships, such as experimental gunsights for the long 18-pounder cannon. Specialist personnel from the Royal Laboratory in Woolwich were on hand to ensure the new equipment worked properly.

To ensure he had better fire control, Exmouth ordered extra butts be attached to the stern of each ship, anchoring them both fore and aft with springs fitted from one cable to another. He also ordered that chain cable be used instead of hemp rope to reduce damage to the mooring from close defensive fire.

By 10 July the ships moored in Portsmouth were ready to sail. Exmouth had been given two companies of specialists from the army including nineteen men under the command of Lieutenant John T Fuller of the Rocket Corps, Royal Horse Artillery.

Also on board as part of Exmouth's staff was, Abraham Salame, an interpreter from the Admiralty who kept a daily detailed account of the expedition. Salame travelled throughout the Eastern Mediterranean working in countries such as Turkey, Arabia, Egypt and Italy in a wide capacity.

The fleet left Portsmouth for Spithead with Exmouth in his flagship, the *Queen Charlotte*. His intention was to head for Plymouth to pick up the rest of the fleet there. However, foul weather forced him to stay for two weeks until 23 July when the gales in the Channel finally subsided. Exmouth had hoped that the expedition would be kept a secret but, stuck as they were for two weeks, word got out that they were heading for Algiers. Soon it was all over the country and on the continent, ending any hope he had of surprising the Algerines.

The ships that left Spithead on 23 July were the *Queen Charlotte*, the *Minden*, *Albion*, *Severn* and *Granicus*. It took them three days to reach Plymouth where, on the afternoon of 26 July, they dropped their anchors in Cawsand Bay to the sound of ceremonial gunfire. Here Exmouth would have the *Impregnable*, *Superb*, *Leander*, *Glasgow* and *Hebrus* joining him, along with a variety of transports and sloops.

To Exmouth's despair he discovered there were manning problems at Plymouth. The crews for all the ships were voluntary and many of the men were neither sailors nor battle experienced. Exmouth needed crews that had the experienced men at their core to balance out the inexperienced land men, loafers and troublemakers who had signed on for one reason or another.

By 28 July everything was ready, so shortly after midday every ship in the fleet raised their anchors and set sail, even though some were still short of a full complement of experienced crew members. 'At noon we sailed from Plymouth, having been joined by the *Impregnable*, a three-decker, under Rear Admiral Sir David Milne; and by the *Minden*, the *Superbe*, and the *Albion*, two-deckers or seventy-fours; and by several other frigates and brigs.'[2] Once at sea Exmouth ordered HMS *Minden* to press on ahead at all speed for Gibraltar to ensure he would have all the supplies, stores and materials he needed when the fleet arrived. But time was against him. Exmouth had to turn his motley crews into well-trained fighting men and he only had a little more than four weeks to do it. He ordered a strict and hard regime of training dominated by gunnery drills. 'His Lordship gave an order to all the fleet, as the seamen had not been at sea for a long time, to put them in exercise of the guns, twice a day without fire, and once a week with fire.' Ships logs record that day-after-day gunnery training took place while the Marines went through their paces on small arms training, 'the value of which became apparent later when they shot down scores of Algerine gunners and sniped the survivors'.

As the men went through their training on the big cannon and small guns they developed speed and teamwork, bringing them up to a standard where they would stay at their posts firing no matter what. While the men trained there were those malcontents who for whatever reason decided life in the Royal Navy didn't suit them and they were undisciplined and mutinous. Just as the logs were full of training entries so they were of floggings – for everything from theft, fighting, bad language, neglect of duty and much more.

Milne was Exmouth's second-in-command and he received Exmouth's orders of battle first and then issued them to the captains of the ships in the fleet. Dated 6 August 1816 the orders were highly detailed. 'All boats will be hoisted out,' Exmouth wrote. 'The Launches prepared for the Howitzers and the Flat Boats for the Carronades and Rockets, and the Jolly Boats must attend the latter with ammunition.'³

He wrote that if the wind was unfavourable for an attack during the day then the launches and flat boats would have to be prepared for a night attack. 'Care is to be taken to afford the crews as much rest as possible, and as the land winds generally prevail very early in the morning, the ships will carefully watch the Admiral's motions at night, and be ready to weigh at dawn.'

The key to his plans was to attack the mole of Algiers, a structure that curves out from the land, forming a harbour between the bay and the shore. The mole had a protected entrance to the harbour and several cannon were mounted along its walls. Exmouth's ship, the *Queen Charlotte*, was to come as close to the mole entrance as possible while the *Superbe* and the *Impregnable* were to anchor as close as they could to the flagship, with the *Impregnable* facing southward and the *Superbe* between the two of them. Exmouth also ordered all the ships to be 'made fast' to each other in order to concentrate their fire.

The *Albion* was to take the place of any of the ships mentioned above that Exmouth stated were 'thrown out. But if the *Impregnable* succeeds in getting her place it appears to me, the *Albion* may be well situated close on her bow presenting her broadside against the only flanking Battery marked "A" of three guns.' The *Albion* was to cover the *Impregnable* and fire on the lighthouse battery outside of the mole. The *Leander* was to anchor as close to the flagship as possible while pouring her broadside onto the town 'until she opens the Mole'. After that, she was to fire on the batteries on the town walls. The *Glasgow* was to fire on the fishmarket battery while the *Granicus* was ordered to occupy any space in the line of ships where she could and take the place of any damaged or destroyed ship. Batteries 7 and 8 were to be attacked by the *Hebrus*, while the *Minden* was to attack other batteries that would be firing on the ships attacking the mole.

Exmouth also had at his disposal an 'explosion vessel' which was to be towed by *Prometheus* to the appropriate place before her fuses were lit and the crew safely back aboard *Prometheus*. The flat-bottom rocket boats were to attack the lighthouse battery and the tower gates.

This was his order of battle and preparations were made when they arrived at Gibraltar on 9 August. Exmouth immediately went ashore to begin work on converting the flat boats into gun and rocket boats. The longboats from the warships were converted to endure the recoil of 12- and 24-pounder guns as well as 68-pounder carronades.

The explosion vessel was HMS *Fly*, a buoy tender that was loaded with more than 143 barrels of powder with fuses. Exmouth's time ashore was busy as he spent many hours meeting with his own officers and officers from Gibraltar, trying to find the best way to attack guns protected by masonry. Several experiments using different calibres of shot and amounts of powder were carried out. All the while, little ships ferried supplies back and forth to the fleet. During the period at sea large quantities of ammunition had been consumed as every ship went through their incessant gunnery drills. All of this was being topped up, along with food, water and a wide variety of other material.

> His Lordship gave orders to the fleet to take off all the cabins which are made on board of every ship, and to keep all the decks clear, from the poop to the head for the management of guns; and that every ship should send on shore the timbers of the cabins, as well as all things that were not necessary for the battle; and that instead of timber, cabins should be made of several partitions of canvass.[4]

While this was taking place the ship's crews were very busy themselves. The sail-makers, for example, made canvas water buckets because the wooden ones had been put ashore. Men lugged away everything wooden that might catch fire: table and chairs, personal sea-chests, cabin bulkheads were all removed and taken away or secured in the hold. The casks for water and powder barrels were inspected, while the guns were checked over repeatedly for wear and tear from the long month of drills by the gun captains. Navigation charts and notes were studied again and again to ensure the fleet would be able to navigate along the treacherous North African coast in any weather. Men not fit for fighting were put ashore. Perkins and Douglas-Morris state that 'the disorder and confusion of Plymouth and Portsmouth had been replaced with a taut expectancy of impending battle'.

Indeed, the motley fleet of ships with their undisciplined crews was rapidly turning into a very capable, honed and tuned fighting force. Exmouth was planning for every contingency. With 1,000 marines and 110 soldiers at his disposal he had the means to make a landing if necessary or if the opportunity arose.

To ensure that his mind was as clear and focused as it could be, Exmouth refused to have any of his relatives or closest friends accompany him on the expedition. He knew the dangers everyone faced. 'Of the hundreds of officers who had clamoured to serve under his command, the Admiral had given preference to those whose death or mutilation would cause professional regret rather than personal grief.'

In all of this there was a fly in the ointment. The second-in-command, Rear Admiral David Milne had no experience in the Mediterranean and was looking upon the expedition as a side show before heading off to his next command, the Halifax station in Nova Scotia, Canada. He had been given orders only a few weeks before to sail to Halifax in the *Leander* but when that ship had been diverted into Exmouth's squadron Milne asked if he could stay with the ship, which was agreed.

At Gibraltar Milne transferred his flag to the *Impregnable*, commanded by Captain Edward Brace who had a distinguished and long career behind him. Brace had been chosen by Exmouth because of his recent experience in the Mediterranean operations at Genoa and Gaeta but he was elderly and sick – the complete antithesis of Milne, which was to prove a problem during the battle.

While Exmouth was in Gibraltar he met with the commander of a small Dutch squadron under the command of Vice Admiral Baron van Capellen. Including his flagship the Dutch Admiral had a total fleet of six ships, five frigates and one corvette. His fleet had been patrolling the Western Mediterranean for several months and when he heard about the English expedition being mounted against Algiers he set sail for Gibraltar to wait for Exmouth's arrival.

When the English fleet finally did arrive van Capellen offered his services and fleet to Exmouth for the coming battle. Exmouth accepted the offer and the combined fleet was ready to sail by 13 August 1816.

Exmouth needed good sunny weather for his crossing to Algiers because in tow behind the larger ships were fifty-five flat-bottomed gunboats, mortar boats and rocket boats. High winds of any kind would have swamped them completely. But the weather didn't hold and for the next twenty-four hours they stayed anchored at Gibraltar.

Just as the weather deteriorated on 13 August HMS *Satellite* arrived, commanded by Captain James Murray, who had just come from Algiers with news for Exmouth. The Algerines were preparing for Exmouth's arrival, preparing for battle.

Chapter 8

The Battle Proper

Friday the 16th – The wind changed from north to east; and in the evening we spoke with the corvette *Prometheus*, Captain Dashwood. He was sent on before to bring off the British Consul from Algiers, but Captain Dashwood could only take off the Consul's family; and the Consul himself was detained by the Dey.[1]

Before the battle Exmouth had given Salame two documents in English to be translated into Arabic and Turkish. One was a letter of ultimatum and a 'Declaration for the Abolition of Christian Slavery' which Exmouth intended to deliver to the Dey and invite him to sign. When the Dey heard of the arrival of the *Prometheus* that had been sent to Algiers from Gibraltar he had the British Consul detained in a room in his own house and also arrested two boats from the *Prometheus* with eighteen men aboard that had come to take the Consul and his family to safety. This story was related by Dashwood to Exmouth who then composed a third letter of ultimatum to the Dey about the immediate release of the Consul and the return of the two boats and their crews.

The fleet stopped at the island of Alboran on 16 August where they waited for a fair wind to take them the rest of the way to Algiers. When the wind changed the fleet set sail again and by the 26th they were in sight of Cap Cazzina, the northern tip of the Bay of Algiers, and by the early morning of the 27th they were in sight of the city itself.

It was at this point that Exmouth gave Salame the orders to move to the *Severn* where he would row across under a flag of truce to the city and hand over the letters and declaration. Before going the officers aboard the *Queen Charlotte* heard that Salame was to deliver the dispatches to the Dey and gathered around him, saying 'Salame, if you return with an answer from the Dey, that he accepts our demands without fighting, we will kill you instead.'

Delighted with their good humour and their bravery he stepped into the boat which was duly lowered into the water and was rowed across to the *Severn*. Captain Burgess, commanding the *Severn*, met Salame as he came aboard. Salame was to go with Burgess under the flag of truce into the harbour, deliver the letters and wait for an answer. Tension was high.

In the bay many foreign ships were anchored and one of them was the French frigate, *La Ciotat*. 'His Lordship then ordered Captain Maitland of the *Glasgow* to visit her, and get some information from the French captain, Lieutenant Ranoir, who pretended every kind of ignorance, and would tell us nothing,' Salame later wrote in his journal. Exmouth later discovered that the French were there to take off the French Consul, his family and any other French nationals.

At 0900hrs Exmouth signalled to the *Severn* to lower its boat and row towards the city. A boat from the *Severn* was lowered into the water with Burgess, Salame and six seamen aboard. 'We took with us, secretly, six muskets, for precaution, to defend ourselves from treachery; and rowed towards the city hoisting our flag of truce', Salame wrote. They were a mile out and Burgess steered towards the harbour entrance.

By 1100hrs they had reached the mole head and saw a boat coming out to meet them. Aboard this boat was the port captain. As the boat approached Salame shouted for them to keep their distance. 'Why are you afraid?' the port captain replied. 'We have not got the plague in Algiers.' 'We are not afraid of the plague,' Salame replied. 'But you have detained two of our boats, with eighteen men, unjustly.'

The port captain made no reply but switched tack and asked how Exmouth was. Salame asked the same about Omar Bashaw and then attached the first letter to the end of a long pole for the port captain to take. Before he took it the captain said, 'Is this for the British Consul?' 'No,' Salame said. 'This is for the Dey to whom I present Lord Exmouth's compliments, and say, that an answer is expected in one hour.' 'But it's impossible to give an answer to such serious business by that time.' Salame replied: 'We shall wait here in the boat two or three hours, that you may have time enough; and, if you do not come by that time we are instructed to return on board directly.'

The port captain replied that two hours was time enough and that he would return with the Dey's answer. Seeing how confused and humble the man was, Burgess moved the boat closer to the captain's and Salame handed the man the letter for the consul asking how he was as well as how the men of the *Prometheus* were. 'They are all quite well, and the consul is in his townhouse' came the reply.

'You must deliver this letter into the Consul's hand, and let me have both answers, of the Dey and of the Consul', Salame said. The port captain promised he would deliver the letters and return with the appropriate answers. The port captain then invited the men to come ashore or onto the mole so they could be in the shade away from the burning sun. But Salame refused. 'I thanked him for his kind offer, the consequence of accepting which, would have been the loss of our heads', he later wrote.

Salame then said, 'The heat of the sun does not affect us but if the Dey wishes to send any of his officers to treat with the Admiral, he would be received with great politeness, and returned in the same manner.' 'I hope it will be so', the port captain replied and then rowed away. Burgess, Salame and the six seamen remained a few yards from the mole, riding the currents in pistol shot of thousands of people who had gathered on the walls and inside the batteries, who hurled insults and abuse at the little English boat. For two and a half hours they stayed in that position in terrible danger waiting for the answer from Bashaw.

While they waited Exmouth used the time to his advantage. Signals passed from ship to ship as he moved his fleet closer to shore, hoving to about two miles from the mole. By 1000hrs the ships had exercised at quarters and loaded their guns. All the British ships in the fleet were cleared for action. The galley fires remained alight for a few hours so that every man could have a meal by 1200hrs as Exmouth ordered. After that the fires were put out. The foreign ships raised their anchors and quickly moved out of harm's way as the British and Dutch fleets moved into their battle stations.

There is no record to tell us what the Dey and his council said during this time but the debate must have been agitated, with people taking many different stands. So many fleets before this one had come and gone without a firing a shot that it was likely Exmouth would back down and leave. Yet the evidence of impending disaster could be seen by looking through the windows as the ships manoeuvred to gain tactical advantage.

The hours ticked slowly by. The Algerines shouted and cursed. Salame and Burgess remained within pistol shot of the people on the mole waiting for the Dey's reply. Burgess anxiously scanned the harbour for a sign of movement from the port captain's boat but he saw nothing. At 1415hrs a flurry of signals went from ship to ship as the fleet moved closer into the harbour. Still there was no sign of the port captain's boat.

Already a half an hour over their deadline at 1430hrs Burgess and Salame decided they'd waited long enough and Burgess ordered the signal of 'No answer had been given' to be raised. As quickly as they could they rowed back towards the *Queen Charlotte*. Salame was anxious to get out of range and back to the ship. 'Knowing their perfidious character, and observing that Lord Exmouth, on his seeing our signal, immediately gave order to the fleet to bear up, and every ship to take her position for the attack, I had great fear that the Algerines would fire upon us', Salame wrote.

When Salame climbed aboard the *Queen Charlotte* and reported to Exmouth he saw the crew anxiously waiting for the order to open fire. But that order would have to wait. Instead, Exmouth ordered the anchor raised and the *Queen Charlotte* to be moved. Slowly, in the light breeze, the giant three-decker began to move forward towards the head of the mole.

Exmouth's battle plans had been elaborate and highly detailed but the light breeze could let him down as the ship inched forward. His plan had been based on long and careful study of the survey map made by Captain Warde. Slowly, the ship moved towards the molehead battery where several hundred Algerine gunners looked on in astonishment. The battery itself was so high that it was higher than the *Queen Charlotte*'s main deck, which meant they could look down on the English sailors but they had to look up at the ship's masts that were high above them. 'There were many thousand Turks and Moors looking on astonished, to see so large a ship coming all at once inside of the Mole, without caring for anything', Salame wrote in his journal.

Exmouth took the flagship to within a hundred yards of the mole head and ordered the anchor be dropped, first the stern anchor then the bow anchor.[2] Salame wrote that the position that Exmouth took with the *Queen Charlotte* was so masterful that only four or five guns could hit them from the mole itself. However, the ship was exposed to other batteries.

The other ships had followed *Queen Charlotte* in sailing in a line astern formation. Exmouth's plan was that each ship would follow in at the minimum safe distance and, when the signal was given to anchor, would do so all at the same time. But two things were against this plan. The first was the rapidly fading breeze and the second was the poor handling of the *Impregnable* by Captain Brace under Rear Admiral Milne's orders. He ordered his sail lowered far too early and so ended up well out of his intended position. When the signal to anchor came Milne obeyed it immediately and ordered Brace to anchor exacly where they were, totally exposed to the lighthouse battery and too far away to pound that battery into submission.

The *Superb* had followed the *Queen Charlotte* closely and should have anchored in a position where she could provide covering fire but instead she anchored too soon away from the mole. However, she was in a position where she could pour her fire onto one of the main batteries without being too exposed in the process.

The *Leander* anchored approximately one hundred yards ahead of the flagship where she could concentrate her fire on the battery located near the fishmarket. The *Minden* anchored near the *Impregnable* but her captain, Paterson, soon realized that the ship was in a dangerous position so he moved in closer to the shore, astern of the *Superb* where his guns would be of use. On the dying breeze the rest of the ships gradually came into their positions but the battle began before they were all where they should have been.

There are no records to indicate where the first shot actually came from. Salame writes that 'a few minutes before three, the Algerines, from the Eastern battery fired the first shot at the *Impregnable*'. Perkins and Douglas-Morris do not mention Salame's reference to the Eastern battery but record various different eyewitness accounts, saying the first shots came from the fishmarket battery at the *Superb* or that the molehead battery fired first, putting a ball into the *Queen Charlotte*'s hull, or that the lighthouse battery was the first to fire at the *Impregnable*, firing three shots in rapid succession (as opposed to the one shot recorded by Salame).

Wherever it came from it was enough for Lord Exmouth to put aside any idea of a peaceful solution. 'Lord Exmouth, having seen only the smoke of the gun before the sound reached him', Salame wrote, 'said with great alacrity, "That will do; fire my fine fellows!"' The quiet of the day was suddenly torn apart as the 24-pounders on the top deck of the *Queen Charlotte* roared in unison. Rocking against the recoil from the deck below came the broadside of the 18-pound cannon while, up in the masts, 12-pound carronades had been hauled up and mounted, their muzzles pointing down at the Algerine gunners on the open top of the molehead battery. Now they spoke as well, sending 300 musket balls ripping into the guns, killing and maiming dozens of enemy gunners.

> This fire was so terrible, that they say more than five hundred people were killed and wounded by it. And I believe this, because there was a great crowd of people in every part, many of whom, after the first discharge, I saw running away, under the walls, like dogs, walking upon their feet and hands.[3]

With slick efficiency the gun crews on the *Queen Charlotte* continued firing, all the weeks of constant drills now paying dividends. The storm from her guns smashed into the enemy guns emplacements blowing the cannon off their carriages. Inside the dark galleries of the gun emplacements men and equipment were pulverized into a tangled mess as the cannon balls found their mark.

But the enemy were not silent. As soon as the guns from the *Queen Charlotte* had opened fire, the enemy guns answered. Though many were being destroyed, the remaining guns on the molehead continued to return the fire. The intensity of the fire from the mole dropped as more guns were destroyed, so Exmouth ordered some of his guns to shift to the battery over the main gate by the city wall that faced the quay. Again, the storm of metal smashed into the emplacements, ripping cannon from their fixtures and carriages sending them plunging into the harbour. The 24-pounders on the *Queen Charlotte* were designed for this kind of close work and their effect was devastating.

The firing began at 1500hrs and the last ship to open fire, the *Impregnable*, did so twenty-five minutes later. The breeze had died to an almost imperceptible level, which meant the thick fog of white smoke from the guns lay like a shroud over the mole area, obscuring the *Queen Charlotte*, *Superb* and *Leander*, except for the very top of their masts. Creeping slowly towards this wall of smoke were the two seventy-four-gun ships, *Glasgow* and *Severn*, both managing to glide past the *Queen Charlotte* and take up their allotted positions near the fishmarket and waterfront. From this point they were relatively safe from enemy gunners and could pick and choose their targets. Within moments of anchoring their guns fired, adding to the noise, confusion and smoke. The other ship of seventy-four guns, the *Albion*, anchored near the *Impregnable*, but her captain soon realized this open position was too dangerous so he moved his ship away, closer to shore, anchoring near the *Minden*. This left the *Impregnable* completely alone and at the mercy of the guns from the lighthouse battery.

While the world exploded all around them the two frigates *Hebrus* and *Granicus* moved slowly on the slight breeze, letting the currents take them to the positions that Exmouth had laid down for them in his original orders. Both ships entered the thick smoke and *Granicus* anchored as close to her correct place as she could, while *Hebrus* ended up too far to port for her guns to be effective.

The whole mole area, outside of the harbour, was crowded with smaller craft as well as the principal ships of Exmouth's squadron. *Prometheus*, *Britomart* and *Cordelia* moved as best they could throughout the battle, not anchoring but firing at targets of opportunity and providing assistance to those ships on station. They tiptoed around the fifty-five smaller vessels which were the mortar boats, rocket boats and gunboats commanded by midshipmen experiencing their first command. These boats moved by oars rather than sails. The rocket and mortar boats fired continuously, sending a hail of projectiles into the town and the harbour where the Algerine fleet was anchored. The crews on the Algerine vessels had no chance, swept away by flying debris and burning splinters as each mortar and rocket exploded.

On the gun decks of the English ships the crews worked like well-oiled machines, keeping up a constant barrage. Covered in smoke, sweat and virtually naked in the oppressive heat they worked for hours, only stopping to drink. Most became deaf, temporarily or permanently, from the continuous roar of the guns. Lines were formed by the gun crews and powder monkeys passing charges, wadding, ammunition and shot to the gun crews. They could barely keep up with the speed of the firing. Salame wrote in his journal that 'I saw two companies of the two guns nearest the hatch-way, they wanted some wadding, and began to call "wadding, wadding!" but not having it immediately, two of them swearing took out their knives and cut off the breasts of their jackets where the buttons are, and rammed them into the guns instead of wadding.'

Salame observed that at no time during the battle did any of the gun crews seem tired, 'not one lamented the dreadful continuation of the fight; but on the contrary, the longer it lasted, the more cheerfulness and pleasure were amongst them; notwithstanding, during the greater part of the battle, the firing was most tremendous on our side'. Even as the guns fired, Salame saw that some of them became so hot that when they recoiled they were thrown out of their carriages 'and so rendered quite useless'.

While all of this was happening the enemy gunners were having an effect. On the ships, flying splinters of wood ripped from the hulls of the ships from the impact of cannon balls tore into men's flesh. Death and injury came from these shards of wood and metal or from limbs being ripped off by cannon balls.

> It was most tremendous to hear the crashing of the shot, to see the wounded men brought from one part, and the killed from the other; and especially at such a time to be found among the English seamen and to witness their manners, their activity, their courage, and their cheerfulness during the battle.[4]

On the deck of the *Queen Charlotte*, Exmouth had several lucky escapes from death. Twice musket balls ripped through his jacket but didn't draw blood. He was hit in the jaw by a splinter and also in the leg by a spent shot that drew blood but didn't maim him. 'It was indeed astonishing to see the coat of his Lordship, how it was all cut up by musket balls, and by grape; it was behind, as if a person had taken a pair of scissors and cut it all to pieces. We were all surprised, at the narrow escape of his Lordship.'[5]

By 1530hrs the Algerines sent a force of roughly forty boats loaded with men, muskets and cannon out from the inner harbour towards the *Queen Charlotte*, *Leander* and *Severn*. Shouting loudly and waving their swords they headed for the three ships. As they rounded the end of the mole, they came into the line of fire of the *Leander* which was anchored in the entrance to the harbour. As they emerged from the smoke, Captain Edward Chatham saw the danger and immediately ordered his gunners to concentrate their fire on the little fleet heading towards them. Within moments broadside after broadside was fired from the *Leander*'s guns. Bits of iron, chain and metal from canister shot tore into the Algerines, sending hundreds of men into the water. Their boats were torn apart by the fire of grapeshot. Men screamed in pain as the shrapnel tore into them. The wooden hulls were pulverized under the intensive fire.

On the deck of the *Leander*, Royal Marines added to the slaughter by pouring accurate and deadly volleys of musket fire into the enemy. More than thirty-five boats were destroyed and the remainder fled back into the protection of the harbour, leaving hundreds of men in the water to be picked off by the marines. As this was dying down, around 1600hrs, Exmouth ordered the barge from the *Queen Charlotte* to board an Algerine frigate that was blocking the mouth of the harbour. Lieutenant Peter Richards, commanding the barge, took a boarding party of Royal Engineers, supported by marines, across to the frigate. Boarding her they laid charges and set the ship alight, losing only two of their number in the process. Within ten minutes of leaving the *Queen Charlotte* they were back aboard. Fire tore through the enemy vessel until she was completely ablaze. The mooring ropes burnt away and she began drifting towards the *Queen Charlotte*. For a few anxious moments Exmouth prepared his crew to move the ship but the Algerine fire ship sailed slowly past them at a safe distance.

Onboard the *Queen Charlotte* Exmouth sent Salame below to get out of the line of fire. He went down to the surgeries (cockpit) to help with the wounded.

> Some of them could not walk. Some could not see; and some were to be carried from one place to another. It was indeed a most pitiable sight; – but I think the most shocking sight in the world, is that of taking off

arms and legs; in preference to beholding which, if I was a military man, I should certainly prefer to be on deck than being with the Doctor in the cockpit.

By 1630hrs Exmouth knew the *Impregnable* was taking heavy casualties. A message had arrived by boat from the *Impregnable* asking for help as they had lost 150 men killed or wounded. He ordered the *Glasgow* to go to the rescue but the lack of any breeze at all meant this ship could only move a short distance, which put her in danger from the fishmarket batteries. In that position she suffered ten killed and thirty-six wounded in a matter of moments, far more than she had in two hours previously.

While most of the enemy batteries in the harbour were out of action, the ones higher up the hillside were still pouring fire onto the fleet. Many buildings around the harbour were ablaze, flames licking through the warehouses on the waterfront. Those not burning were heavily damaged from cannon balls smashing into them.

Throughout the bombardment the rocket boats and mortar boats had become better at choosing their targets, judging distance and were now pouring fire down more accurately than ever before. Most of the Algerine fleet burnt fiercely from the effect of this saturating fire. Installations on shore within range of the rockets were now a mass of flame and rubble.

Exmouth decided he had to do something about the lighthouse battery so he ordered the *Fly*, an explosion vessel loaded with 143 barrels of gunpowder, to be run ashore at the base of the battery in order to blow it up. Once again, Rear Admiral Milne made an error in judgement which essentially made the attempt a wasted effort.[6]

The first lieutenant of the *Queen Charlotte*, Lieutenant Richard Flemming, had been in charge of gunboat no. 5 throughout the afternoon which had been anchored near the *Queen Charlotte*. He was now put in command of the *Fly* that was being towed by the *Cordelia*. Flemming went aboard quickly, along with Captain Reid of the Royal Engineers. However, Milne sent Captain Herbert Powell to direct them to the place where the explosion ship should be moored to create the best effect. Flemming's orders were to take command, while Powell's were to direct the vessel to the right place. However, Powell was giving Flemming conflicting orders and despite their efforts the ship was run aground in the wrong place, and exploded on a minor battery that had been knocked out of action some time earlier. It had no effect on the lighthouse battery.

The five Dutch frigates were also in the thick of the fighting. It was their job to suppress the batteries around the shore, particularly the fishmarket batteries, to avoid the leading English ships getting caught up in cross fire. On the way in they destroyed one of the outlying forts, Fort Babazoun. They too took heavy casualties.

Hour after hour the bombardment went on. The American Consul, William Shaler, described the scene in his journal as he watched from his window in the American Consulate. 'Shells and rockets fly over my house like hail,' he wrote. 'The fire is returned with constancy from several batteries situated at the North West corner of the town and from four heavy guns directly below my windows. These batteries are exposed only to an oblique fire and apparently have not suffered much.'[7]

Despite the shells landing all around him, Shaler continued to make notes. 'At half past seven the shipping in the port is on fire. At half-past eight, the cannonade endures with unabated fury on the part of the English and is returned from the batteries in this quarter. The upper part of my house appears to be destroyed, several shells having fallen into it whole rooms are knocked to atoms.'[8]

Finally, at 2300hrs a signal was sent by Exmouth to the rest of his fleet to withdraw 'after observing the destruction of the whole Algerine navy, and the strongest parts of their batteries,' Salame wrote. 'With a favourable breeze, we cut our cables, as well as the whole of the squadron, and made sail.'

With the firing all but over, Salame went up on deck to join Exmouth. He could see the devastation lit by the burning fires:

> The blaze illuminated the entire bay, and the town with the environs, almost as clear as in the day time. The view of which was really most awful and beautiful; nine frigates, and a great number of gun-boats with other vessels, being all in flames, and carried by the wind to different directions in the bay. I observed how, in these nine hours time, our shot had effected so horrible a destruction of their batteries; instead of walls, I saw nothing but heaps of rubbish, and a number of people dragging the dead bodies out.[9]

Exmouth, his voice hoarse, turned to Salame who could see that he had two slight wounds one on his cheek and the other in his leg. 'Well my fine fellow Salame,' Exmouth said mildly. 'What think you now?' Shaking Exmouth's hand Salame replied, 'My Lord, I am extremely happy to see your Lordship safe, and I am so much rejoiced with this glorious victory, that I am not able to express, in any terms, the degree of my happiness.'

From the higher batteries the Algerines continued a much more slackened pace of fire as the fleet slowly extricated itself from the harbour, which took two hours in all. Although a steady breeze was blowing, so many ships had their sails and rigging in tatters that they had to be towed away by more fortunate vessels. The last of the Algerine guns stopped firing at 0100hrs on 28 August. In place of the roar of the guns now came cataclysm of thunder and lightning. The fleet anchored five miles out in the bay.

As dawn broke on the morning of 28 August the devastation was clear. While Bashaw did his best to rally his defences and his troops in case of another attack, the resolve of the defenders was waning. Shaler wrote in his journal that his consular house was virtually destroyed. He wrote that 'every part of the town appears to have suffered from shot and shells. The Marine batteries are in ruins and may be occupied at any time. Lord Exmouth holds the fate of Algiers in his hands.' Shaler also wrote that 'The combined fleets are at anchor in the bay, apparently little damaged.' He, along with the Algerines, being five miles away, could not see the condition of the fleet close up: the overcrowded surgeries filled with men with appalling injuries, the torn sails and damaged rigging, that the ammunition was all but exhausted and that onboard some ships there were few men left to man the guns. But none of Exmouth's ships had been sunk in the fire; no wrecks lay smoking in the harbour save those of the Algerine fleet which had been destroyed.

So from a distance of five miles the fleet appeared to be unscathed. Exmouth played on this perception and sent Salame and Burgess once again, under a flag of truce, with a letter to the Dey offering peace, provided the Dey released the British Consul, the officers and men he'd seized and the Christian slaves he held. If he didn't accept the peace Exmouth offered, the letter said that 'I shall renew my operations at my own convenience.'

To signal agreement the Dey's batteries were to fire three guns. Salame and Burgess once again rowed out to the molehead and handed over the letter from Exmouth. Salame's impression of the destruction caused on the batteries and the mole was recorded in his journal.

I was quite surprised to see the horrible state of the batteries and the mole since the preceding day. I could not now distinguish how it was erected, nor where the batteries had stood; as well as many fine houses which I had seen in the city the day previous. And I observed too, that there had not more than four or five guns mounted on their carriages and that of all the rest, some were dismounted, and some buried in the rubbish. Besides this, the entire bay was full of the hulks of their navy, smoking in every direction, and the water out and inside of the mole was all black, covered with charcoal and half-burnt pieces of wood. But the most shocking and dreadful sight was, the number of the dead bodies which were floating on the water.

This time, though, there was an answer and less than two hours later three guns were fired, signalling the Dey's acceptance of terms.

The Swedish Consul was to act as go-between in the negotiations. The following day the British Consul was set free and reported to Exmouth aboard the *Queen Charlotte*, telling him of his harsh treatment. The men of the *Prometheus* who had been seized by the Dey's forces were returned to their ship. The process of releasing Christian slaves began. A negotiating party under the direction of Captain James Brisbane of the *Queen Charlotte* was sent ashore. That day two more British warships arrived, the *Ister*, under the command of Captain Forrest with Rear Admiral Sir Charles Penrose aboard, and HMS *Wasp*, Captain Woolridge commanding.

Penrose was now available to take some of the strain off Exmouth's shoulders and took over the task of visiting the Dey and finalizing the peace treaty. On 30 August Exmouth handed his report on the action and subsequent results to Admiral Milne, ordering him to set sail for London and give the report to the Admiralty. The anchor of HMS *Leander* rose out of the water, the sails were raised and caught the fine easterly breeze and she sailed towards Gibraltar. From there she would head for Portsmouth. However, the wind changed and the *Leander*'s passage home was a slow one. To ensure the report got there quickly, Exmouth also ordered Captain Brisbane to take it over land. He sailed for Spain in the *Heron* and from there travelled overland to Boulogne where he found a ship to take him across the Channel and he arrived at the Admiralty on 15 September. He was the first to arrive in London with the news of the battle and the victory. Milne arrived on 27 September.

There were seven main terms of the peace treaty. The first was that any prisoners taken in a future war between Algiers and any European power were to be treated as prisoners of war and not as slaves. The second term was for the Dey to formally renounce the practice of Christian slavery forever. He was also to release all Christian slaves, regardless of their nationality, to Exmouth's officers. The fourth term was that the Dey was to repay the Italian States all the monies they'd paid to Algiers in tribute, which amounted to approximately $382,000. The Dey also had to make reparations to the British Consul of $30,000 for the loss of his own possessions. Next, the Dey had to make a formal, personal and abject apology to the Consul for his treatment while in captivity. Finally, the Dey was to sign the new peace treaty that would signal a lasting peace between Algiers, England and the Italian States and each side was to fire twenty-one guns to signal the return of normal relations.

In all 1,641 slaves were released, eighteen of whom were English and the rest from a wide variety of nations but by far the highest number were Sicilians and Neapolitans. The Dey handed the $382,500 over to Exmouth, along with the personal reparations to the British Consul. In short, the Dey agreed to all terms of the treaty and under Penrose's direction they were carried out. By the evening of 3 September all parts of the treaty had been resolved and agreed and at midnight of the same day the British fleet set sail for Gibraltar. Exmouth left behind the *Prometheus* under the command of Captain Dashwood who also had elements of the Dutch squadron as company.

Lord Exmouth returned to England a hero on 6 October when he sailed into Portsmouth, a little more than two months after he'd left on the expedition. Some estimates on the numbers of Algerines killed are over 8,000, while others say the casualties were even higher. On the British ships 128 were killed and 690 wounded, while the Dutch ships suffered thirteen killed and fifty-two wounded. Though his ships had been severely damaged, none had lost their masts; none, including the little boats, had been sunk.

The devastation of Algiers had been almost complete. With the exception of two ships, which the Algerines had scuttled in the harbour to avoid the destruction by fire and shot, virtually her entire fleet had been destroyed. William Shaler reported that most of the city lay in ruins. But six months later he wrote to Washington that the city's defences had been rebuilt and that the Dey was working hard to restore the prestige and power of Algiers. In less than two years he had managed to rebuild the city but he fell out of favour with his own people and was strangled to death in the public place of execution on 16 September 1818.

Within a short period of time the piratical ways of the Algerines were re-established and were only permanently stopped when the French invaded and occupied Algiers in 1829 after relations between the two countries fell apart. It took the French three weeks to gain Algiers and take the city, forcing the surrender by the Dey which the rest of Europe had been unable to achieve in three hundred years.

Yet, if we believe Shaler's entry in his journal the day after the bombardment, had Exmouth pressed his advantage and landed troops ashore he might well have taken the city; that is something we'll never know. But Exmouth had done what he had been ordered to do and in that respect the Battle of Algiers was a victory for the Royal Navy.

When Algiers became a French possession her corsair activities ceased, but another state along the Barbary Coast was soon to replace her. This was Morocco and the pirates concerned were the notorious Riff pirates who would compel the Royal Navy to once again use force.

Chapter 9

Black Charlie and the Reef (Riff) Pirates

Late in 1848 the Channel fleet, on its way to Ireland, was diverted to Gibraltar. After the invasion of Algiers by the French and their subsequent occupation of that country, the Barbary corsair activity had diminished substantially. Both Tripoli and Tunis had along with Algiers ceased their activities and renounced Christian slavery. Morocco, on the other hand, had not. This was the reason why the fleet was diverted to Gibraltar. The Barbary pirates, from the mountainous district of the Moroccan coast, known as Riff or Reef pirates, had taken a British ship which was one of many. The fleet, commanded by Admiral Sir Charles Napier, aboard his flagship HMS *St Vincent*, was on its way to save the crew, the ship and exact some form of punishment on the pirates. 'The usual process of these pirates, after murdering the crew of a captured ship, or transferring the crew of a captured ship, and transferring the cargo to their boats, was – and perhaps still is – to sink her on the spot, obliterating thus all trace of their cruel deed.'[1]

Over the centuries the generations of tribes from this inhospitable area had operated with impunity largely because of the inability of foreign powers to mount an effective offensive against them, because of the limited technology of the times and because of the rough terrain. But with newer and bigger ships, much larger guns, heavy bombardment could be brought to bear on the miscreants. The situation was exacerbated by the fact that the Sultan of Morocco was unable to do anything about the lawless people in his territories and he suggested that the people making the complaints should take the law into their own hands and deal with the pirates themselves. 'It follows that a declaration of war against the Sultan, as the responsible party, is the only manner of obtaining redress for the repeated outrages committed by the pirates of this part of the Barbary Coast.'[2]

The result of war would be a few towns destroyed along the coast, many innocent people killed and the culprits fleeing into the mountains, as happened when the French attacked Tangier in 1844. The Sultan on hearing the cost of the French attack said that if he'd been paid half that sum by the French he would have destroyed the town himself.

This part of the Barbary Coast along North Africa which the Reef pirates occupied extended from the Straits of Gibraltar to Cape Tres Forcas. 'It is a most inaccessible and precipitous nature, being formed by mountain ramifications of the Atlas; whilst in a few rocky creeks along this dangerous and ironbound coast, the pirates draw up their boats, and await the opportunity of attacking any defenceless vessel that may come within their reach.'[3]

For many decades the physical geography of the region had protected the pirates, with many of their outrages going unpunished. This was the situation when the British merchant brigantine the *Ruth* was captured in the area. Two years later another English merchant ship was taken, *The Three Sisters*, which was the reason why the Channel fleet had now been diverted. In addition to the ships being taken, the treaty between England and Morocco had been broken and many merchants had lost considerable sums; some form of action was needed. On 25 November 1848 Lord Auckland wrote to Admiral Napier giving him his orders. 'I have written to the Foreign Office and said that you will be ready to do to the Emperor (Sultan) of Morocco whatever may be desired.'

The first action Napier was to carry out was a sweep of the coast from Tetuan to Melilla, using small boats to destroy all the pirate boats encountered. The second act was to blockade the ports on the western coast and his third was to attack Mogador and knock it to pieces – but only as a last resort. 'My recommendation', Auckland wrote, 'is that you be instructed to send a steamer to Mogador, with such just demands as may be determined upon, and with an intimation that you have a strong force to insist upon a compliance with these damans, in such manner as may be necessary, and to see what comes of this.'

The official instructions from the Foreign Office that came to Napier through the Admiralty and were dated 28 November 1848 were vague in comparison to Auckland's letter. While bad weather held up the fleet at Spithead, Napier received his official instructions enabling him to take whatever measures he felt were best for 'chastising the pirates' but he was to use what force he could that would not bring the two sides into full-scale war. However, in a letter from Lord Palmerston of the Foreign Office, dated 5 December 1848, Napier was told that 'we feel full confidence not only that you will accomplish whatever the force under your command may be equal to, but also that you will not undertake more than that force can be fairly expected to do'.

Palmerston wrote that he understood the severity of the weather conditions during the winter months so a delay until the spring when the winds changed enabling the fleet to sail south would be beneficial if it meant saving the lives of sailors as well as ships that might be lost in the stormy seas. Any political inconvenience would be far less important than the loss of life. 'If you and the Admiralty should, upon considering the matter, think that it would be advisable to wait till the spring brings better weather', Palmerston wrote, 'I shall be perfectly content to wait until then, and would much prefer doing so, rather than run any unnecessary risks.'

Lord Auckland, who was the First Lord of the Admiralty, was not only Napier's superior but also a friend. This can be seen in the letters and dispatches that they wrote to each other. Napier relied on Lord Auckland to provide him with the support he needed and to keep him informed of the political and social climate back home.

When the fleet left Spithead in the middle of December and arrived into Lisbon on the 4 January sad news was waiting for Napier. Lord Auckland had died. Gone was not just a professional friend but also the valuable communications on which Napier relied. A letter dated 4 January 1849 from Captain W A Hamilton relayed the sad news to Napier. 'Here it is difficult to realise the loss of the head and hand (and heart as well) that so gently, yet so admirably, conducted this great machine. It has, comparatively speaking, and for the moment, paralysed its working, and a heavy cloud accompanies this momentary want of action.'

In Lisbon, Napier replied to Hamilton in a letter dated 16 January where he stated his understanding of his orders. 'I am only allowed to chastise the Reef pirates – that, I presume, can only be done by burning all their boats.' Shortly after he wrote this letter, Admiral Napier's squadron left Lisbon and sailed for Gibraltar, braving rough and stormy seas throughout the passage. By 31 January the fleet was anchored at Gibraltar and Napier wrote to Lord Auckland's successor, the Right Honourable Sir Francis Baring, very briefly laying out his plan of action. He was sending the steam-driven warship HMS *Stromboli* to reconnoitre the coastline, look for the pirate strongholds and also provide detailed weather information, before sending the rest of the fleet. 'I hope you approve of my keeping the '*Regent*' here till an answer comes, as it might weaken our demands if she went, and I have taken care to let it be known that I expect two more line-of-battle ships.'

The tone of Napier's letter was friendly and open. Fortunately, Sir Francis Baring replied with a letter dated 22 January 1849 in an equally warm tone that asked Napier to communicate with him in the same friendly, confidential matter that he'd done with Auckland. Baring also stated that he relied on Admiral Napier's prudence in not taking hostile action against the Moors without instructions. He said that Napier's conduct would always be met with support.

Armed with this Napier proceeded with his operations against the pirates. We have seen the reasons for these operations against the Moors boiling down to two main categories: breaking the commercial treaty between Morocco and Britain and the outrages committed by the Reef pirates on British and other nations' shipping.

The stretch of coast was supposed to be under the Sultan of Morocco's control. However, the Spanish had a presence there as well. They had a fortress at Melilla which was only a few miles from Cape Tres Forcas. The Reef pirates openly declared they were at war with the Spanish because they had been driven from their land in Spain in the late fifteenth and early sixteenth centuries. From all our documents and correspondence it is clear that the Reefians almost continually attacked the Spanish fortresses there and that the Spanish were unable to stop them without using a large force of troops and occupying the territory. Instead, they hoped the British would pick up the gauntlet.

The capture of the brig *The Three Sisters* was the straw that broke the camel's back as far as Britain was concerned. On 2 November 1848 the Reef pirates captured the merchant vessel and ran it ashore at Cape Tres Forcas, near Tramontana Bay. Luckily the crew and the master managed to escape the pirates, who brought up more than 500 men to defend the new prize. When word of the capture reached Gibraltar, the Royal Navy steamer, HMS *Polyphemus* commanded by Captain McCleverty was dispatched to get the crew and take the ship back.

When he arrived off the coast, McCleverty could see *The Three Sisters* anchored in close to the shore. Barking out orders he felt the rumble of the steam engine beneath his feet as the *Polyphemus* turned towards the shore. Moments later, musket balls flew through the air smashing into the hull. McCleverty immediately ordered his gunners to return the fire and seconds later the guns fired, sending a mixture of grape and shot into the pirates who scattered quickly. This was his chance. McCleverty ordered the boats to be lowered and rowed towards the shore to tow the merchant vessel out to sea.

However, the pirates hadn't gone far and now, hidden behind the rocks, waited for the boats to come in close before they opened fire. Lieutenant Allen Gardner, commanding the British boats, searched the coast for signs of movement from the pirates. Suddenly, they began firing as the boats came in range. Gardner ordered the boats to continue towards *The Three Sisters* while ordering those men with guns to return fire.

Shot flew in all directions, whizzing overhead, smashing into the water, splintering the wooden hulled boats. One man cried out, hit by a musket ball as the boats reached *The Three Sisters*. Fire from the pirates was intense and more men were hit. Lieutenant Waxey was wounded as he led a team that attached the lines to the merchant ship. Quickly Gardner ordered the boats to tow the merchant ship away out of range and back to the *Polyphemus*. When the boats returned safely to the warship with *The Three Sisters* in tow, McCleverty discovered Lieutenant Waxey and seven other men had been wounded in the engagement. He wanted to punish the pirates in any way he could but 'in consequence of the impracticable nature of the coast, refrained from attempting a landing, for which prudent conduct we find he was highly praised'.[4]

On the evening of 17 February 1849 four warships, the *Sidon, St Vincent, Vanguard* and the *Powerful*, in company with the steamers *Stromboli, Gladiator* and the *Polyphemus* with the *Reynard* and the *Plumper*, set sail for Cape Tres Forcas to begin actions against the Reef pirates. On arrival Napier despatched the *Polyphemus* to Melilla.

At dawn the following morning the fleet moved to the shoreline and began sailing westward.

A few people here and there appeared on the cliffs, and lighted fires; and when they reached the spot where the *Three Sisters* was captured, about forty or fifty men were seen high up among the mountains, as also a few miserable huts and two fishing-boats on the beach, but nothing I thought worth attacking it would have been useless to have started to attack the few Moors we saw as they would have retired higher up in the mountains and to destroy their fishing boats I thought that too insignificant operation for the squadron to perform and was not an adequate chastisement for the offences committed and might embarrass the Government in any future operations against them which might be construed by the Sultan as a second punishment for the same offences.[5]

The fleet continued westward and saw another three fishing boats but nothing worth attacking, the country being thinly populated and sparsely cultivated. From there, Napier moved the fleet back to Cape Tres Forcas and continued sailing to Melilla where a few people were seen who took pot shots at the *Sidon*. 'The governor told me he had made two sorties and then immediately decamped to the mountains, when he stopped, they halted. Also the Spaniards took long shots at them.'

The Governor at the Spanish fortress at Melilla stated that the pirates could get together 8,000 to 10,000 men in a couple of days. Napier's only option then was to make a landing. But his own description of the place shows how difficult such an operation would be. 'Their fortifications of which is estimated on the Eastern side of the promontory is about 3 leagues distant from the sea on the West side', he wrote.

If a landing was made on both sides Napier reckoned it would cut off the people at Cape Tres Forcas from the rest of the country but it would be a long, arduous operation, requiring large numbers of troops and equipment, 'as they would take to the foothills and retire from hill to hill in a country they are acquainted with of which we are totally ignorant and even if we were not attacked in the war the success would be very questionable'.[6]

In the west of Cape Tres Forcas there are patches of cultivation which can be easily got to and to the east near Melilla the country is well cultivated but it would be a question of policy whether so doing might not mean the apprehension of affronting the Spanish against their natural enemies the Moors though the Governor of Melilla informed me that there are some of the Sultan's officers in the neighbourhood and that the inhabitants are of the very worse description. I have no doubt the Moors of Melilla would be too happy to co-operate in the operations.[7]

Napier felt the only way to hurt the people of the area was 'by landing in the long days when the corn is ripe and setting fire to it and seizing their cattle / their homes are not worth destroying and taking care to let them know why we have done so'.

Napier had expected to find targets to attack and destroy when he arrived off the coast but instead he found nothing. In his account he wrote that 'whether, knowing we were at Gibraltar, they had taken the precaution to remove their boats into the country I cannot say, nor could I obtain any certain information as to the position of their large towns or villages, but presume, if they have any, that they are inland'.

Having been totally unsuccessful he sailed the fleet back to Gibraltar where he left on 16 March for England. Though *The Three Sisters* had been recaptured, its crew safe with no casualties, the mission had failed. The pirates continued their actions against any ships and vessels that found themselves becalmed or ventured too near to their coast, plundering several ships over the years from a variety of nations and either murdering the crew or taking them into slavery to be ransomed off.

The next British vessel to be caught in the pirates' snare were the brigantine *Violet* in 1851 and the schooner *Amelia*. In these cases the masters of the ships were murdered and the members of the crews who did not escape were taken into slavery. When news of this outrage was received at Gibraltar the Royal Navy sent HMS *Janus* to get the crews back and punish the pirates. Commanded by Captain Powell, the *Janus* arrived off the coast where the two captured vessels lay, total wrecks. Several small boats from the shore headed out towards them and Powell ordered his gun crews to open fire. The boats loaded with pirates had no chance against the might of the *Janus*'s guns and were all destroyed. Powell then directed his fire onto the shore and pounded the pirate boats that were hauled up on the shore, destroying all of those as well.

Continuing along the coast, another larger force of pirate boats was seen moored along the shore. Powell had intelligence as to the whereabouts of the crew from the Spanish Governor in the area and so knew that he had arrived at the place where the British sailors were being held. Powell ordered his own boats to be launched to attack and destroy the enemy vessels and get the crew back. Under furious fire from the pirates who had collected in overwhelming numbers Powell was wounded, along with seven of his men, but they did manage to get some of the crew of the *Violet* back to the safety and freedom of the *Janus*.

What happened to the rest of the crew? In this case they were ransomed rather than rescued. From the documents available it appears that no rescue attempt other than Powell's was made to get them. 'I am happy to inform your Lordship that the four captive seamen of the *Violet*, whose fate has been in such long and anxious suspense, have at length been ransomed and safely arrived here. They will proceed to England by the earliest conveyance.'[8] The four crew members had been languishing in captivity for months while the ransom had been negotiated. The ransom came about through the offices of Sir Robert Gardiner, Governor of Gibraltar, who robustly negotiated their release through the British Consul at Malaga, the Spanish Governor at Melilla, the British Consul Mr John Drummond Hay at Tangier, as well as the British Consul at Tetuan. 'I think it a duty to bring their praiseworthy conduct under your Lordship's special notice.'

Two years later, another British vessel was attacked by the Reef pirates. We know the information in detail through the letters of John Drummond Hay in Tangier. In a letter to the Earl of Clarendon dated 29 August 1853 he provided a copy of the statement from the master of the *Vampire* John Sand. 'It would appear the description of the site whence the piratical vessel put off, that it came from the village of Beni-Boogaffer in Akkalaya the inhabitants of which district committed the piracies on British vessels in 1846, 1848 and 1851, as also on those of other Foreign Nations.'[9]

In his statement made at the British Vice-Consulate office in Oran, Sands stated the *Vampire* was the property of Mr Bramley Moss Plumber of Gibraltar, where the ship was registered. He declared that he'd 'left Gibraltar on the 10th of August 1853 around 5 p.m. bound to Oran with a cargo of manufactures and Tobacco and that on the 11th a heavy Easterly wind forced us to make for the Reef Coast which we sailed along until the gale subsided on the 12th around 10 p.m. and a dead calm accompanied with intense fog came on'. Sands was nervous and apprehensive. He was in dangerous waters and could see nothing in any direction. Without any wind all he could do was sit and wait. The vessel 'remained at a stand opposite a tongue of land on the Reef Coast called the Cape de la Tres Forcas. On the 13th at about noon, the fog cleared away leaving the vessel on the same spot exposed to the sight of the Pirates who infest that part of the Coast.'

Sands did not communicate his growing fear to the rest of the crew. He hoped the wind would pick up before anything happened but 'at about 5 pm the same day he saw a sail with several oars put off from the Coast on the west side of Cape de la Tres Forcas and make directly for the vessel, evidently with the intention of plundering her', Drummond Hay wrote in his letter. The pirates did not just row quietly towards the *Vampire*, they came on wind and oar, shouting, yelling, cursing and firing their muskets to intimidate the crew.

When the Reef Boat was within one hour's reach of the vessel, most fortunately for the Master as well as for the crew, a fresh Westerly breeze came on, and enabled the *Vampire*, a fast sailing vessel, to get out of the reach of the Marauders, who on seeing that they were left behind, stopped rowing and afterwards turned back towards the direction of the coast from whence they came. The *Vampire* arrived at the port of Oran yesterday at 5 pm.[10]

As we have already seen, the British government were quite happy to send Royal Navy warships into the area to rescue crew members of captured

British vessels and at the same time pound the pirate boats and villages into dust. However, that kind of punishment never really worked and while the navy was willing to mount a landing against the pirates to punish them once and for all, the Foreign Office was not so keen. Nevertheless for the consuls and vice-consuls on the spot there was something that could be done, which Admiral Napier had outlined a few years earlier. Indeed, Sir Robert Gardiner, Governor of Gibraltar, wrote to the Duke of Newcastle in a letter dated 3 September 1853, saying that it was time Her Majesty's government did something effective to stop the piracies being committed on British and other nations' vessels along the Reef Coast. 'I think attention will be again drawn to the subject by the growing frequency of the aggressions of these lawless hordes against Her Majesty's subjects.'

Gardiner wrote to the government in January 1852 about the release of the four captured crew members of the *Violet*. In that letter he also recommended specific actions for dealing with the pirates. He thought the letter with these suggestions had been referred to the Lords of the Admiralty but because of a change in government hadn't been acted upon. He decided to write again. The first thing he mentions is that troops in any prolonged land operations should not be drawn from the garrison at Gibraltar.[11]

For his plan of operations Gardiner stated that 'A landing for the purpose of destroying their crops as a means for the annihilation of the Pirates would of course be attended with greater or less facility according to the extent of the force employed.' He suggested that the operations would require a 'considerable advance into the country'. But the results would be questionable if the operations were not frequently repeated. 'The object in view cannot be that of more retaliation on these lawless people, but to afford security for our Merchantman.' He believed that security could be achieved without direct engagement with the pirates by simply destroying their crops and boats.

In this letter, he reiterated his conversation with one of the crew members from the *Violet* who had told him back in January 1852 that there were no coastal defences, that the population of the area was thin but that the people were generally armed, the villages were small with scattered huts for the people living there, the main crops were wheat, corn, barley and beans, and the harvest time was May. Gardiner wrote that his informant told him there were large numbers of cattle, goats and sheep and these large 'flocks of cattle appeared a contradiction to his impression of a thinly scattered population'. He also suggested that the operations to land a force should not be a combined one, 'that the operation, whatever may be decided upon, may be left to ourselves'.

He suggested that any nature of cooperation with France would have to be treated with great care and seriousness in punishing the pirates. He also pointed out that there should be 'an understanding with the Sultan of Morocco so as to secure his assurance to our descent on his Territory before we undertake any Expedition to the Reef Coast'. He goes on to cite the incident of the capture of *The Three Sisters* in 1848 by the Reef pirates when the Sultan said

> he had no power or control over the Riff Pirates and actually suggested our taking the law into our own hands. Let application be made to the Sultan for redress to England, indemnification to the sufferers, punishment to his lawless subjects, but let us not land on his shores without his concurrence so that the French can not attempt to justify such attacks as they made in 1851 on Rabata and Salee, by citing a precedent in the examples of England.

In late July 1854 another incident took place that so stirred the imagination and passion of the British people that it was mentioned in Parliament when the Earl of Hardwicke asked the then Secretary of State for Foreign Affairs, the Earl of Clarendon, what was being done about the piratical acts being committed against British shipping. What brought this to Hardwicke's attention was the taking of the British brig the *Cuthbert Young*.

According to the Hansard entry of that debate in Parliament Hardwicke put his question by saying that 'our commerce on the highway of the Mediterranean had of late been much exposed to attack by a body of men known as the Riff Pirates who amounted in number, I believe, to 4,000 or 5,000 and who occupied a situation on the coast of Morocco, about 120 miles from Gibraltar'.

The Earl continued by saying that, while they lived under the immediate rule of their own chiefs or sheiks,

> they were tributaries or subjects of the Emperor (Sultan) of Morocco, and had lately become known as being most dangerous to the trade of all nations. The matter was of the more importance inasmuch as the position they occupied was on the direct highway of the commerce to the East and the Mediterranean, and it was of the highest importance that some measures should be taken to check their piratical proceedings.

He believed they had first been heard of in 1851 when they'd attacked the *Violet* which he said,

> was treated in the manner customary with pirates, having been attacked and plundered, the master wounded, and the mate killed. The Government on that occasion sent a vessel of war to inquire into the circumstances, with a view to revenge the attack and bring away the plunder if possible. That vessel was received in a warlike manner.

This was the action of the *Janus*, commanded by Captain Powell, where Powell himself was wounded and managed to get some of the crew back to safety.

> That was in 1851; but as late as June or July last a vessel coming from Malta to England, named the *Cuthbert Young*, of Newcastle, was treated in the same manner, and the *Prometheus* was sent out to recover her, and to do what she could against the pirates. I do not know if she succeeded or not, one statement being that she brought back the hull of the captured vessel, and another that she did not succeed.

Hardwicke suggested that these events showed that the pirates were ready for anything and that the government had only dealt with it by warning vessels to beware of that part of the African coast. He had served in the Mediterranean himself for many years and knew that it was not easy passing through the Straits of Gibraltar to keep clear of the Reef Coast because the current went in that direction:

> and vessels were driven on it whether they would or not; the consequence of which was, that it proved a capital trap for those men, giving them a position in which they could deal with the vessels as they liked. It appears to me that something more is necessary to be done than the course taken by the Government of giving notice at Lloyd's that it was a dangerous coast; and if the Government were not prepared to deal with those people by any measures of a warlike character, there should be at least a steam cruiser constantly there as a sentry for the protection of trade. The question I wish to put to my noble Friend is whether the Government intends to take any, and what, steps for the safety of trade with respect to these pirates?[12]

The response from the Earl of Clarendon to Hardwicke's question was non-committal. He said the subject had long occupied Her Majesty's Government as there had been four or five cases of piracy since 1847 but the difficult of dealing with these pirates was

> that they occupy a portion of the territory of the Emperor of Morocco, and are his subjects. In that state of affairs, an application had been made to the Emperor to prevent the continuance of these depredations; but the Emperor professed his inability to do so, when Her Majesty's Government then informed him that they would undertake to do it irrespective of his assistance. In the case to which my noble Friend had alluded – that of the *Cuthbert Young* – the vessel which was ordered to look out for the pirates immediately went to the coast and recaptured the vessel, which was defended by the pirates, who were fired at and shelled, and there is reason to believe they sustained considerable loss but I can assure my noble Friend that the attention of the Government has been directed to the subject, and there is a vessel now at Gibraltar a warship specially charged to watch that coast for the protection of vessels passing through those Straits.[13]

Unlike the other ships that were captured, the incident with the *Cuthbert Young* was well documented and had a favourable outcome, which may be why it had so much notice.

In the 24 June 1854 edition of the *Gibraltar Chronicle*, the details of the taking of the brig were recorded. It made for interesting reading:

> The British brig *Cuthbert Young*, of Newcastle, Captain John George Marshall, of 293 tons register, coppered and copper fastened, out 25 days from Malta, in ballast and beamed to Falmouth for orders was unfortunately becalmed and driven by the force of the current to within ten miles off Cape Tres Forcas, on the coast of Riff, on the night of Wednesday last, the 21st instant, where, to the astonishment of the master and crew, they were suddenly alarmed by the fire of musketry, and immediately afterwards observed a number of boats approaching which proved to be full of pirates.

There was no moon that night so there was little light other than on the ship. Onboard the *Cuthbert Young* it must have been pandemonium as these shouting, swearing, yelling pirates, firing their muskets, rowed as fast as they could for the becalmed ship. Without wind in their sails there was nothing the crew could do, as the article reports.

By 10 o'clock, finding little chance of escape, the night being rather dark and the pirates increasing their fire and closing upon the brig, the stern boats was lowered, six of the crew got in and pushed off in the greatest confusion; twenty minutes elapsed before the remaining portion of the crew could launch the skiff, when they jumped into it and made away as fast as they could, hotly pursued for an hour by two piratical boats who kept up a constant fire on them until they were out of reach. It was not until 5 p.m. on the following day (seventeen hours after leaving the brig) that the skiff was fallen in with by the Austrian bark *Vincense*, Captain P. Fachietti, who took them on board and treated them with every kindness, they being in a state of great exhaustion, not having tasted food during that time. Captain Fachinetti was on his way to Swansea to take in a cargo of coals, and put in here yesterday merely to land Captain Marshall, James Lang (first mate), William George Hardy (second mate), W. Tock (Cook) and W. Wanless (apprentice). The stern boat with the other six (including two boys the safety of whom was Captain Marshall's first thought) has not, we are sorry to report, been heard of.

The article was sent by Mr Drummond Hay, British Consul at Tangier, to the Earl of Clarendon, Secretary of State for Foreign Affairs, as part of a letter he wrote to the Earl dated 29 June 1854. In this letter Drummond Hay stated he'd received correspondence from Sir Robert Gardiner advising him of the taking of the *Cuthbert Young*. 'On the receipt of Sir Robert Gardiner's letter, I addressed a letter to the Moorish Minister for Foreign Affairs, Sayed Mohammed Rhatub and I beg to submit, herewith, to your Lordship a translation of this letter and of Sayed Rhatub's reply.'

Drummond Hay suggested in his letter to the Earl that 'Her Majesty's Government would hereafter treat the Reef People as being responsible for their own acts without appealing to the Sultan, who had confessed his want of power to control the lawless tribes of Reef'. He also stated that the Spanish Chargé d'Affaires said the Sultan of Morocco had ordered the Moorish Governor at Tetuan to release six pirates from the Reef district who were implicated in several incidents of piracy on Spanish vessels. They had been detained as hostages by Sayed Mohammed Rhatub at the request of the Spanish Chargé d'Affaires until a Spanish sailor boy still a captive in the hands of the pirates was sent to Tetuan. 'Under the circumstances of the case, I thought it my duty to give every support in my power to my colleague', Drummond Hay wrote 'and to let the Sultan understand I should consider myself justified in holding him responsible for these acts of piracy, if it was discovered, that his Majesty neglected to chastise the pirates when he had it in his power, or that his officers returned to connive in allowing the guilty to escape with impunity.'

Drummond Hay included a copy of the letter he'd sent to Sayed Mohammed Rhatub dated 25 June 1854 advising him that, as the Sultan had formally declared in 1852 that he couldn't enforce his power on the Reef district and that he wasn't responsible for their outrages and wouldn't make any reparation,

> that Her Britannic Majesty's Government would treat the Reef people as independent and as being responsible for 'their own acts'. On this account I do not, with the sanction of Her Majesty's Government, demand immediate reparation from the Sultan for this outrage of the British Flag. My object, however, is to request that a messenger be dispatched immediately to the Reef, with directions to obtain information regarding the six men, who may possibly have been taken prisoners, by the Pirates if they were compelled from the smallness of their boat to seek refuge near land.

He then goes on to tell Rhatub that he has discovered that six of the crew of a Reef boat that committed an act of piracy on a Spanish vessel were the same pirates who had been

> at the request of the Spanish Charge d'affaires and with your consent arrested and detained, as hostages at Tetuan, as a guarantee for the security of a Spanish boy still held in captivity by the pirates, but that not withstanding this arrangement, an order was being recently received from the Moorish Court to let these Reefians at liberty, without waiting for the release of the Spanish subject or making any communications to the Spanish Charge d'affaires.

Indeed, these six pirates were set free by one of the Sultan's officers in the Reef district, which Drummond Hay communicated to the Earl of Clarendon in his 29 June letter.

Why concentrate on the situation with the Spanish boy and the six Reefian pirates? This incident illustrates the mentality of the Moroccan government from the Sultan down, and the mentality of the Sultan's officers in charge of the Reef district. Here is what Drummond Hay said about it in his letter to Rhatub:

> If the government of Morocco shows its indifference to the just demands of a colleague, conniving as it were in allowing parties

implicated in a piratical act to escape, I should then consider it my duty to hold the Sultan responsible for the outrages which have been or may be committed by the pirates of Reef on the British Flag, as these pirates will doubtless become more daring in their acts when they perceive that the Moorish government allows these outrages to pass with impunity, even when it may be in its power to chastise them.

Drummond Hay included the reply he received from Rhatub in his 29 June letter to the Earl of Clarendon. It said that as soon as he had received Drummond Hay's letter asking for a courier to be sent to the Reef district to find out any news of the six crew members from the *Cuthbert Young*, Rhatub immediately dispatched a messenger to the area, 'directing him to give us the information you require and when his answer reaches us, you shall be informed of the contents'. Rhatub also stated that he'd sent a courier to the Sultan which included Drummond Hay's letter and the details of the taking of the *Cuthbert Young* so 'that its contents may be known to his Royal Mind and you shall have the answer when it comes, if it pleases God'.

It is here that Rhatub in his letter to Drummond Hay states that he did not know the six Reefian pirates had been released and had only heard about it from the Spanish Consul at Melilla, 'but as soon as I learnt it I wrote to the Sultan and manifested my dissatisfaction in a very distinct manner. I pray God that the answer may be such as we desire.'

As the letters went back and forth the British government decided to send the steam-driven warship, HMS *Prometheus* to Gibraltar to deal with the situation. The ship arrived a day after the master of the *Cuthbert Young* turned up at Gibraltar.

I frequently expressed my views to her Majesty's Government regarding the manner and necessity of destroying this nest of pirates, and the danger of the outrages on the British flag becoming more frequent, should not some chastisement be inflicted on the lawless tribes of the Reef Coast. The site where the piracy on the *Cuthbert Young* was committed is exactly the same where three British vessels have been captured, besides six or seven vessels of other nations, during the last eight years.[14]

A few days after its arrival in Gibraltar, the *Prometheus*, under the command of Captain Edward Rice, set sail for the Reef Coast. The account of what took place was published in the *Gibraltar Chronicle*, 28 June 1854.

Her Majesty's steamship *Prometheus*, Commander Rice, which left our Bay on Sunday evening last, for the Riff Coast in search of the *Cuthbert Young*, made the land at day break on the following morning, and ran along the coast until 5 p.m. where the brig with loose sails was seen in a creek among the rocks at anchor, and a very great number of pirates were likewise observed on the beach opposite where the vessel was, armed with long bright-barrelled firelocks.

The article stated that, as soon as the *Prometheus* arrived, the pirates started firing at the ship. Rice ordered his gun crews to return the fire. The cannon roared, plastering the shore with shot and shell 'causing great havoc amongst them, and a hawser proceeded under the cover of the steamer's fire, to board the brig, speedily succeeded in clearing the decks taking possession of her, the crew also destroyed two large boats which were lying on the beach, and after accomplishing that arduous task left at about half past seven that evening'.

But the *Cuthbert Young* was a hulk; the pirates had ripped out the cabin bulwark and taken it away along with the galley, spare spars, sails and anything else they could find to remove, with the exception of the anchor and the chain cable, 'which they in vain tried to possess themselves of had been removed. It is understood that three of the *Prometheus* crew have been slightly wounded. No tidings of the missing boat belonging to the *Cuthbert Young* has yet reached us from any quarter.'

Far greater detail can be seen about the action in Commander Rice's own report to the Secretary of the Admiralty dated 28 June 1854 which he wrote when the *Prometheus* was back in Gibraltar. Addressed to the Lords Commissioners of the Admiralty, Rice told them he left Lisbon on 22 June and proceeded towards Gibraltar as they had ordered him to do. However, on the afternoon of the following day,

> when we were about six miles S.W. of Cape St. Vincent, I fell in with Her Majesty's Steam Ship *Melina*. On learning from her commander that she had despatches for Admiral Dundas, and that her coal would not be sufficient to take her either to Gibraltar or Cadiz, I kept company with her until the next morning, when, as it blew hard from the eastward, with a heavy sea, I was unable to take her in tow until the afternoon, when it moderated.

Rice managed to get the *Melina* to Cadiz where he left her on 25 June at 0600hrs and then proceeded to Gibraltar, arriving at 1700hrs.

Having immediately communicated with Captain the Hon. George Grey (delivering to him their Lordships' letter), I was informed by him that, on the night of Tuesday last, the 20th instant, an English brig, called the *Cuthbert Young*, of South Shields had been captured and plundered by piratical boats, about 10 miles to the N.W. of Cape Tres Forcas, but that the master and crew, 12 in number had escaped, and arrived at Gibraltar.[15]

Captain Grey sent the master, Mr Marshall, on board, as also a pilot, for the Riff Coast, and at 8 o'clock the same evening I proceeded to sea.

The anchor from the *Prometheus* splashed into the water near the Spanish Fort of Albucema the following morning. According to Rice, this is on the Reef Coast in the district of Beni Oriaga. Here he learnt from the Governor of the fort 'that the boy referred to by their Lordships' letter had been given up and sent to Tangier, unhurt in the charge of two soldiers of the Sultan of Morocco, four days previously, having been confined five weeks in the neighbourhood of Albucema'.

The Spanish vessel captured by the Moors was laden with water, oil, and Spanish Government stores for the fort of Albucema. She was taken at night, and subsequently destroyed on the shore of Beni Oriaga, in sight of the Spanish garrison just out of gun shot. The Moors sent to offer to sell her, the cargo, and the boy, to the Governor of Albucema for 6,000 reals. The Governor declined and detained the messenger as a hostage for the security of the boy, and he is still a prisoner but to be released.

Rice was also told by the Governor of Albucema that he, the Governor, thought the Spanish government was going to station a small force of armed vessels at Penon Valez, Albucema and Melilla for the suppression of piracy. With this information in hand, Rice steamed away from Albucema, heading along the coast in search of the *Cuthbert Young*.

At 4 P.M. we found her anchored about 200 yards from the shore, in a rocky inlet, 10 or 12 miles S.W. of Cape Tres Forcas, near the spot marked Zera on the chart. I steamed in towards her and as we neared her, the Moors opened fire on us with volleys of musketry from the rocks, among which the brig was anchored. As the brig was in 3 fathoms of water I could get close to her, and Lieutenant Visconti and a party of men were sent to make a hawser fast from our bows to hers, and to slip the cable. The cable could not be unshackled, the anchor was therefore hove up, and at 6 o'clock we backed out of the cove with the brig in tow.

Soon after the Moors began firing, and were assembled in considerable numbers round us, we opened fire on those ahead, and on the port bow from the pivot gun forward, and on those on the starboard side and starboard quarter, from the quarter deck guns, with grape, canister and short range shells. The mini muskets were also used with success.

Under the direction of the *Prometheus*'s senior lieutenant, Lieutenant Edye, the fire was kept up as the operation to secure the *Cuthbert Young* took place. Edye barked out orders to the gun crews, training his telescope on the targets, giving co-ordinates to his gun captains. The guns on the *Prometheus* rained down a barrage of fire remorselessly on the pirates, as the operation on the shore to secure the *Cuthbert Young* continued. Shells pounded the pirates sheltered in their rocky positions on the shore, destroying their boats, smashing into the rocks, dispersing many of them, wounding and killing many more.

Meanwhile Lieutenant Visconti and his team managed to secure the hawser to the *Cuthbert Young*, weighed anchor and managed to pull out of range with 'great steadiness' according to Commander Rice:

During the hour and a half we were employed in getting the brig away, the Moors kept up a constant fire, which, from the nature of the ground, they were, from some quarters further in shore, able to do so with comparative safety. I am happy to say that we had but one casualty, John Hays, stoker, wounded in the head by a musket ball, but not dangerously.

In his report to the Admiralty, Commander Rice said that the *Cuthbert Young* was largely intact, 'with the exception of the destruction of some of the internal fittings and spare sails'.

With the *Cuthbert Young* secured in behind the *Prometheus*, Rice ordered a course back to Gibraltar. They left the area at 1930hrs that same day and arrived at the Rock at 0100hrs. However, the trip back was eventful indeed when the starboard engine broke down and the *Prometheus* had to limp for Gibraltar on only one engine. 'I find that the defects of both engines, as detailed in the report of Mr Thomas Murray, Chief Engineer, herewith enclosed, will detain us at this place three or four days. As soon as ready, I shall return to Lisbon agreeable to their Lordships' orders', Rice wrote in his letter.

On 3 July 1854 Drummond Hay wrote another letter to the Earl of Clarendon telling him that the *Prometheus* had returned to Gibraltar and Rice had told him that while he was in the Reef district he had heard that on the night of 27 June an unknown ship had been attacked by pirates when it was passing the coast not far from Cape Tres Forcas.

Commander Rice's informant apprehended the crew had been taken prisoner by the pirates. Under the circumstance of the case, Commander Rice said he hesitated, about proceeding to the piratical district to attempt to recover this captured vessel, as he had done in the case of the *Cuthbert Young*, fearing the pirates might murder the captives, if still alive, when exasperated at the loss of their booty. He therefore requested me to ask the Moorish Government to send some officer with him in the steamer, who might assist in a parlay with the Reefians and in ransoming the captives.

Drummond Hay refused the request saying that it would take too long to request the Moorish Minister to send someone with Rice back to the Reef Coast. He also said that he believed

the fact of an officer of the Sultan arriving in the district of the pirates would also probably interfere with the success of any parley with them for the purpose of ransoming the captives. In 1851 the British sailors, captives in the hands of the pirates, were given up, at my interception, by a Reefian chief, though the pirates, and this chief had rejected frequent applications from the Sultans' principal officer in Reef for the release of the Captives.

It was in this letter that Drummond Hay also told the Earl of Clarendon that the Spanish sailor boy had been finally recovered from the pirates through the 'Moorish Court which was solely owing to the detention at Tetuan, as hostages, of certain Reefians from the piratical district'. Drummond Hay had a plan, which he outlined in his letter to the Earl and which he recommended to Commander Rice who said he would do follow it. Rice was to go directly to the

Spanish Fortress of Melilla which is within a few miles of the piratical district; there, he would be able to learn, whether the crew of the captured vessel had previously escaped, or were in captivity or had been murdered. If they are in captivity Commander Rice could then have a parlay with the pirate chiefs at or near Melilla, or he might visit in Her Majesty's Steam Ship *Prometheus* and with a flag of truce, warily approach the shore, for the purpose of a parlay with the natives. To assist Commander Rice in carrying out this purpose I obtained a letter from the Spanish Charge d'affaires for the Governor of Melilla requesting that every information and assistance be afforded him for effecting the object he had in view.

Commander Rice wanted someone with him who knew the area and could speak the language. Drummond Hay sent his brother James Drummond Hay to be as of much assistance as possible, 'accompanied by a Moor in my employ who is a native of Reef. I strongly warned them all to be on their guard against treachery in any parley with the pirates.'

Drummond Hay told Commander Rice that he could ransom the captives for as much as £20 a head if necessary 'but that I thought if the parley was carefully conducted much less would be required'. Drummond Hay then warns that, because the *Prometheus* had returned so early, he hadn't taken down any of the details that Commander Rice communicated to him so the account he wrote to the Earl of Clarendon might not have been entirely accurate.

I have dispatched a courier with a letter to the Moorish minister, reporting this fresh outrage and requesting him to send me every information he may receive on the subject overland, and do all in his power to recover any captives in the hands of the pirates. If I hear there are British subjects, or even the subject of any other nation, in the hands of the pirates I shall dispatch a trustworthy messenger to the piratical district to look after the captives, and prevent if possible their ill-treatment, and I shall also address a friendly letter to the Reefian Chief, Shereef Al Hadary, through whose mediation and influence I obtained the release of the British subjects in 1851.

Rice carried out the plan and returned to Tangier on 6 July having spoken with the Spanish Governor at Melilla 'who informed him he had not heard of any vessel having been attacked or taken by the Pirates since the capture of the *Cuthbert Young*. This information was confirmed by the statements of some Reefians, who had visited the Spanish Garrison and had some conversation with my Reef servant.'

After leaving Melilla, the *Prometheus* cruised close along the shore looking for any sign of a captured vessel, but saw nothing except several large Reefian boats. The pirates appeared in numbers and started shooting at the ship.

I have no doubt the recapture of the *Cuthbert Young* and the chastisement inflicted by the *Prometheus* will have produced a beneficial effect upon the Pirates, but I trust some more formidable expedition, may be seen hereafter to inflict great injury upon the lawless tribes of that coast as may more effectively deter them from their outrages. Your Lordship will pardon me for observing that I think Commander Rice deserves the greatest credit for the manner in which he has carried into effect the object of his visit to these waters.[16]

Chapter 10

The Reefians (Riffians)

I believe I am right in surmising it has been especially on account of political reasons Her Majesty's Government have hitherto abstained from chastising the Reefians as they deserved for the frequent piracies committed by them on British Vessels, knowing that it would have involved the necessity of a British force invading the territory of Morocco. (John Drummond Hay, British Consul at Tangier, April 1856)

The British Consul at Tangier wrote several letters to the Secretary of State for Foreign Affairs outlining the situation that was occupying most of his time – the outrages committed by the Reefians on foreign vessels, especially British ships.

Since Admiral Napier's failed expedition to the coast the consuls and governors had begun championing his recommendations that a force be landed and the pirates' houses, cattle, boats and crops be burnt and destroyed to punish them. By 1854 this had still not taken place. The government had sent the steam warship *Prometheus* to Gibraltar for the purpose of patrolling the Reef Coast. In the summer of the same year the Earl of Clarendon wrote to Drummond Hay asking for his recommendations on dealing with the pirates. He replied in a letter from Tangier dated 8 August 1854. 'I would beg you to refer to the despatch marked No 1 of the 7th of January 1852 addressed by me to Viscount Palmerston, transmitting a memorandum regarding the number of boats and of armed me in the Riff district, and offering suggestions as to the best mode of chastising them.'

In that letter he included a report from Captain Gifford written in 1852 (see Annex A) that detailed the habits, haunts and countryside of the Reef Coast. Drummond Hay wrote:

For the effectual punishment of the pirates, I think a force ought to be landed and that the village of Beni-Boogaffer, which is within half a mile of the beach, should be if possible burnt and the cattle and other property of the pirates destroyed or carried off, for the main object will be to effect such a heavy loss upon these outlaws as may deter them from attacking for the future British vessels. Where as the mere destruction of their boats would not gain that object, for even one hundred of their large boats, would not be equivalent in value to the profit they might make on the plunder of the cargo of one British vessel of two hundred tons.

In the same letter Drummond Hay tells the Secretary of State that he believed the Sultan would be more than happy for the British to succeed in punishing the pirates. Six years earlier Admiral Napier went to the Reef Coast to recover *The Three Sisters*, her crew and punish the pirates but, as Drummond Hay wrote, 'He had, unfortunately not done so, but had listened to propositions put forward by the Chiefs of Akkalaya of a similar nature to the present, though their twenty thousands dollars had been offered in compensation for the seizure of the two British vessels, "Three Sisters" and "Ruth".'[1]

Instead of punishing the pirates, as Drummond Hay thought Napier was supposed to do, he came to an arrangement where the pirates promised they would stop their piracy and build honest trade with the British and other foreign vessels, but a few days after Napier's fleet left the area they struck again, taking a Spanish vessel.

One of the tribal chiefs that Napier had been negotiating with was chief of the tribe of Beni-Said. Shereef Al Hadary was friendly towards the British and had helped Drummond Hay on a number of occasions when dealing with the pirates. In the case of the missing sailors Drummond Hay asked if Al Hadary would become security for 'the good conduct of the Akkalayans, he declined saying they were a lawless people under no control and whose promises were not to be trusted'.

At the beginning of July 1854 Drummond Hay sent a messenger into the Reef country to find out what happened to the six missing sailors from the *Cuthbert Young*. That messenger returned on the 12 August 1854 with a letter from Al Hadary. Immediately, Drummond Hay sent a letter to the Earl of Clarendon bringing him up to date.

This letter is in reply to a few lines I addressed to the chief asking for tiding of the British Sailors, and expressing a hope he would use his powerful influence in releasing them from captivity, as he has so generously done in the case of the captives of the 'Violet'. My messenger appears to have departed the day before the French steamer 'Newton' visited that coast.[2]

The Reefians held Al Hadary in great respect, even saw him as a holy man according to Drummond Hay, who refers to him as 'an honest Moor'. Indeed, Drummond Hay tells the Earl in his letter that it was Al Hadary that 'interceded with me, after the last piracy on behalf of the Akkalayans'.

In this instance Al Hadary was offering to mediate between the British and the pirates of Beni-Boogaffer. 'My messenger, who is a trustworthy Riffian, confirms all that is stated in the Shereef's letter.' The messenger told Drummond Hay that he was at a conference where the piratical chiefs begged Al Hadary to

make peace between them and the English, but he said the conditions they insisted on, would be that they should continue to stop and search all vessels passing their coast but that, should the British vessels have on board certain pre-arranged signals they would be allowed to pass, after search, without further molestation and that vessel of all other nations, except the French, would be captured.

The response from Al Hadary was vehement abhorrence of the acts of piracy the tribes committed and the conditions that they were demanding. Nevertheless, the pirates wouldn't give way.

Nothing was agreed, there was no news of the missing sailors and the pirates would continue to attack foreign shipping plying the coast. But Drummond Hay ensured that every avenue that could be pursued was in order to stop the outrages from the Reef Coast.

In conversation with the Moorish Authorities, I have always urged them to counsel the Sultan to endeavour to subjugate the Reef Country, as the lawless acts committed by its inhabitants in their demi-independent state, might produce questions, which, could seriously affect the safety of other part of the Sultan's dominions, and foreseeing, as I have always done French interference and ambitious views in the quarter, when time and opportunity may render the annexation or conquest of the Reef Country favourable.[3]

Mr Drummond Hay's trusty Reefian messenger saw firsthand how the pirates operated when on the 1 August the messenger saw a square-sailed vessel becalmed in the water just off the coast. 'Three boats, with some seventy or eighty armed men, immediately put off after her, but when they had approached within a short distance, the wind freshened and the vessel escaped capture. He said the flag appeared to be Spanish, but he was not certain.'

Far greater detail is listed in the letter and Drummond Hay apologizes for taking up so much of the Earl's time with so much information which he says might seem 'very trifling matters'. The point he was driving home was that the information in Al Hadary's letter and the firsthand experiences of his messenger were 'further evidence of the futility of the proposals of these pirates and the policy of our admitting French interference, in such affairs unless much stronger reasons have been put forward than those I am acquainted with'.

Interference was also coming from the direction of Algeria and Paris. Algeria was a French possession and the French were interested in the Reef country. They had invaded Algeria back in 1829 after more than 109 French survivors of two shipwrecks were massacred by the Algerines and their heads put on display. Now a French Governor oversaw a Muslim government, making the nation a possession of France. The French Algerine frontier was not far from the Reef country and, while the English and the French were at this point in time allies, the French kept up a constant communication with Al Hadary and other key players in the district.

When the *Cuthbert Young* was taken, the French government ordered the French imperial steam sloop, *Newton*, commanded by Captain Chalier, to assist in the search for the captured brig and to rescue any of the crew taken into captivity. Chalier left Cadiz around 27 July bound for the Reef. 'After taking on board an interpreter at Tangier, he went direct to Melilla and having connections with the governor of that place returned along the Coast to the Westward.'[4]

As the *Newton* steamed along the coast she was fired at occasionally by the pirates and wherever opportunity offered itself, she returned the fire with some effect.

Near the place from which the *Cuthbert Young* was taken, a shell was thrown at some men hauling a boat up the beach, which killed two of them and destroyed the boat. Four leagues to the west of Zera Captain Chalier landed and communicated with a merchant, supposed to profess much influence amongst the tribes and pointed out to him the certain retribution which would sooner or later befall his people if they continued their piratical acts.[5]

This information comes from a letter that Commander Rice of the *Prometheus* wrote to the secretary of the Admiralty. Rice said that the following day, when the *Newton* returned to the place where the *Cuthbert Young* had been taken, three Reefians swam out to the boat, two of whom Chalier allowed on board.

> They asked if the vessel was French or English and on being told French, they begged Captain Chalier to act as their intercessor with the English Government to obtain pardon for the Capture of the *Cuthbert Young*. He told them he would only speak with their Chiefs, whereupon they returned to the shore and soon came off in a boat with 12 others amongst whom were 3 Chiefs.

This information was given to Rice by Captain Chalier when they met in Tangier. Chalier told Rice the pirate chiefs expressed their sorrow for having taken the *Cuthbert Young*,

> for which they had been already punished, and feared they might be yet more so, and as they did not know how to communicate with the English government that Captain Chalier would do so for them and act as their intercessor. He said he would do what he could for them, but that they must be prepared to pay for the damage they had done and submit to the conditions that would be imposed on them, that the chiefs must go with him to Tangier as security for the good conduct of the Tribes and to learn the terms on which their pardon could be obtained.

The chiefs reluctantly agreed to go to Tangier after killing an ox on the deck of the *Newton* in honour of their good faith. 'They expressed their desire to trade with us, and that we should come to visit their Country peaceably,' Commander Rice wrote in his letter.

But almost a year later, the pirates struck again, at two British vessels this time. Drummond Hay wrote to the Earl of Clarendon on 24 May 1855 providing what little information he had.

> Herewith are two printed paragraphs, which I have extracted from the Gibraltar Chronicle of the 18th and 19th instant, reporting two further acts of piracy committed on British Vessels in the beginning of this month, on the Riff Coast. I have no further information on the subject from other channels, but there is no doubt that the pirates who have committed these outrages belong to the Beni-Boogaffer tribe, being the

same people, who captured the British vessels in 1846, 1848, and 1851, beside several Spanish vessels, and, very lately, a French brig as reported to your lordship by Vice-Consul Reade.

He ends his letter by saying that, the weather being fine, the time was perfect for the English, Spanish and French to form a combined expedition to 'destroy this nest of pirates, who continue to become, every year and day more daring in their acts'.

The first of the ships to be plundered was the *Lively* of Horton that had left Hartlepool on the 7 April with a cargo of coal for Malta. The master of the brig was James Napier and the crew consisted of ten men. Napier made a statement at the Port Department at Malta on 9 May 1855. A copy of the statement was sent by Governor Reade to Lord Passmure dated 11 May 1855.

In his statement, James Napier said that on 2 May around 1400hrs they were 'in the latitude 35.33 North and 3.18 West Long' near Cape Tres Forcas when they saw a large boat with about fifty or seventy men pulling fourteen oars on each side, flying a black flag, heading directly for them. As the boat got closer, Napier decided to abandon ship, so he and his crew quickly climbed into their boat and left the *Lively* but instead of heading for the ship, the Reefians chased his boat for half an hour until they turned away and went back to the *Lively* where they hoisted their black flag. Later that afternoon, Napier and his crew were picked up by the bark *Empress of Hull* from London that was bound for Constantinople.

The incident concerning the *Lively* was reported in the *Gibraltar Chronicle* but with a twist. The paper reported that the *Lively* was brought into Gibraltar by the captain and crew of the brig *Conference*, of North Shields with a cargo of coke for Cartagena, which was the second act of piracy that Drummond Hay referred to in his letter.

By the statement made by Captain Peter, of the latter vessel, it appears that, having had to abandon his own ship on the 2d inst, near Cape Tres Forcas, in consequence of an attack made upon her by the Riff Pirates, and seeing another vessel about 8 or 10 miles in the offing, he pulled towards her, found, on getting on board, that it was the *Lively* of Stockton, and that she was totally abandoned. He consequently took charge of her and brought her safely to this Port. Before he left the *Conference*, the pirates were nearly on board, and he saw nothing further of her afterwards.[6]

Once again the *Prometheus* was dispatched to try to deal with the pirates. Commander Rice reported the engagement to the Secretary of the Admiralty in his letter of 27 August 1855. The *Prometheus* arrived at the Reef Coast near Melilla and began cruising along the shore towards Zera Bay where she hove to. Rice had seen something on shore. He called for the engines to be disengaged. 'Observing some of the large piratical boats hauled up in shore and what appeared to be part of a Ships cargo and while examining the place the ship touched slightly on a sand bank', Commander Rice wrote.

The moment the steamer arrived the pirates began gathering on the shore and Rice expected them to open fire with their long muskets. Instead, through his telescope, he saw them hoist a flag of truce. 'Which I answered not being my intention to have attacked them on this occasion.' Even through the steamer was gently touching a sand bank it was slowly drifting towards the shore and was in range of the pirates.

Suddenly, they opened fire. Musket balls peppered the *Prometheus* as the pirates fired. Rice immediately called for full reverse and as the engines engaged and pulled the ship off the bank taking her out of range of the pirates' musketry, a chance shot 'killed the boatswain as he was standing at his duties on the forecastle. This being an outrage which required punishment I immediately hauled down the flag of truce and prepared for action.' Rice called out for a course correction, barking orders so the steamer moved forwards and backwards as necessary for the crew to get her guns trained on the shore.

'Fire!' the gun captain shouted and the guns from the *Prometheus* opened up, sending volley after volley of shot and shell onto the shore. Rice then decided to deploy the rockets that were onboard the *Prometheus* and these joined in the bombardment, 'destroying huts and boats with shell and killing and wounding several of the pirates'. As the firing continued, the crew of the *Prometheus* could see the pirates bring down a 'small gun' which Rice supposed was a 6-pounder 'and after the first Shot was fired we directed the long gun on it, diverting the men from it and silencing its fire'.

Finally, at 1730hrs Rice ordered the guns to stop firing and as the last shot died away he scanned the shore. The huts and boats were utterly destroyed and on fire. The pirates left alive had fled into their rocky hiding places along the beach. 'From what I have now seen', Rice wrote in his letter, 'I think the only plan to be pursued in this instance is keeping out of musket range and destroying their boats; thus depriving them of their principal means of annoying trade and at the same time without making war, dispersing them as much as possible.' The nature of the shore was such that it was so rocky that they could see several sheltered enclosures where the pirates could have a degree of security while firing on any vessel that came within musket range. However, a warship like *Prometheus* could stand off out of range and fire with impunity, destroying their boats, smashing their huts – even their rocky shelters could be pounded into rubble by shot, shell and rockets.

Having once again inflicted serious damage on the pirates, Rice ordered a new course and they steamed away down the coast. Rice concluded his letter to the Secretary of the Admiralty by recommending that the 'measure of destroying boats whether hauled up or afloat and of taking every opportunity of inflicting damage on them be rigorously pursued until they are brought to bear'.

From his office at the British consulate in Tangier, in early December, John Drummond Hay wrote another report to the Earl of Clarendon, this time with some good news about the Reef Coast. 'Seed Mohamed Khateeb sent me this morning, a letter he had received from the Basha and from the information given in this letter and from the language held also to me by Khateeb, in a late interview, it would appear that a severe chastisement has been inflicted by the Basha on the pirates of Beni-Boogaffer.'[7]

The letter stated that the Pasha, Ben Abdel Malek, had a force of about 4,000 cavalry and the same number of troops with which he attacked the pirates.

> He is a Riffian himself by birth, and it would appear his little army was supported by several of the inland tribes of Reef, who are not benefited, in any way, by the piracies committed on European vessels and yet are constantly kept in dread of an invasion of their territory on account of the outrages perpetrated by their pirate brethren.

This was good news indeed and exactly what Drummond Hay had been trying to bring about for some time – getting the Sultan to take responsibility for the Reef territory. The troops and cavalry the pasha commanded had come from the Sultan so now it appeared that the pirates had been brought to bear at last. 'I do not suppose the whole Riff territory have now acknowledged their complete submission to the control of the Sultan, but I have no doubt, if the Basha continues for some years as their Governor, a great change will take place in the country and that piracy on that coast will be put down.'[8]

However, Drummond Hay wanted to see for himself just how much had changed since the pasha's attack on the area. He also wanted to try to bring about complete peace to ensure the tribes of that area gave up not only plundering foreign vessels but also attacking the Spanish garrisons at Melilla. In early April 1856, the British Consul from Tangier climbed aboard HMS *Miranda*, commanded by Captain Hall, and sailed for the Reef Coast. Drummond Hay made a diary of his voyage some of which he shared with the Earl of Clarendon in a report which he sent on his return. 'The result of the cruise along the Reef Coast has been satisfactory. The *Miranda* steamed, for the greater part of the voyage within musket shot of the land, and instead of the inhabitants engaging, as heretofore, in hostilities against us we were saluted everywhere, and especially in the piratical districts with the most friendly demonstrations.'[9]

They touched land at three places along the coast, Penon de la Gomera, Albucema and Melilla, 'and were very courteously received by the Governors of the first and last mentioned Spanish Garrisons'. These governors were instrumental in setting up interviews with the chiefs of the Reef tribes and while he stated that he felt no real confidence

can be placed in the statements or promises, made by those lawless people, I think some good and certainly no evil results may be brought about by the language, which I have held to the chiefs, as also by the result of my interviews with the Spanish Authorities. I have been enabled, also by this trip, to make myself acquainted with the Riff coast and the position of the Spanish fortresses.

Concerning the conflict between the Reef pirates and the Spanish garrisons Drummond Hay stated it was in Britain's best interest to urge the Sultan and his Moorish government to stop the frequent attacks on the Spanish. 'It can hardly be expected that the wild inhabitants of Riff, notwithstanding their late chastisement by the Sultan, will continue for any time to respect our vessels or flag, or make much distinction between an Englishman and a Spaniard, when engaged in constant conflicts with the latter, both by sea and by land.'

Both the British and the Spanish wanted to ensure Morocco remained an independent nation and that the Reef territory was clearly controlled by the Sultan. 'But should the Spanish Government as I believe had been their intention at one time, march a large force into the Riff country to chastise the pirates, I fear it would be establishing a precedent for other Powers, who might hereafter find like plausible reasons or excuse for similar expeditions.' He felt that if Britain and Spain cooperated in stopping the attacks on the Spanish and ensuring no further piracies took place on all foreign vessels they could help the Sultan 'make every effort and sacrifice to effect the complete subjugation of the Riff district'.[10]

When Mr Drummond Hay came ashore from the *Miranda* at Tangier, the voyage to the Reef country over, he must have had a real sense of satisfaction. He had seen firsthand how effective the punishment had been by the pasha on the pirates. Not once had the ship been fired upon and everywhere they went they'd been greeted as friends and allies. Though there was still much to do he must have felt some quiet confidence that things were beginning to settle down at last. It was not to be.

On 14 May 1856 the pirates attacked the British barque, *Hymen*, capturing the crew and destroying the ship. Outraged, Drummond Hay wrote a letter to Seed Mohamed Khateeb informing him of this new act of piracy.

I have received information from the Senior Naval Officer at Gibraltar that a British barque, called the *Hymen* had been captured by the prates of Akkalaya on the 14th instant. I do not possess further particulars regarding this fresh outrage on the British flag by the lawless subjects of the Sultan except that it would appear the crew had been detained in captivity, and that a tribe in the neighbourhood of Melilla had offered, in a friendly manner, to assist in effecting the liberation of the captives.[11]

Drummond Hay's bitter disappointment is clearly shown in this letter.

The partial chastisement inflicted last year on the tribe of Beni-Boogaffer has not had the desired effect, which had been anticipated by the Moorish Government, of stopping these piracies. I have now, therefore, to state distinctly to Your Excellency, that, if the Sultan of Morocco desire to avert a foreign invasion of his country, and the occupation, hereafter, by a Foreign Power, of the Reef territory, there is no alternative but the complete subjugation of the people of Reef, by His Majesty. To effect this it will be required that the Basha should not only inflict an immediate chastisement on the piratical tribes but that he, the Basha, should remain permanently as Governor of that province, with a large Moorish force under his command, and that castles, or forts, should be built at the principal villages on the coast, and Moorish officers be appointed to reside there with orders to prevent any boat in Reef from putting to sea for the other purposed than those of carrying on a lawful coasting trade, or carrying on board arms, or ammunition of any kind whatsoever.

He made it clear that he expected the Sultan to mount an immediate punishment of the pirates by once again providing the Pasha with the necessary force to do the job, as well as expecting the Moorish government to pay whatever compensation was necessary to the British for loss or injury. He ended his letter by saying that, if nothing was done by the Moorish government, 'Her Majesty's Government will at once take the affair into their own hands. The Moorish Government must always bear in mind that the possession of a territorial domain is attended with responsibility for the acts of the people dwelling within it and a denial of such responsibility involved a renunciation of territorial domain.'

So now it seemed all was lost. The outrages were continuing and all Drummond Hay's work seemed to have been for nothing. But this time it was different. He had heard from the Pasha that friendly tribes who wanted peace in the region were prepared to help ensure the captives were safe and sound.

The following day, 30 May 1865 Drummond Hay sent another report to the Earl of Clarendon where he stated that he felt that from the information he had gathered from the Pasha, from a short note from one of the captives and from the Senior Naval Officer at Gibraltar, that the captured crew of the *Hymen* were safe, 'that my labours have not all been in vain and that I left some good seeds in my late visit in *Miranda* which have perhaps saved these poor sailors from being barbrously murdered'.[12]

Shortly before penning this letter to the Earl of Clarendon, Drummond Hay met with Khateeb and the Pasha to discuss the situation and he reported that the Pasha Ben Abdel Malek was desperate to get back to the Reef and hit the pirates hard.

He says that if the Sultan will give him the troops, and ensure all of them are properly paid and fed he will destroy the tribe of Beni-Boogaffer and establish the Sultan's Government in Riff. I confess as I said on the first expedition that the Sultan always risks being worsted by the Riffians, unless there is division amongst them which there would appear to be, but I know the Basha is sincere in his language and so is Khateeb, but this will not suffice for the future security of British life and property.

Again, Drummond Hay pointed out to the Earl in his letter that Britain should mount an expedition to destroy the pirate boats, hamlets, crops and cattle without getting involved in full-scale war. 'My Despatches in 1846, 1848, 1850 and 1852 will confirm this.' He conceded that Britain had been occupied with the Crimean War during those years and so had not been willing to get involved with another long-drawn-out conflict of attrition but he wanted to bring to the Earl's attention a confidential letter he had written to the Governor of Gibraltar regarding French intentions in the region.

You know a French vessel was taken some fourteen months ago by the Riffians. The French have made little stir in the matter with this Government, until they perceived we were doing all we could to tranquillise the Riff and get the Sultan to accept his domain over his lawless subjects.

Drummond Hay wrote that, through a Spanish colleague, Senor Carlos de Espanna, he'd received a confidential letter from the Spanish Governor of Melilla that

he understands the French are preparing a force on the Algerine border to invade the Riff. This of course may be mere conjecture of the Spaniard, but yesterday when I happened to be conversing with my Swedish Colleague regarding the piracy on the English Vessel, he observed that it was to be regretted the British Government had never sent an expedition to destroy the pirates, as the Sultan he said, had not the power to control the Riff people, but he added you will soon have satisfaction through another channel.

Drummond Hay's Swedish colleague was the Swedish Consul Mr D'Ehranoff who was very friendly towards the French officials in Tangier with whom he spent a great deal of his time. 'He had been informed (he did not say by whom) that a French expedition was about to penetrate this summer into the Reef Country, and he had seen the plans which had been prepared for the expedition', Drummond Hay wrote. 'I merely replied by saying, I am certain the British Government will neither desire to hold any territory themselves in Reef or allow any other nation to occupy permanently any position of that territory.'[13]

If this information was true the implications would have far-reaching effects and would put the lives of the English captives in jeopardy. 'The fanatical feelings of the people would be roused by the first rumour of an invasion of their land by the Christian and the English hostages might be sacrificed.'

The British response was to send the steam warship HMS *Ariel* commanded by Captain Manse to try to recover the captives and bring them home to safety. At the same time the Pasha, on Drummond Hay's request, sent a mounted courier to the Reef to encourage the friendly chiefs to do all they could to liberate the English prisoners,

> with threats of vengeance to the pirates, if any of the captives be injured. With this horseman I sent an intelligent Moor with a letter to the master of the *Hymen* and gave the man some money to provide for the wants of the captives, and directed him to remain with them, until they should be liberated, if the pirates would allow him to do so. I gave him also, a letter from my Spanish colleague to the Governor of Melilla, wherein the latter is requested to provide, if necessary, any comforts for the captives, in case they should be detained by the Riffians for any length of time.

Drummond Hay was then advised by Khateeb that couriers had been despatched to the Sultan and the Viceroy at Fez and that plans and preparations were being made for the Pasha to depart for the Reef country and put the pirates down once and for all. 'He is to be joined by a large force from Fez, whence he will proceed to the Reef. This expedition is sent by the Sultan, in consequence of the representations I lately made, regarding the state of Reef, the conflicts with the Spaniards and the necessity of the Sultan's rendering himself, if he wishes to avert a Foreign invasion, master of the Reef.'

In the same long letter to the Earl of Clarendon where all of this was detailed by Drummond Hay, he also stated that the Sultan's orders to the Pasha were

> to act with more rigour than he did last year, and he declared that he would make such an example of the pirates and rebels, as he hoped would deter them from committing like outrages for the future. He called upon Seed Mohamed Khateeb in my presence to urge the Sultan to provide him with a sufficient force, as he said his good will and good intentions would be null, if he had not the means of carrying out the object they have in view.

Before Drummond Hay sent his 30 May despatch to the Earl of Clarendon he included some further news. He added that he received through the courier that had been sent to the Reef district news of the crew and master of the *Hymen*. Mr Richards, the master of the vessel had been allowed to write a short note to the consul to let him know they were all safe and to provide details of their capture. 'It would appear that the vessel had, in the first place been wrecked; but I conclude Mr Richards had carefully worded his letter from a fear that the pirates might have found some one who could read it to them, and thus destroy the letter which spoke of their misdeeds.'

It took seven boats filled with pirates to plunder and wreck the *Hymen* and bring off all the crew. She had been carrying a cargo of coal which the pirates didn't want and so abandoned her after rampaging through the cabins, destroying them and taking anything of value from the ship. Members of the friendly tribe Beni-Said wrote to the Pasha that they had brought the vessel ashore and tried to salvage whatever they could so they could send it to Khateeb for delivery to whomever the items belonged to.

As far as the captives were concerned, one of the Beni-Said tribe and a few friendly men of the Beni-Boogaffer tribe managed to save the crew and bring them into the hands of the friendly chief, Seed Mohamed Al Hadary, 'the chief who saved, in 1854, the sailors of the *Cuthbert Young* who were subsequently liberated by myself'.[14]

The news of the possible French invasion of the Reef territory meant that it was urgent the captives be liberated as soon as possible because no doubt there would be a reaction to this news by the people of the district. Getting the captives into friendly hands was a huge step forward. Now, Britain had to ensure their safety by sending another warship to the area. If the French did decide to make a move they might reconsider if there were British warships off the coast.

Drummond Hay sent a despatch by express boat to Gibraltar asking the senior naval officer there to send another warship into the area to get the prisoners back in case Commander Manse in HMS *Ariel* was unsuccessful.

I now despatch the British Vice Consul, Mr Reade, and a Moorish Officer, with letter from the Basha to the friendly chiefs to deliver over the captives in case their liberation has not been affected by the *Ariel* which the Basha seems to think is probable, as the Chiefs may hesitate about delivering the Captives before they receive a written communication from the Basha, approving of their friendly conduct.

HMS *Retribution* was duly sent to the Reef, carrying Mr Reade and two Moorish officers to get the captives back. However, Drummond Hay was able to advise the Earl of Clarendon a few days later that HMS *Ariel* returned on 6 June 1856 'with Mr Reade bringing all the persons who had been onboard the *Hymen* at the time she was captured'.

Drummond Hay states in his 8 June report to the Earl of Clarendon how fortunate it was that Mr Reade and the two Moorish officers sent by the Pasha arrived in time at Melilla because 'Commander Manse had not been able to effect the liberation of all the men and was about to return here to obtain letters from me for that purpose when the *Retribution* arrived at Melilla.' Drummond Hay reported that, according to Mr Reade who was the British Vice-Consul at Gibraltar, he had some initial difficulties in obtaining the release of the captives but after some tough negotiation was able to do so without paying any ransom and without agreeing to any conditions,

> which it would appear from a subsequent parlay he had with the Chiefs of some of the piratical tribes, it had been the intention of the latter to impose.
>
> The prompt release of the Englishmen without any demand for ransom contrasts strongly with what occurred last year, when a French Brig was captured by the same pirates and an officer of the French Consulate who had been sent in a Government Steamer to the Reef, was compelled to pay 16000 francs for the liberation of the French crew.

This had happened before the first expedition by the Pasha to put down piracy had occurred, still Drummond Hay believed that the subsequent attack of the Pasha on the pirates and all the effort that he and the Royal Navy had made to suppress piracy had some effect. 'I think it will be admitted our labours to check the outrages of those lawless people, have not altogether been thrown away, for not only have we affected, in the present instance, the prompt liberation of the Englishmen, but they have been comparatively well treated and no one has been murdered.'

Drummond Hay went on to commend the friendly services of Chief Seed Mohamed Al Hadary who had been instrumental in bringing about the successful release of the English prisoners of the *Hymen*, along with the actions of the friendly chief of the Beni-Boogaffer tribe, Said Mohamed El Gram, 'who rescued the men from the pirates and delivered them into Al Hadary's hands. El Gram is the Chief of Beni-Boogaffer appointed by the Basha of Reef.'

In acknowledgement of everything he had done for the British prisoners, Drummond Hay told the Earl he had sent Al Hadary, 'as a mark of our goodwill, and in return for his hospitality to my countrymen, two small Bales, containing articles of British manufacture to the Value of £21. I have requested Al Hadary to give some portion of these articles to El Gram for his services, as he, Al Hadary praised El Gram's conduct.' He also sent to Al Hadary a certificate which he had signed and sealed which stated all that Al Hadary had done for the British captives and compelled, 'in the name of her Majesty's Government, all British officers to whom the certificate may be presented to treat Al Hadary and his family as friends of the English'.

In that same letter Drummond Hay stated he had asked Commander Manse to return with HMS *Ariel* as soon as possible to the Reef country to continue to cruise off the coast while waiting to see if the British government was going to do anything to punish the pirates who were continuing their outrages even though the captives had been freed.

The owner of the *Hymen*, Mr Richards, had been a passenger aboard his own ship when she was taken and when he'd been liberated he gave Drummond Hay

an exact account, as he states, of the value of the *Hymen* and the property on board lost by and plundered from himself, master and crew. I shall address a note without loss of time to See Mohamed Khateeb, demanding eighteen thousand dollars as a compensation for the losses of the British Subjects. From this sum will be deducted the value of the few articles saved from the wreck by Al Hadary which are now deposited in the Moorish Government Magazine and will be sold by public auction for the benefit of the proprietor or whomsoever it may concern.

Drummond Hay then turned his attention to Commander Manse of HMS *Ariel*. Apparently, Manse had sent a letter to the senior naval officer at Gibraltar concerning the capture of the *Hymen* and the subsequent liberation of the crew. In it he stated that the conduct of Chief Said Mohamed El Gram was not as friendly or forthcoming as Drummond Hay made out.

Drummond Hay states he didn't agree with the Commander in his report to the Earl and suggests that his views came from his lack of knowledge of the Reefians and their position vis-à-vis the Sultan. 'Also from Commander Manse's ignorance of the language and from the fact that all the information he obtained came entirely through the Spaniards or their Interpreters.' Manse's recommendation was to have El Gram punished because he was the governor of the Beni-Boogaffer tribe and because he refused to deliver up the Englishmen when demanded by the Commander of a British Ship of war, but Commander Manse was not then I suppose aware, that the Riffians of that district, for the last two hundred years, have not submitted to the Sultan's control and that El Gram has only the mere name of the Basha but has no troops or police to enforce his command on the robbers, amongst whom he resides, nevertheless with such a shadow of authority, this chief rescued the British mariners from the hands of the pirates and from being murdered and he fed them at his own expense.

Perhaps Manse felt that he had no need to get any local information on the tribes and the local politics of the tribes because he represented the mightiest force on the planet, the Royal Navy, with which Britain had built her empire.

Rather than go blustering in, demanding the release of the prisoners or else, Drummond Hay knew the politics of the place and knew how delicately one had to deal with the people to achieve one's aims. So as far as he was concerned, El Gram had acted in a friendly way in good faith. Manse did not have the full facts and was not aware of Al Hadary's part in the affair and so not aware of Al Hadary's glowing recommendation of El Gram.

I have in compliance with Al Hadary's request recommended El Gram to the Basha, who promised if he succeeds on his expedition to strengthen El Grams hands. Commander Manse with whom I have twice had some conversation on the subject now takes, I believe, the same view as myself, but I think it right to offer this explanation or your Lordship might be surprised to find such a divergence of opinion, viz that I should praise the very Chief, whom Commander Manse, by his cruder observations selects as the fittest person to make an example of on this occasion.

Twenty days after Drummond Hay sent his letter of 8 June to the Earl of Clarendon announcing the liberation of the English prisoners, he sent another one, this time outlining operations by HMS *Ariel*, commanded by Manse against the Reef pirates. On 19 June 1856, HMS *Ariel* steamed for the Reef coast and arrived just as the sun was setting. Calling for All Stop, Manse let the ship drift quietly towards the shore. The anchor splashed suddenly into the water and held fast, bringing HMS *Ariel* to a standstill in the Bay of Botoya.

Manse and a team of crack armed men climbed into the ship's boat and rowed away from the *Ariel* towards the shore. Moving down the beach, they spied three large pirate boats drawn up on the shore. They were about half a mile east of the River Kort. With guns drawn they moved quickly and quietly as darkness grew to the boats and captured them without firing a shot. 'No combat took place with the Riffians as the few men who guarded the boats, took to flight', Drummond Hay wrote in his letter.

Manse then continued along the shore, having posted men at the three boats with instructions to take them, intact back to the ship. West of the river his team came upon another large pirate boat 'near which he found two men sleeping. He captured these men and a quantity of bees wax and a musket, which were in their possession.' These men were in the territory of the friendly tribe, Beni-Said, which Commander Manse was not aware of. He took the two men prisoner. The whole operation and the length of the shore they travelled had taken most of the night and by the time they returned to the *Ariel* dawn was peering over the horizon.

In a loud thunderclap, the *Ariel*'s anchor was hauled up from the sea. Manse ordered the engines engaged and the slowly backed out of the bay and steamed off down the coast, firing at two more pirate boats that had been hauled up on the shore. 'He sailed for Gibraltar, where, he left the three captured Riff boats and came over here bringing with him the two prisoners.'

On 21 June Drummond Hay met with the Pasha in Tangier just before he left for Fez where he was joining a company of cavalry destined for the Reef. 'He is to be joined by a force of five or six thousand horsemen. His orders, he tells me, are to inflict a severe chastisement on the Akkalaya tribes, than on his expedition of last year. The day of the Basha's departure, I rode out to take leave of him and we were joined by Commander Manse of HMS *Ariel* who had just arrived from Gibraltar.'

Hearing about Manse's actions on capturing the boats and prisoners without bloodshed, the Pasha was very satisfied indeed 'as he said it could not be expected that a British vessel of war should respect the Riff coast until the Sultan had established his government there and had repressed piracy'. Of course, the Pasha would have preferred Manse to have destroyed all the boats, the huts and killed as many pirates as he could, as he felt that now the pirates would go to great lengths to conceal the boats that remained while they went into their hiding places. 'On Commander Manse showing some Arabic documents to the Basha, which had been found on the person of one of the two captives, the Basha discovered one of his own letters to Seed Mohamed Al Hadary and other papers which convinced him, as also myself, the captured Reefians belonged to the tribe of Beni Said.'

Drummond Hay promised the Pasha he would set the prisoners free 'and restore to them the property which Commander Manse had found in their possession. On my return to Tangier I received satisfactory evidence from the men, and from credible witnesses that they belonged to Beni-Said.' The two Reefian prisoners said they were sleeping near to a broken boat that was a pirate boat at the time of their capture which, by association, made them look like pirates. 'It appears the limits of the Beni Said commence from the western bank of the River Kort.'

Drummond Hay did indeed set the prisoners free and returned their possessions to them. He wrote a friendly letter to Al Hadary outlining 'how it had come to pass that any aggression had been made by one of HM ships on the friendly tribe of Beni-Said. I enclose for your lordship's information the reply of the Basha to me.' This letter was taken by one of the freed Beni-Said prisoners to Al Hadary.

> The other captive is too old and infirm to return by land, so I shall take care of him and send him back by sea by the first opportunity. I further enclose for your Lordship's information the translation of a letter addressed to me by Al Hadary, acknowledge the gifts I sent him and giving me some information regarding the pirates of Akkalaya, who, by his account, would appear to be in great consternation at the approaching expedition of the Basha.

In his letter to the Earl, Drummond Hay then turns his attention to Commander Manse, saying that he had asked Manse to only attack the pirate boats at sea, as he felt that any conflict with an insufficient British force

> would lead to an erroneous impression regarding the power we have of effectively chastising the pirates for their outrages, and moreover might place these people on their guard, and thinking under the success of any larger expedition, sent either by the British Government or the Sultan less effectual. yet under all the circumstances of the case, and considering the gallant and prudent manner in which the capture of the three boats were made without bloodshed or conflict of any kind

whatever, I may be permitted to express a hope Commander Manse's conduct on this occasion will receive your Lordship's commendation, without any reference to his having separated himself from my suggestions.

Although two Beni-Said men had been captured it was Drummond Hay's belief that this would not cause enmity between the Beni-Said tribe and Great Britain.

One of the men is a chief and master of a Beni Said boat, and he tells me, that when he reports the kind treatment he has received, he is certain, his Chief and tribe will be convinced the English are their friend, and that the Beni Said will refrain from all connection with the Beni-Boogaffer in case the latter are attacked by the Sultan or even by a British force.

A short time later, a small headline in the London *Times* appeared reading, 'Riff Pirates Massacred.' The story states that the tribes had gathered at the Spanish fortress of Albucema to pay a fine of '20,000 when they were attacked and massacred by the Basha's cavalry. Twenty-five heads were collected and sent to the Sultan.'

Like other engagements over the decades of the Royal Navy's operations pirates of the Barbary Coast the skirmishes with the Reef pirates showed that Britain was trying to do the right thing but was not applying sufficient force. If Admiral Napier had landed a force and burnt their villages and crops and destroyed their cattle how much different would the events have been afterwards?

Yet looking at Drummond Hay's correspondence it is possible to say that the Royal Navy's presence and actions did make a difference. The operations by HMS *Janus*, HMS *Polyphemus*, HMS *Prometheus* and HMS *Ariel* created divisions amongst the tribes. Many were desperate for peace with Britain and the diehards were isolated. This isolation made it much easier for the Pasha to inflict severe punishment on them and for the sultan to impose some control on the territory.

This improvement was, however, to be short-lived, for Spain and Morocco would go to war in 1859 and Morocco would be defeated at Tetuan where the Reef territory would come under Spanish control. From that point on Spain would find itself in a continuous guerrilla war with Reefian Berbers until the establishment of the Republic of the Rif in 1921.

The rest of Morocco would increasingly come under the French sphere of influence. The Conference of Madrid in 1880 guaranteed the independence of Morocco but as French influence grew in the area and as the Germans attempted to counter this influence, Morocco eventually became a French protectorate in 1912. In 1956 the Reef region was returned to Morocco when she gained independence.[15]

Chapter 11

Twenty-First-Century Piracy:
The Mayhem Continues

Throughout this book I have looked at different ways in which the Royal Navy dealt with piracy in and around African waters. Lord Exmouth bombarded Algiers; Admiral Napier was tasked to go and destroy Reef pirate boats, crops and cattle, but didn't. How the navy has dealt with pirates has depended greatly on politics and politicians. Over the last 300 years or so, British politicians have used the Royal Navy to exact revenge and punishment on the Barbary pirates, the Riff pirates and the pirates like Roberts cruising on the West African coast. Naval bombardments, engagements at sea, burning boats on the shores, along with diplomatic expeditions, have been the rule of the day.

No British government has sanctioned the action of landing troops to put an end to piracy on the African coasts. Instead, governments have used their warships to punish pirates for their outrages. But the punishment has had only temporary effect and, as we have seen, the pirates very quickly rebuild and are soon back up to their old tricks. Piracy has never really gone away.

Angus Konstam tells us that piracy is essentially robbery on the ocean and the men who undertake this activity are not the romantic pirates of Hollywood but just criminals prepared to use violence to get what they want. 'Piracy thrives where law and order is lacking.'[1] As we have seen, the Royal Navy has been fighting piracy for centuries and not just off African waters but in other hot spots around the world, such as the Caribbean and the Atlantic coast of America right up until the eve of the Second World War. During the Golden Age of Piracy the Royal Navy had some real success in capturing pirates. Between 1700 and 1725 Blackbeard was killed and his crew captured off an island in North Carolina's Outer Banks, while Roberts was engaged off the coast of West Africa and fifty-two of his men were hanged after being tried in Cape Coast Castle.

After dealing with the Reef pirates, the Royal Navy was involved in pirate hunting off the Cuban coast during the 1820s. In the 1830s they went after pirates operating out of Singapore and the following decade they were hunting down pirates operating in the many inlets and bays around Hong Kong. Indeed, by the early nineteenth century, pirates operating in the Far East were endemic and for more than 100 years, in the Far East, hunting down piracy was one of the navy's main tasks.[2]

In one instance, billed as the Sunning Affair by the *Illustrated London News*, some forty pirates had disguised themselves and boarded the British steamer *Sunning*, which was out of Shanghai bound for Canton. The men hijacked the ship, and took over, ordering the crew to steer for a remote anchorage. They never reached their destination because the crew broke free, got the revolvers out of the weapons cupboard and stormed the bridge. Once there, they held it while the pirates did everything in their power to try to take it back. Unsuccessful in this, the pirates then set fire to the ship. Fortunately, before the fire could spread, the gunboat HMS *Bluebell* arrived, a boarding party was sent over and the pirates were captured, the fire put out and the *Sunning* was then towed to safety. From 1926 onwards a wave of piracy plagued the Chinese coast and was part of a miniature crime wave.

To take care of the problem the Royal Navy dispatched a squadron of gunboats, spearheading the war against the pirates by the international community. This wave of piracy lasted until 1935 when the navy finally managed to get rid of the last few holdouts – a very similar situation to the piracy problem from Somalia today.

Of course, we still have this romantic view of pirates as loveable rogues like Jack Sparrow – not a young man holding a loaded AK47 assault rifle, or a grenade launcher. The reality is that piracy often includes rape, extortion, kidnapping and murder. So how can piracy be stopped? Historical experience tells us the best way to stop it is to increase the risk of them getting captured at sea by increasing the number of warships patrolling the area and depriving them of a safe haven on land from which they can operate with impunity. Angus Konstam tells us that because of the state of near anarchy in Somalia the policing of piracy at sea is hugely important. The Royal Navy has centuries of experience in combating pirates and uses its vast expertise to deal with the threat of increased crime on the high seas.[3]

To get an idea of how bad the situation was, at the time of writing, in Somalia we can look at some statistics from the International Maritime Bureau for 2008 which stated that there were more than 100 attacks by pirates on merchant shipping that year. There were forty successful hijackings and fourteen ships were held for ransom by Somali pirates, with more than 200 crew held as hostages.[4]

The statistics for 2009 are just as startling. There were more than 147 incidents of piracy, with thirty-two vessels successfully hijacked and more than 500 crew members taken into captivity to be ransomed off. The pirates fired upon more than eighty-five vessels according to the International Maritime Bureau.[5]

In the past pirates would seize merchant ships and take the best one they captured for their own. Usually, this meant they would seize a ship that had more cannon than their own, that had better and more sails, so it would be faster, and had enough room in the hold for a wide variety of captured loot. Today, tactics of the Somali pirates are somewhat different. They use high technology, such as mobile phones, global satellite tracking systems, radios and small speedboats with powerful outboard motors. The pirates are armed with AK47 automatic rifles and rocket-propelled grenades.[6] Often, these small, fast speedboats are launched from much larger 'mother ships', much as the pirates in centuries past would launch rowboats filled with men, carrying muskets and sabres, and they would row furiously towards their prey. Today's pirates also have intelligence from contacts in various ports that tip them off to the sailing times of the large tankers and freighters that ply the shipping lanes around the Horn of Africa.

However, it can be difficult to understand how a small speedboat filled with armed pirates could capture a massive tanker or freighter. Remember that the speedboat is much more manoeuvrable than the huge ships it is after and therefore can move very quickly and be alongside the victim in a matter of minutes. Then the pirates use rocket-propelled grappling hooks and irons to secure ropes and ladders to the ship. The pirates have no qualms about firing their rocket-propelled grenades at the ship to scare the captain into stopping. Once the ship is captured, it is taken to the Somali port of Eyl and the hostages, crew and any passengers, are then taken ashore and held until ransom is paid.[7]

Sounds familiar doesn't it? The tactics are very similar to those used by the Barbary Coast pirates and the Reef pirates and for similar reasons the Somali pirates are difficult to stop. First of all, the area they operate in is roughly a quarter of the Indian Ocean, which makes it difficult for modern navies to police such a vast area. The pirates move quickly and often under the cover of darkness so by the time a surprised crew can react it is far too late.

Secondly, once a ship has been captured, using a military solution to stop them becomes far more difficult because of the hostages the pirates have made of the crew and any passengers. In 2010 there was still no international legal system, or court, set up to bring the pirates to justice. The UN Security Council in December 2008 took steps enabling countries to pursue pirates on land as well as at sea by approving a resolution that extended the powers that nations had to enter Somali waters to capture pirates.

At the time of writing the biggest problem was the lack of government control within Somalia itself. Torn by years of conflict, the Somalia government had been unable to enforce law and order. As a result piracy flourished. Desperate poverty and lack of security inside Somalia was a normal state of affairs; there were no jobs and half of the population depended on food aid. One of the most violent and poorest countries on the planet, Somalia had been hit by severe drought for many years and food was scarce. Hunger and violence were the norm for the majority of the population. The risks of turning to piracy were negligible but the rewards were great.[8]

In 2009, the international community was largely fighting the problem of piracy on the ocean only, much the same way as the Royal Navy dealt with the Barbary Coast pirates and the Reef pirates. The problem is and always has been on the land. The BBC published a story on their web news pages in April 2009 that detailed the difficulties in dealing with piracy. 'In Somalia there is virtually no authority to carry out the kind of policing that could effectively disrupt pirate operations.'

The internationally recognized government of Somalia, at the time of writing, was involved in a fierce struggle to gain control of the country from well-organized and equipped militia in the south. Government troops had been fighting for years to gain control of the capital city, Mogadishu, so 'combating pirates must seem a somewhat lower priority'.[9]

Most of the pirates attacks came from the northeast region of the country, known as Puntland, where what little local government existed was overwhelmed by the chaos and instability of dealing with the continued mass exodus of refugees fleeing the war and heading for Yemen in boats of any shape and size. Unscrupulous pirates undertook to smuggle the refugees into Yemen but in many cases dumped them overboard before they reached the shore for fear of being caught.[10] Many of the refugees seeking sanctuary drowned before ever getting to the shore while those that did make it ended up as second-class citizens in Yemen which is already a poor country.

BBC News published a story on the web in April 2009 about piracy being a symptom of a much larger problem inside Somalia and stated that the average income was approximately $650 per year: 'the lure of up to $10,000 for a successful pirate raid is obvious'. As with all pirates, money was the driving factor. It was estimated that the pirates had received ransom payments of more than $150 million in 2008 alone.

According to a report by Simon Cox published on BBC News web pages on 29 January 2009, piracy had become a mini-industry with the money trail leading back to London. In 2008 pirates had been paid $35 million in ransom money for the release of ships they had captured and hundreds of crew members they had held captive.[11] Behind the release of the captives there are batteries of negotiators, security teams and lawyers, all based in London, the world's capital for the maritime industry. Cox wrote in his report that the players involved in paying the ransoms preferred to remain in the shadows. He described the chain of events ultimately leading to the ransom being paid by a light aircraft or helicopter dropping it via parachute onto the captured ship.

Once a ship owner knows that a ship from their fleet had been captured, the first thing he or she does is to contact a law firm that specializes in ransoms at sea and kidnapping. There are no rules to this game but, as Cox stated, 'at the end of the day it's somebody from the owner's side talking to someone from the pirate's side, negotiating their way to a final settlement'.[12]

Since the rise of piracy off the Somalia coast and around the Horn of Africa a trend has been set of the payment of ransoms, so when the pirates captured a vessel and took the crew hostage they were sure the companies would pay up. Cox stated that one of the key elements of a successful conclusion is to call in a specialist negotiator to try to reach a reasonable price for the ransom. This could mean daily contact with the pirates for several months before an agreement was reached. 'The going ransom rate is $1m–$2m.'[13]

Perhaps the best way to describe it is as a commercial transaction but with a twist. 'They have hijacked the ship, the crew and its cargo and they want a certain amount of money for its release although human lives are involved and the consequences of something going wrong are quite significant.'[14] Once the agreement has been reached an even bigger headache begins – getting the money to the pirates. In the case of the *Sirius Star* oil tanker captured by pirates in November 2008 the money was dropped by aircraft but most of the time the pirates got their money by drop-off boat, which was not without its own set of problems.

The people who carry out the drop-offs by sea carry huge amounts of cash with them and often fend off attacks by other pirate gangs themselves before getting near to the people they are trying to pay. They also have to ensure that the navies patrolling the area know what they are doing – it is vital that 'you're not going to be looked at as a pirate vessel … then you might get taken out by a naval vessel'. The law firms do not provide this service for free. Their fees plus those of risk consultants, security advisers, overheads and the cost of hiring the team to deliver the money could mean 'doubling the ransom amount'.

However, in his investigation, Cox stated that some believed there were darker elements involved rather than just purely criminal activities. There could be ties between the pirates 'and the radical Islamist group al-Shabab'. They worked together because they had a common enemy in the international community and this relationship was only getting stronger through time.[15]

The costs of tighter security, higher insurance premiums, ransom payments to pirates, extra fuel and so on mean that the costs of piracy have been passed on to the consumer by the shipping companies increasing their prices to pay for the increased cost. 'Piracy is estimated to have cost the world an estimated $60–70m in 2008.'[16]

Over the years the response from the international community to increased attacks on merchant shipping has been to send warships into the area to patrol. But some of the merchant ships have started taking things into their own hands to thwart piracy, for example, the Italian cruise ship, the *Melody*, that managed to stop an attack when its security men fired their guns in the air. Six pirates in a speedboat approached the *Melody* and opened fire, spraying the vessel with some 200 rounds. But as they tried to board the ship the security men fired their weapons into the air and other crew members poured water on the pirates. Passengers took action as well by throwing chairs overboard in an attempt to hit the pirates.[17]

Fighting modern-day pirates is proving to be as elusive as fighting pirates has ever been over the centuries. Even with the larger naval presence in the area and more United Nations resolutions giving these navies greater powers to chase the pirates the effect hasn't halted piracy. Ship owners in 2009 began to take steps to try to stop pirates from boarding their vessels. The pirates come to the most vulnerable spot of a ship where there is the least distance between the water level and the height of the deck. Then, using grappling hooks and ladders, they climb aboard quickly and take the ship. Some ship owners put barbed wire at these points, which in some situations has been effective.

Other solutions have included using long-range acoustic devices that provide clear warning of attack 'and in some instances, damage the hearing of potential unwelcome boarders'. Providing more lookouts has also proved to be effective, while many ship captains use very sensitive radar to alert them to incoming visitors.

Perhaps the biggest difference between merchant ships of today and the ones of the East India Company or the Royal Africa Company of the last centuries is that the latter were armed, with several cannon. Indeed, Bartholomew Roberts's ship the *Royal Fortune*, was a merchant vessel before it was captured by Roberts and it was heavily armed. Most merchant vessels today are not armed but a BBC report in April 2009 stated that many ship owners were seriously considering taking that step.[18]

Although the source of piracy lies on land, as described above, piracy is still largely being fought on the high seas and, as in centuries past, right in the thick of it has been the Royal Navy. In November 2007 a small piece on the Ministry of Defence (MOD) News pages was published about Type 23 frigate HMS *Richmond* foiling a people-trafficking gang. *Richmond*, an anti-submarine frigate, working in consort with the Yemeni coastguard, tracked two suspicious dhows during the day. Using long-range sensors they could see that the vessels were acting suspiciously so they maintained a cat and mouse game, keeping just off the horizon so the smugglers couldn't see them.

As night came, they followed the vessels that were steaming away from Yemen back towards Somalia when they struck. Moving in quickly the crew from the *Richmond* coordinated the close-quarter interception with the Yemeni coastguard and captured the dhows. 'Using the "stealthy" features of the Type 23 Frigate', said Commander Piers Hurrell, Commanding Officer HMS *Richmond*, '13 suspected human smugglers were arrested and two vessels seized. The message this sends to others involved in this illegal activity is quite clear.' *Richmond* was part of a UK, US and German operation that was working closely with the Yemeni government to ensure the maritime environment in the Gulf of Aden was being used according to international maritime law, with the purpose of reducing piracy and smuggling.[19]

Another Royal Navy frigate, HMS *Cumberland*, was heavily involved in fighting piracy during a four-month deployment in 2008. She returned home to her base in Plymouth late in December having had a highly successful tour where she intercepted four pirate vessels and seized three rocket-propelled grenade launchers, more than twenty assault rifles, ammunition and hand guns. She also confiscated several small skiffs from the pirates and sank them by gunfire.

Originally deployed to be part of the Standing NATO Maritime Group 2 which was to be stationed in the Arabian Gulf to carry out defence diplomacy missions, the task force was diverted by NATO to the Gulf of Aden after passing through the Suez Canal. Her new task was to carry out escort duties for the World Food Programme and conduct counter-piracy operations.

The crew of HMS *Cumberland* had spent the summer training intensively for operations, including dealing with piracy scenarios and maintaining maritime security patrols, so by the time the re-task came from NATO they were ready for their new assignments. Working together with the rest of the task force, other coalition ships and maritime patrol aircraft, including her own Lynx helicopter, HMS *Cumberland* was very effective at countering pirate activity in the area. Using a suite of sensors to pinpoint vulnerable merchant ships which would most likely be attractive to the pirates as easy targets, the ship would patrol that sector. Any reports that came in that sounded suspicious would see the Lynx quickly launched and then the helicopter and the ship would head towards those co-ordinates. Usually, the Lynx was the first to arrive on the scene, flying low and close to ensure the people on the vessels below could see the helicopter's machine gun, which signalled that they meant business.

As the helicopter circled, her crew relayed information back to the ship, from the number of pirate ships in the area to the extent of the attack, if one had taken place and so on, keeping *Cumberland* fully aware of the situation. As the frigate came on the scene, through a series of aggressive manoeuvres, closing in on the pirates, almost running them down, she would fire flares, sound horns, flash lights and send continuous radio calls clearly demanding the pirates stop what they were doing and heave to.

If that didn't work then the ship's fire hose would be deployed, blasting the pirates' vessels with high pressure water to disrupt their activities, while overhead the Lynx continued to circle, providing top cover. All the while, the ships' Royal Marine boarding teams prepared to launch their Pacific 24 fast inflatable boats in order to board the pirate vessel. In one incident when the Marines of the Fleet Protection Group Royal Marines, 45 Commando, boarded a pirate vessel and began searching it they discovered a cache of weapons along with ladders, grappling hooks and other standard pieces of equipment used for piracy. The pirates were arrested and taken into custody.[20]

In February 2009 a report appeared on the MOD news website about HMS *Northumberland* patrolling off the coast of Somalia searching for pirates. Part of an EU anti-piracy task force, *Northumberland* and the rest of the task force were charged with protecting an area of operations spanning one million square miles. The operation, known as Op Atalanta was primarily charged with escorting aid to the World Food Programme. Earlier in the month *Northumberland* safely escorted three aid ships into Somali ports without incident. The capture of the *Sirius Star* in November 2008 illustrated the vast distance the pirates covered, so patrolling such a large area, even for the most modern navies, proved to be difficult. 'Clearly you can't police all of that with warships all of the time', said Rear Admiral Philip Jones.[21]

The key to success for the task force was to prioritize the hot spots in the area, where the pirates are most likely to attack, and then to coordinate the anti-piracy efforts with the rest of the task force and with other naval forces in the area. Part of the operations team Lieutenant Commander Nick Gibbons illustrated how the success of the pirates was due to their lack of sophistication. 'A small potential fishing boat with four or five people on it could one day be fishing, but tomorrow could be climbing on board a 300,000 tonne tanker.'[22] This flexibility makes it difficult to identify the pirates.

Cracking down on piracy is a serious business. The Gulf of Aden sees more than 25,000 ships a year pass through it, carrying a significant amount of the world's trade and much of the world's oil. 'It's of huge interest to a whole range of global trading nations to keep those sea lanes clear and to make sure the pirates can't interrupt that traffic', Rear Admiral Jones explained.[23]

Throughout the rise of piracy over the last few years from Somalia, Royal Fleet Auxiliary ships have played an important role in disrupting pirate attacks on merchant shipping. For example, in April 2009, RFA *Wave Knight* stopped two attacks by pirates on vulnerable merchant vessels in the Gulf of Aden and released thirteen hostages who had been captured by the pirates. The ship was part of the Combined Maritime Forces that have been operating in the Gulf of Aden and in Somali waters for some time. The RFA fleet provides everything from fuel to food for Royal Navy ships and is vital in keeping the navy's warships properly supplied.

In this instance, a distress signal from a merchant vessel was received at 0800hrs on Saturday 18 April 2009. The message from MV *Handy Tankers Magic* said that they were under attack from pirates. Changing course for the co-ordinates provided by the tanker, *Wave Knight* put on all speed. They found when they arrived on the scene that the attack had already broken off but they caught sight of the skiff fleeing the scene and followed it to a fishing dhow which the pirates were using as their mother ship.

As *Wave Knight* approached, Captain Pilling, commanding, deployed the ship's own weapons team and a Royal Navy armed force protection team who trained their weapons on the dhow providing cover. Over the radio, Pilling demanded that the dhow stop and, eventually, faced with the firepower from *Wave Knight* the vessel hove to. During the chase *Wave Knight*'s radio operators had been in contact with a Dutch warship, HNLMS *De Zeven Provincien*, operating within NATO's Standing Naval Maritime Group 1 task force, keeping them informed of what was happening. Shortly after the dhow stopped, the warship arrived on the scene. The Dutch ship sent its boarding teams across to the dhow where they discovered not only were the pirates aboard but thirteen hostages as well. These fishermen had been held for more than six days and were relieved to be free. The seven pirates aboard were not caught in the act of piracy, even though they had hostages, and so they were released by the Dutch after their weapons had been seized and destroyed.

Wave Knight's second run-in with pirates began two hours later when their radio room received another distress call from the MV *Front Ardennes*. Again the ship changed course and headed for the new co-ordinates at high speed. This time she arrived in time to stop the pirate skiff from boarding the merchant vessel. Pilling ordered the weapons teams to be redeployed along *Wave Knight*'s deck as the ship bore down on the pirates. Over the radio *Wave Knight* sent repeated warnings to the pirates for them to break off the attack but they didn't. Finally, Pilling ordered his teams to open fire and the air was split with crack of warming shots being fired. Thoroughly frightened, the pirates fled the scene and Pilling ordered a course correction. For six hours *Wave Knight* followed the pirate skiff, all the while keeping in radio contact with ships from the NATO task group, HMCS *Winnipeg* and USS *Halyburton*. Helicopters from both warships flew close to the skiff as *Winnipeg* arrived to relieve *Wave Knight* on station. The skiff was boarded by teams from *Winnipeg* who found weapons and ammunition which they destroyed and they released the pirates, having no firm evidence to hold them.

Throughout this operation, *Wave Knight* provided landing facilities and fuel for the helicopters from the NATO warships. Pilling manoeuvred his ship in close to the pirates, stopping them from escaping and enabling the Canadian team from the *Winnipeg* to board the pirate ship. 'Our primary role is refuelling and aviation operations, but we are fully capable of conducting anti-piracy operations in and around the Horn of Africa', Captain Pilling said. 'We have been on station for over a year providing support to many nations, and we remain committed to helping ensure maritime security.'[24]

In June 2009 the Type 23 frigate HMS *Portland* was on counter-piracy operations in the Gulf of Aden when sailors from the frigate boarded two skiffs which they suspected were pirates. They were using a weapon that few pirates have ever had at their disposal – air power. In conjunction with a Spanish maritime patrol aircraft, the crew of HMS *Portland* identified and chased the two vessels and, after catching up with them, sent a boarding team of Royal Navy and Royal Marines personnel in their rigid inflatable boats to intercept the two skiffs. With powerful outboard motors the navy boats rapidly closed the gap between them and the vessels, forcing the pirates to heave to. All the while, the ship's helicopter, a Lynx armed with snipers and a machine gun, flew overhead providing cover.

The insertion teams from each of the navy boats climbed aboard the respective skiffs and began a quick search of each vessel. They discovered grappling hooks, extra barrels of fuel, rocket-propelled grenades, automatic weapons and ammunition. These were no fishing boats and the ten people aboard were not fishermen. Despite the weapons and other items there was nothing linking the pirates directly to an attack or act of piracy so they were set free but not before the navy had confiscated their weapons. As the navy boats returned to the ship HMS *Portland* fired a shot into one of the skiffs, completely destroying it.

Portland was part of a multinational task force, Combined Task Force 151, set up to carry out anti-piracy operations within their designated area. Consisting of forces from Turkey, the UK, the US, South Korea, Singapore and Denmark, the role of CTF 151 is to actively suppress, deter and disrupt piracy, ensuring the freedom of navigation for all nations using these busy shipping lanes as well as protecting global maritime security.[25]

In December 2009 the Type 22 frigate HMS *Cornwall* ended her stint as flagship of the Standing NATO Maritime Group 2(SMG2) on anti-piracy operations off Somalia as part of the NATO operation Ocean Shield. She arrived back in Plymouth on 10 December 2009 after a successful four-month deployment where no merchant vessels were captured by pirates in the Gulf of Aden while the frigate was on patrol. The operation was a success because of the hard work, pride and dedication of the crew of HMS *Cornwall*, according to her commanding officer, Commander Johnny Ley who said, 'the ship's company have been absolutely first rate and they have continued to deliver in spades. It's down to them that we have not missed a single day on task.'

In April 2009 the ship steamed away from her home at HM Naval Base Devonport in Plymouth tasked to undertake large-scale naval exercises with NATO allies in air defence and submarine-hunting. In addition to these exercises she was to undertake some high-profile diplomatic port visits in the Mediterranean. All of this was thrown out of the window when the task force was ordered further east.

The piracy problem was getting worse and something needed to be done. At Crete, Royal Navy Commodore Steve Chick came aboard and took command of the task force, making *Cornwall* his flagship. At the same time, the crew began a short period of mission-specific training. When all was ready, the task force sailed to the Gulf of Aden to begin patrolling the 500-mile stretch of water between Africa and the Arabian Peninsula. However, once they arrived it became clear to Commodore Chick that, although there were naval forces from a variety of nations in the area, to be more effective against the pirates better coordination was needed.

In conjunction with other task force commanders from the EU, Chinese and Indian navies in the area, a regime of close cooperation was implemented that resulted in far less duplication, enabling the combined task forces to deal more effectively with piracy. 'By co-operating and co-ordinating our activity much better, I think we're being much more efficient. Routinely, examples are given maybe where a Japanese [ship] has detected a skiff, a NATO helicopter might react to it, and a European Union or a coalition ship then goes and boards it.'[26]

Throughout her 226-day deployment, HMS *Cornwall* steamed 43,453 nautical miles and refuelled twenty-two times at sea while under way. Throughout this period the ship's Lynx helicopter flew 155 separate sorties, which works out to a cumulative total of 214 hours airborne, or nine days in the air. The missions for the helicopter were varied, covering everything from tracking pirate strongholds along the Somali coast to providing casualty airlift and evacuation from merchant ships. Throughout the entire deployment the ship's crew trained hard to keep the frigate's operational effectiveness at the highest possible levels through a series of operational readiness exercises where three Seawolf supersonic anti-aircraft missiles, 30,000 rounds of machine gun shells and 246 main gun shells were fired.

The Royal Navy frigate HMS *Chatham* was involved with counter-piracy operations when it successfully intercepted a pirate mother ship in April 2010, east of the Gulf of Aden. The ship had launched its Lynx helicopter for a standard sweep when the crew reported a suspicious vessel. Changing course, HMS *Chatham* steamed towards the position while the Lynx remained on station, eyeing a hijacked Indian-registered dhow, the MSV *Viskvakalayan*. It wasn't long before they spotted weapons aboard and for the next three days, *Chatham* shadowed the pirate ship.

On the third day, the frigate closed as the dhow slowed, her fuel almost exhausted. Small fast boats, with crack teams of marines aboard, were quickly embarked from *Chatham* and sped towards the dhow, which was now very close to the frigate. Royal Marine snipers trained their guns on the dhow. A small skiff sped away, filled with the pirates heading back to Somalia as fast as they could. Onboard the Indian vessel, her master and fourteen crew were free thanks to the efforts of HMS *Chatham*. The marines climbed aboard and provided medical assistance to the relieved crew. The pirates had a weapons cache of AK47 assault rifles and rocket-propelled grenades and the information that came from the crew of the MSV *Viskvakalayan* indicated that the pirates had probably tried to capture a merchant ship earlier but had been unsuccessful.[27]

In April 2010 an article appeared on the BBC News online web pages that indicated the pirates had changed tactics. Rear Admiral Peter Hudson, the Royal Navy admiral in charge of the EU naval task counter-piracy task force, told the BBC in an interview with Nick Childs that the allied navies would have to increase their cooperation and concentrate their forces to counter the new threat. Pirate activity in the region is rapidly expanding. Indeed in March 2010 alone, the amount of activity was double that of the period between September and November 2009 where there is a traditional calm period between monsoon seasons.

Most of the pirates' new tactics were centred in the southern part of the Indian Ocean known as the Somali Basin. Admiral Hudson said that the pirates had switched to using swarm tactics where they were trying to flood an area with action groups. 'By correctly positioning our aircraft, putting our ships in the right area, we've managed to break up, dismantle, disrupt over 20 of those groups', the admiral said during the interview. He also indicated that there had been a significant rise in the number of suspected pirates held in jails in Kenya and in the Seychelles but while the naval presence was working, there was still an appetite for piracy. He suggested there could be 'a handful or thousands' of people involved in the different aspects of the area's piracy operations.

For the allied navies the Gulf of Aden has been their main area of success and their main focus, which has forced the pirates further south. The EU also has escort of World Food Programme ships carrying food aid to Somalia as one of their key objectives, which has resulted in twenty warships having to cover a region ten times larger than Germany.

 So why can't the allied navies with all their sophisticated technology, wipe out the pirate threat which boils down to heavily armed men in small motor boats? Admiral Hudson believed that part of the answer to that question is the sheer size of the area. 'However, international co-operation has increased', the admiral explained. 'Our priority is to act more closely together to reduce the risk in key areas. So we will be using the dialogue we have with the region, maritime patrol aircraft and our intelligence assets as well as our partners India and China, to make sure we can concentrate our efforts in a more sophisticated manner.' In the interview he acknowledged that naval force alone could not be able to stop piracy completely but that it must be dealt with from inside Somalia by the international community.[28]

While the Royal Navy has performed admirably and in many cases successfully in putting down piracy over the centuries, it has been hamstrung by policy. We see this in the incidents concerning the Reef pirates where time and again the consuls on the spot demanded a force be landed to deal with the pirates. The historical precedent for this is the French invasion of Algiers in 1829 which effectively ended the Algerine corsair activity.

The French occupied Algeria and took it as a possession but is it really necessary to occupy the nation that the pirates operate from? Occupying Somalia in order to stop piracy could prove to be a disaster and force the international community into a long protracted guerrilla war of attrition. But if a force went in there that was strong enough to provide security to the elected government, deal with the insurgents, re-establish law and order and start rebuilding the country then maybe the piracy might stop.

Annex A

Survey of the Riff Coast

The following survey report was written by Captain Gifford, commanding HMS *Dragon* out of Gibraltar, on 22 January 1852 to the admiral of the Mediterranean. This report was part of the preparations the Admiralty was undertaking for mounting an expedition to the Reef territory to crush the pirates. Admiral Napier's advice about landing a force strong enough to burn the pirate's crops, destroy their boats and cattle was being considered and Gifford's report figured heavily in their thinking.

The Riffians are a numerous, daring, warlike and brave race of people, accustomed to bloodshed; and attaching little value to human life, an insulting word is often answered by the death blow.

They commit their piracies as far as twenty miles from the land in boats pulling, usually eight to ten oars, and carrying from thirty to thirty-five men and they attack with a settled plan as if they had long been accustomed to these outrages.

The object to be attained is to stop the piracies and to open a communication with the people to prevent them from carrying out these atrocities in the future; at the same time to affect this without weakening the tribes more than is absolutely necessary as they form a strong and sole barrier to French encroachment along the coast.

I would therefore confine the first lesson to the part where the last piracies were committed vis from Cape Tres Forcas to Cala Tera about thirteen miles of which I will now give a slight description. The very extreme of Tres Forcas is a small sheltered beach which leads up to a pretty valley surrounded by an amphitheatre of hills with very low bush on them, and apparently there is no exit but across these. I observed considerable corn fields, two horses, some donkeys, twenty head of cattle and flocks of goats and sheep and several houses, low and built of stone and earth. From this the coast westward is high and rocky and precipitous without cultivation for full three miles, when a little is observed up a narrow ravine with a small sandy beach to the sea. Three quarters of a mile from this is the pirates creek, which Commander Powell attacked but could not land, we observed one boat, but there might be many more concealed, the natives collect in number on the rocks commanding it as if it was a place they wished to defend. Round the southern point of this creek was anther sandy beach which led to a narrow valley opening with larger dimensions as it ascended amongst the hills, where it was lightly and richly cultivated with terraced gardens and over a large extent of ground, here was a village and numerous detached houses, it would be difficult of attack without a large force.

The coast again became steep and rocky, for two miles where there were several sandy patches and in different places two boats, nor was there much cultivation for some distance, about eight miles from the cape was the little bay and sandy beach on which the *Violet* as placed, and where Commander Powell landed and destroyed some boats, a most daring and gallant act, there were several sandy and sheltered spots and the land protruded out forming a promontory, we observed several boats in different places. The land all about was very highly cultivated and over great extent of moderate height but undulating, and intersected with some gullies and ravines, no bush cover, and no large hills within four or five miles, several villages about two miles from the shore, and numerous detached houses. Rounding the promontory we observed a few horses, mules, donkeys, much cattle, flocks of sheep and goats, and a deep open bay called Zera, with six boats at the bottom, near which a stream with steep and high banks in places, runs into the sea, on the right of the bay the land again became high and mountainous close to the sea, it was a sandy rise with very low bush, and back near the villages we saw olive trees and numerous armed parties watched us. It had all the appearance of a very populous and flourishing district. This is the country I would propose to attack and my plan would be for 'Janus' to attack with 250 men and utterly destroy the valley at the extremity of Tres Forcas. Commander Powell knows the exact position and arriving there in the grey of the morning would make some prisoners a most especial point thereafter and make strong demonstrations against the pirates creek but only open a fire from the vessel. Land one division in Violet Bay and another in Zera Bay about four miles apart and make a rush for the villages where the two divisions would unite utterly destroying everything and otherwise guided by circumstances.

Should the weather look threatening, take possession of the promontory and a few howitzers with sappers and mines ought to secure it against the attack of any number of Riffians and after finishing here attack Pirates creek and if possible the villages over it. Steamers and crews search everywhere and destroy boats.

To ensure success; 1st the weather must be settled, 2nd the expedition must be fitted out in secrecy and 3rd carried out with alacrity for the 1st to give a sight to expect what Providence alone can control, I would fix the expedition for harvest time about the middle of May, as a week sooner or later according to the season, at that period you would do the pirates the greatest injury and give them the surest lesson, nor would the tribes of the interior leave their harvest in such great numbers to assist them.

2nd, Secrecy, from the numerous villages and houses and from the fact of every male carrying a musket the pirates would soon muster in large numbers. The expedition should therefore consist of 2,000 fighting men including some artillery and a few sappers and miners and 400 men to carry the wounded. This is entirely independent of the crews of the vessels as steamers are very short handed. To effect this quickly, I would employ the marines of the Mediterranean and Lisbon fleets, and one regiment from Gibraltar or Malta, at which Island all preparation should be made, here it would be known on the Reef coast immediately. At the time fixed for carrying it out rendezvous off Cape de Gate or in Almeria Bay from Lisbon and Malta, and down on the Reef coast in the night, attack at daylight.

3rd Clarity: the affair must be well considered and matured before hand, therefore the two naval and military chiefs should have a complete understanding, visit the coast as soon as possible together and arrange their plans, signals, points for disembarkation and re-embarkation. Steamers must be employed and were I to command, the shipping I should wish would be the *Dragon*, *Dauntless*, *Retribution*, *Encounter*, *Firebrand*, *Fury*, *Courage*, *Spiteful*, *Janus* and *Modiste* on account of her light draught.

No combined movements with another nation but if absolutely indispensable to have one with Spain. Let them start from Almeria Bay together one carry the above, at sea and then cooperate around Melilla according to circumstances, either by transporting our troops there by sea, or joining their column by land, Zera Bay not being from more than ten or twelve miles from that place.

The previous preparations and which I consider absolutely essential and sacred on the men to undertake the expedition without, would be ten or twelve flat boats, eight to carry 80 to 100 men, but no occasion to carry guns – two life boats, large and of good construction to ensure communications at the commencement of bad weather – four light mountain 12 pounder Howitzers, stretchers for carrying the wounded, combustibles for burning the crops, some entrenching tools, and a few tents – the men must be dressed in a dark colour and black belts, and be provided with conical bullets to give them a chance for the Riffian mode of fighting, will be from a distance, and while they are as (and their muskets have long reach) they will fire deliberately, and not a single shot will be thrown away, as you close I conceive they will never make a stand unless at their villages to protect their women and children.

It is absolutely necessary to have an interpreter and Mr J Drummond Hay who has seen many there and knows the language has volunteered his services.

In the mean time a vessel should frequently visit the coast in moderate weather, and it should be given out generally that the Government have given up all idea of attack, but intend to watch the coast as the means of preventing piracy, and Mr Drummond Hay should be instructed to spread it as much as possible to Tangier and Tetuan.

Proclamations should be drawn up stating that the destruction was made to punish the pirates, that our only wish is to injure those who go entirely against all laws of God and man, in murdering and robbing innocent people, who are quietly and peaceably proceeding on trading voyages; and not to hurt any other portion of the Riffians, and that we would not do so, could we distinguish the good from the bad.

About the time of starting send down to the Sheriff who saved the lives of our men to say that in consequence of his kindness we do not touch that part of the coast where he resides, nor do we intend doing so unless we find they come to attack us or continue to commit acts of piracy. Mr Drummond Hay could probably manage this.

This expedition as recommended by Captain Gifford never took place.

Reef Pirate Activity and the Navy's Response

What follows is a chronology of the activities of the Reef pirates over several years and the responses of the Royal Navy and British government.

In August 1846, Captain Sir T Nicholson was called upon to report as to the best mode of punishing the Reef pirates. He proposed that a steamer should run along the coast and destroy all the boats from Cape Forcas to twenty miles to the westward. He states he had approached the shore without difficulty, having expectation that destroying the hamlets would require a considerable force.

In February 1849, Admiral Napier reported he had proceeded to the Reef Coast, with five steamers to inflict punishment on the Reef pirates for the plunder of *The Three Sisters*, and found nothing worth attacking. He suggested an expedition should proceed and burn their crops at the proper season. Admiral Napier also proposed that the Reef people should be called up to pay 20,000 dollars as compensation. The Consul at Tangier objected to the plan, a long correspondence ensued and it was eventually dropped by the Foreign Office.

On 23 January 1852, Captain Giffard of HMS *Dragon*, was sent to recover the crew of the English Brig *Violet* plundered by the Reef pirates and suggested that 2,000 men, conveyed in ten of Her Majesty's steamers, should proceed to the Reef Coast at the harvest season and destroy some of the villages belonging to the pirates, and burn their crops.

On 30 April 1852 Admiral Sir W Parker proposed a plan for destroying the boats of the Reef pirates, by proceeding secretly to the coast, with 500 men in four or five steamers, taking as many boats as they would need to facilitate the landings.

On 15 July 1852 the Foreign Office requested the Admiralty come up with a plan for a combined attack on the Reef pirates, the governments of Tangier and Spain having promised their cooperation.

On 11 January 1853, the Foreign Office, having come to the conclusion that a combined attack on the Reef pirates would be inadvisable, required the Admiralty to state the best mode of mounting actions against the pirates. The Admiralty stated it was too late in the season to mount large operations on the Reef Coast.

On 21 September 1853 the Foreign Office reported an attempt on the British vessel *Vampire*.

On 15 June 1854 the Foreign Office reported an act of piracy against a Spanish vessel. The next day, 16 June 1854, the *Prometheus* was ordered to make a demonstration of force off the Reef Coast.

Ten days later on 26 June 1854, Captain Jury reported the capture of the *Cuthbert Young* by Reef pirates, and stated he had despatched the *Prometheus* in search of her crew. The same day, 26 June 1854, Commander Rice of HMS *Prometheus* reported having recovered the *Cuthbert Young* and inflicting considerable damage on the pirates who tried to prevent him from retaking the vessel.

On 14 July 1854 the Foreign Office requested the Admiralty, with reference to the *Cuthbert Young*, that measures should be taken to punish the pirates. The following day 15 July 1855 the Admiralty replied that without military forces the navy were insufficient for the purpose. The same day, 15 July 1855, the Foreign Office transmitted a long report from the Consul at Tangier, on the case of the *Cuthbert Young*, in which he stated it was the Spanish government's intention to mount a small expedition to punish the Reef pirates.

On 16 August 1854 Commander Rice reported that the sloop *Neston* had proceeded to the Reef Coast, in consequence of the attack on the *Cuthbert Young*, and that her captain had taken to Tangier three of the Reef chiefs, who begged his mediation to reconcile them to the English.

Ten days later, 26 August 1854, the Admiralty requested the Foreign Office to state whether any steps should be taken to enter into communications with the chiefs through a consular agent or through a naval officer. The Foreign Office transmitted a report from the Consul at Tangier of the terms proposed by the Reef chiefs through Captain Chalier and stated that it would be improper to trade with them unless they gave some guarantee of their good faith and further good behaviour, such as payment for the plunder of the *Cuthbert Young*, hostages to be left at Tangier, or the destruction of all their boats. These terms the chiefs would or could not accede to. The Consul further stated that since May 1846 no less than seventeen acts of piracy had been committed by the Reefians. The Foreign Office entirely agreed with the view taken by the Consul and informed the Spanish government who expressed some disappointment but a readiness to cooperate against the Reef pirates.

On 6 December 1854 the Foreign Office reported an attack on Gibraltar by Reef pirates.

On 10 May 1855 the Foreign Office reported mounting cases of piracy by Reefians.

On 21 May 1855, Captain Heath of *Medusa* reported the seizing of the English Brig *Lively* by Reef pirates. He proceeded to the Reef Coast but finding nothing but the remains of a vessel returned after firing a few shots at the pirates.

Seven days later, on 28 May 1855, the Foreign Office transmitted a report from the Chargé d'Affaires at Morocco, on the capture of a French vessel by Reef pirates, who stated that it substantiated his opinion that no reliance could be placed on their promises.

On 16 June 1855 the Foreign Office transmitted a report to the Admiralty from the Chargé d'Affaires in Morocco on outrages on the Reef Coast, and recommended that a small fleet be sent there to punish the pirates.

On 21 June 1855 the Foreign Office requested a ship of war to be sent to the Reef Coast for protection of trade and *Prometheus* was ordered to Gibraltar to visit the Reef Coast frequently.

Conversation between British Consul at Tangier and Reefian Pirates

After the pounding from the *Prometheus* during the rescue of the *Cuthbert Young* some of the Reefians from the village of Beni-Boogaffer were afraid that the British might come back again and destroy the village. Three of the chiefs decided to visit Drummond Hay and Al Hadary set up this meeting through the French interpreter, Mr Catelle, who brought the three men to the consul's house in Tangier.

Drummond Hay relayed this conversation to the Earl of Clarendon and said that the three men told him that it was their village that had committed the piracy on the *Cuthbert Young* and on the *Violet* in 1851. 'I then asked them, what they had to say to me', Drummond Hay wrote.

'We know the English had always been friends to the Sultan and of the Moors and we wish also to be friends, that the past should be forgotten, peace should be made', the chiefs said, adding that British vessels from then on would not be molested. 'God disapproves of our acts, we have quarrelled amongst ourselves over the booty and killed each other.'

'These people', said the chief pointing to the Captain and Mr Schmidt, 'have offered their mediation through Sayed Mohamed Al Hadary and now we rely upon them and you, to restore, friendship between us and your tribe [meaning the English] we will also give you this in writing!'

To this, Drummond Hay replied, 'The French are also our allies and friends and the captain of this French vessel has friendly intentions, towards us and you in listening to your prayer and bringing you here, and friendly acts ought always to be regarded in a friendly light, I do not blame you therefore, for having come, but words are like the froth of the sea and what is written on paper can be destroyed. You are a lawless sect without a government submitting to no control and having no laws. These same proposals which you now make were made to by you to the British Admiral some years ago, except that you endeavoured to deceive him in addition, by offering twenty thousand dollars, you have also made other proposals through the good man and chief Sayed Mohamed Al Hadary but, when I asked for some pledges or at least, if he would guarantee your promises, he answered you were a lawless set and that he never could be surety for your keeping to your promises. If you want to make proposals let them be based on pledges of sincerity and let hostages be offered and then I might submit them to my government, for I can come to no arrangement with you as I am only an agent of my government in this country but not a chief as you may have supposed. I will mention to you however, what you might propose, though I would not insure its acceptance. Bring hard cash in hand, in compensation for the robberies you have committed on British vessels and offer also to place three or four hostages for five or six years in the hands of the English to reside here and should a piracy be again committed on your coast, as soon as the news is arrived by ear, these hostages would be handed over by us to the Sultan to be dealt with as pirates, which would probably be to have their heads cut off. If you did not want to give hostages, deliver up all your large boats to the British, keeping only your two or four oared boats for fishing, and should you ever be forced to build another large boat without our permission the pact between us would then be at an end and we should attack you.'

To this the Reefians asked who would pay the compensation and who would pay for the maintenance of the hostages for they 'only belong to Beni-boo-gaffer and could only be responsible for our village and that as their village is the easiest to attack for an invading force they were desirous to make friends and were sincere about it, but could not answer for the others'.

After a long parley they made no offer for compensation nor for hostages nor for giving up the boats but finished by saying, 'if they had attacked and plundered our vessels, that we have killed many of their people in battle, but that all would be forgotten if I liked to take their promises well and good and that Al Hadary would be surety for them, but if not they had nothing more to say and their affairs were in the hands of God'.

Mr Schmidt interposed by saying he was sure Al Hadary would not be security for them. 'I then told them to go back to their tribe and say that words verbal or written without material guarantees of their good faith were worthless, that they, the Chiefs might be or not be honest men and keep or not keep to their intentions but that their words or acts would be no security for the acts of their people unless we had good and substantial proofs of the honesty of their intentions. I further added that hitherto we had not inflicted any chastisement on them as we had been especially desirous never to act in a hostile manner against any territory to which the Sultan of Morocco could lay claim, and that it had been Gods' will but that they had seen what one small British steamer with a few men could do, that we had hundreds of steamers at our disposal and that now the "cup of patience was filled to the brim."'

There the parley ended and the Reefians withdrew.

Annex D

Letter from Seaman John Foster

The brief note below to Mr Richards, owner of British Barque *Hymen*, from Seaman John Foster, was written when Foster was held hostage by the Reef pirates to assure the British authorities that the hostages were being treated well and asking that they be ransomed.

I send you these few lines to inform you that the Barque *Hymen* of Liverpool, from Liverpool, bound to Ancona with a cargo of coals was captured by two boats belonging to Beni-Boogaffer. The Chief of the pirates gang plundered everything from the ship and left her, taking the crew and Captain amounting to fifteen in number. The Carpenter and three Seamen are together and the others we have not seen since we come ashore. The vessel is now ashore a total wreck and we have no means of getting away from here unless you send of us, if you will be so kind to do so. The man we have been with has behaved very well to us.

Annex E

Pirates Executed at Cape Coast Castle by Admiralty Court

The following pirates from Roberts's crews were executed at Cape Coast Castle in April 1722 after being tried and sentenced by an Admiralty court made up of officers from HMS *Swallow*, local merchants and the governor of the castle, General Phipps. Their bodies were strung up 'within the flood-marks' as examples to anyone who might be thinking of turning pirate. These men served aboard Roberts's own ship the *Royal Fortune*, or aboard the *Ranger*.

Name	Age	Home town
William Magnes	35	Minehead
Richard Hardy	25	Wales
David Sympson	36	North Berwick
Christopher Moody	28	
Thomas Sutton	23	Berwick
Valentine Ashplant	32	Minories
Peter de Vine	42	Stepney
William Phillips	29	Lower Shadwell
Philip Bill	27	St Thomas's
William Mains	28	
William Mackintosh	21	Canterbury
William Williams	40	near Plymouth
Robert Haws	31	Yarmouth
William Petty	30	Deptford
John Jaynson	22	near Lancaster
Marcus Johnson	21	Smyrna
Robert Crow	44	Isle of Man
Michael Maer	41	Ghent

Daniel Harding	26	Croomsbury in Somersetshire
William Fernon	22	Somersetshire
Jo. More	19	Meer in Wiltshire
Abraham Harper	23	Bristol
Jo. Parker	22	Winifred in Doresetshire
Jo. Philips	28	Alloway in Scotland
James Clement	20	Jersey
Peter Scudamore	35	Bristol
James Skyrm	44	Wales
John Walden	24	Somersetshire
Jo. Stephenson	40	Whitby
Jo. Mansfield	30	Orkneys
Israel Hynde	30	Bristol
Peter Lesley	21	Aberdeen
Charles Bunce	26	Exeter
Robert Birtson	30	Ottery St Mary, Devonshire
Richard Harris	45	Cornwall
Joseph Nositer	26	Sadbury in Devonshire
William Williams	30	(speechless at execution)
Agge Jacobson	30	Holland
Benjamin Jeffreys	21	Bristol
Cuthbert Goss	21	Topsham
John Jessup	20	Plymouth
Edward Watts	22	Dunmore
Thomas Giles	26	Minehead
William Wood	27	York
Armstrong	34	London, executed onboard the *Weymouth* at Whydah
Robert Johnson	32	
George Smith	25	Wales
William Watts	23	Ireland
James Philips	35	Antigua
John Coleman	24	Wales
Robert Hays	20	Liverpool
William Davis	23	Wales

Source: Captain Charles Johnson, *A General History of the Most Notorious Pirates* (1724).

Annex F

Chronology Leading up to the Battle of Algiers

1529: The harbour at Algiers is fortified and a corsair fleet is created.

1541: Emperor Charles V commands a powerful international force that arrives at Algiers and destroys the city. It is rebuilt by the Algerines.

1581: Formal trade relations are established with England when Queen Elizabeth appoints an ambassador to Algiers and England recognizes fully Algiers as a sovereign state.

1602: Despite the trade relations between Algiers, English ships are being taken by corsairs and Queen Elizabeth writes to the Dey complaining of acts of piracy on English vessels.

1620: Sir Robert Mansel is sent by King James I in command of a squadron of eighteen ships from Plymouth to stop the Corsair activities. He threatens to bombard Algiers but doesn't and returns to England having achieved very little.

1621: In less than a year forty English ships are captured by the corsairs and King James I decides to send Sir Thomas Roe to Algiers to negotiate a new treaty.

1623: An embargo on exporting ammunition to Algiers is put in place by the English government and there is a lot of debate about finding possible solutions to the Algiers problem which amounts to nothing.

1631: The entire population of Baltimore, a small Irish fishing village, is seized by Algerine corsairs and held captive in June of this year. In the city of Algiers the British Consul reports that there are more than 25,000 Christians held as slaves in appalling conditions.

1640: Several English merchant vessels are seized by corsairs who cruise off Exeter, Plymouth, Dartmouth and Barnstaple. At Penzance the corsairs land and capture sixty villagers while Parliament raises a tax for ransoming hostages held in Algiers in response.

1654:   Admiral Robert Blake is put in command of a squadron of ships and sent to Algiers by Oliver Cromwell and imposes a new treaty which is supposed to endure forever and cannot be broken.

1660:   To implement the previous treaty the new King Charles II sends Lord Sandwich, commanding a squadron of ships that arrives in the harbour at Algiers and fires on the city but causes little damage.

1664:   The Royal Navy becomes directly involved in Algerine affairs when Captain Nicholas Parker of HMS *Nonesuch* is appointed consul.

1668:   Several English slaves are released after Sir Thomas Allin arrives in Algiers with nine warships and two fireships and threatens to destroy the city.

1669:   Allin returns with a larger fleet, after Samuel Pepys convinces Charles II that the current treaty with Algiers is a humiliation to England. Allin opens fire on the city's defences but achieves nothing and sails away.

1670:   Allin returns again with a combined Anglo-Dutch fleet under Admiral van Ghent and engages with several Algerine vessels at sea, sinking six. Sir Edward Spragge, commanding a squadron of Allin's ships, attacks Algiers, sailing into the harbour blasting several Algerine ships and harbour installations causing severe damage and sinking several ships. However, within months the damage is repaired, the fleet rebuilt and the Algerines begin their pirate activities again.

1674:   189 English slaves are redeemed when Sir John Narbrough arrives in Algiers commanding a small squadron. He spends 62,300 pieces of eight to get the slaves freed.

1676:   The Royal Navy ketch, *Quaker*, is captured by Algerine corsairs.

1681:   An attempt to put down the corsairs by Admiral the Hon. Arthur Herbert fails and he is obliged to revert to the old treaty still giving the Algerines the right to seize and search English ships.

1682:   The French Admiral the Marquis Duquesne brings his squadron into the harbour and bombards the city of Algiers twice, firing 6,000 shells and killing more than 800 people. In retaliation the Dey fires captured Christians out of Algerine cannon.

1688:   A French force of twenty warships under the command of Marshal Duc d'Estrees arrives and pounds the city of Algiers for ten days, launching more than 13,000 mortar bombs and destroying most of the residential area but they fail to knock out the Algerine gun batteries. At the same time, England takes advantage of the situation between France and Algeria to improve its own diplomatic and political standing.

1689: England tries a new tack when William and Mary send messages of friendship to the Dey but it doesn't stop corsairs from continuing to seize English ships.

1694: A fleet of fourteen warships under the command of Sir Francis Wheeler is sent to the Barbary States as a show of force and a testament to the power of the Royal Navy. However, all but three are lost in a storm.

1699: A new treaty is signed when Vice Admiral Aylmer arrives in Algiers.

1703: Another treaty is signed when Admiral George Byng arrives with another squadron but English ships continue to be captured by the Algerine corsairs.

1722: A Quaker ship bound from Plymouth for America is seized by corsairs. George Fox, in a letter to the Dey, says that slavery is not permitted according to the Koran and the Algerines return the ship and the crew.

1739: Another attempt is made to release English slaves when Admiral Haddock arrives commanding another squadron and with gifts of goodwill from King George II for the Dey. His demands for the release of English slaves fall on deaf ears and he leaves empty-handed.

1747: A ship with seventy-seven officers and men of the Hiberian Regiment, along with their wives and children, is captured by Algerine corsairs and they are all sold as slaves. Nothing is done to repatriate them.

1749: When an English vessel carrying £25,000 for the Postmaster General of Great Britain is seized by corsairs, Commodore the Hon. Augustus Keppel attempts to recover it but fails.

1767: During the negotiations for the purchase of cattle and grain needed for the garrisons at Gibraltar and Minorca, Commodore Spry is humiliated by the Dey.

1784: A multinational force of eighty-three ships from Spain, Portugal, Naples and Malta arrives in the port of Algiers and proceeds to bombard the city at long range for several days, causing very little damage.

1796: The English bring captured French ships into the harbour at Algiers to get help from the Dey in their fight against Napoleon and the crews of the French ships are sold into slavery.

1801: The release of twenty-three English ships and 266 crewmen is negotiated by the British Consul, John Falcon without Britain having to pay any ransom.

1803:   Commodore Edward Preble of the United States imposes a treaty on Tripoli after the US declares war on the Barbary States but the US continues to pay tribute to Algeria and Tunis.

1811:   In order to ensure vital supplies get to Wellington's troops fighting in Spain, the British government sends assurance of friendship and valuable gifts to the Dey.

1812:   The Algerine problem is momentarily put aside when Britain and America go to war against each other. At the same time, a professional soldier, John McDonell, is appointed British Consul at Algiers.

1814:   At the Congress of Vienna pressure is applied on Britain to take action against Christian slavery which the Congress condemns.

1815:   A lasting treaty is signed by the US and Algiers.

1816:   In April Lord Exmouth arrives in Algiers and manages to ransom some Sicilian and Sardinian slaves before sailing on for Tripoli and Tunis. In May Exmouth returns again to try to negotiate a better result but ends up quarrelling with Omar Bashaw, the Dey, who immediately has John McDonell, the British Consul, arrested. Exmouth returns to England and is given command of an expeditionary force in July. He returns to Algiers and bombards the city in company with a Dutch fleet on 27 August.

1817:   The Algerines have repaired most of the damage and start their piratical activities again.

1818:   A resolution to suppress the corsairs is passed by the Congress of Aix la-Chappelle.

1819:   Algiers is visited by a combined Anglo-French fleet demanding that all forms of slavery should be immediately renounced by the Algerines. They respond by challenging the two admirals Freemantle and Julien to attack after manning their defences. The fleet does not take up the challenge and sails away having achieved nothing.

1823:   Corsair activity is increasing dramatically.

1824:   Tensions erupt when a fierce sea battle between two Royal Navy ships and a corsair ship takes place. The Dey renounces all treaties and declares he is going to resume all forms of Christian slavery after the French send a squadron of five warships to exert pressure. Great Britain declares war on Algiers and two British warships, HMS *Regent* and HMS *Naiad* under the command of Vice Admiral Sir Harry Neale, blockade the port. More ships arrive, including HMS *Revenge*, a powerful Royal Navy warship, and on

12 July there is an exchange of fire between the British blockading fleet and the Algerine shore batteries. The British move in closer and continue the bombardment of the city, defensive installations and batteries. One of the warships, a steamer, has her funnel shot away. The Algerines come out with several hundred pulling boats, forcing the British fleet to move away. Vice Admiral Neale calls a halt to the bombardment and opens negotiations with the Dey, ending up with a treaty being signed where the terms were exactly what the Dey had wanted before Neale's arrival. The fleet steams away having achieved nothing.

1829:   During a formal audience the Dey is grossly insulted by the French Consul and both men lose their tempers and come to blows. French sailors in the city are massacred and beheaded by the Algerines as relations between the two countries rapidly disintegrate. The heads of the sailors are used as footballs by the mob in the streets. A few weeks later two French vessels are wrecked after running ashore in thick fog. The dazed survivors are attacked by the Dey's troops and all 109 are murdered and their heads are displayed in Algiers. Enraged, the French equip a powerful military force and land at Sidi Ferrudj on the coast. The beachhead is supported by a French squadron while another French squadron blockades the port. The French concentrate on landing stores, ammunition, troops, artillery and a battering train. At one point, the Algerines send a scratch force of soldiers to attack the French encampments but they are beaten back by the French and the soldiers scatter in panic into the hills. With everything ready, the French advance on Algiers destroying any resistance in their path. When they reach the city they begin bombarding the landward city walls until the Dey surrenders and the campaign is over, the French taking only three weeks to do what no other force had done in three hundred years. The French force the Dey and his entourage into exile in Naples, while the rest of his cabinet, ministers, administration and mercenaries are also shipped off by the French Navy to Italy and to the Levant. The French set up a Muslim cabinet under a French governor and Algeria becomes a possession of the French.

Notes

Introduction

1. This deposition, now held at National Archives at Kew, is from Commander Antonio Alloy and was witnessed by G Adderley, Naval Commissioner and Justice of the Peace for Gibraltar, 23 Oct. 1834.
2. See Peter Earle, *The Pirate Wars* (2004), p. 10.
3. Ibid., p. 26.
4. Ibid., pp. 11–12.
5. Ibid., p. 27.
6. Calendar of State Papers Domestic, 1603–10, 8 Aug. 1609, held at National Archives at Kew.
7. Earle mentions this in his *Pirate Wars*, p. 28.

Chapter 1

1. Calendar of State Papers Domestic, Charles II, 27 Aug. 1677, vol. 396, no. 51.
2. Letter from Lorenzo Paulucci, Venetian Secretary in England, to Giovanni Sagredo, Ambassador to France, 23 May 1655, in Calendar of State Papers Relating to English Affairs in the Archives of Venice, London, vol. 30, p. 73.
3. See N A M Rodger, *The Command of the Ocean: A Naval History of Britain* (2004).
4. Letter from Captain George Crapnell, *The Merlin*, Cagliari Bay, Sardinia, to Thomas Smith, Navy Commissioner, Calendar of State Papers … Venice, 17 April 1655, p. 41.
5. From a report by Lorenzo Paulucci to Giovanni Sagredo, Calendar of State Papers … Venice, 14 June 1655, p. 85.
6. Lorenzo Paulucci to Giovanni Sagredo, Calendar of State Papers … Venice, 5 June 1655, p. 80.
7. Ibid.
8. The information comes from Piero Mocenigo, Venetian Ambassador in England, to the Doge and Senate, Calendar of State Papers … Venice, Aug. 1669, p. 98.
9. Ibid.
10. Piero Mocenigo to the Doge and Senate, Calendar of State Papers … Venice, 11 Ocy. 1669.
11. The prolific Mocenigo wrote to the Doge again, Calendar of State Papers … Venice, 1 Nov. 1669.

12. Piero Mocenigo to the Doge and Senate, Calendar of State Papers ... Venice, 3 Jan. 1670.
13. Calendar of State Papers Domestic, Charles II, *Longon Gazette*, 31 Jan.–3 Feb. 1670.
14. Piero Mocenigo to the Doge and Senate, Calendar of State ... Venice, 11 April 1670.
15. Thomas Allin to Mr Wren, Calendar of State Papers Domestic, Charles II, vol. 278, Sept. 1670.
16. Sir Thomas Allin to Sir J Williamson, 10 Aug. 1670, Calendar of State Papers Domestic, Charles II, Battle of Cape Spartel, British History Online and National Archives at Kew, no. 50.
17. Sir Thomas Allin to Sir J Williamson, 26 Aug. 1670, Calendar of State Papers Domestic, no. 133.
18. This information is from Tomas Rudio, Venetian Secretary in Spain, Madrid, to the Doge and Senate, Calendar of State Papers ... Venice, 26 Sept. 1670.
19. Taken from Calendar of State Papers Domestic, Charles II, pp. 394–5, 422. *London Gazette*, 22–6 Sept. 1670.
20. See Calendar of State Papers Domestic, Charles II.
21. Bernardo Navagero, Venetian Proveditore of Zante. to the Doge and Senate, Calendar of State Papers ... Venice, 13 Nov. 1675, p. 580.
22. Ibid.
23. From the account of an action by Sir John Narbrough's fleet against the fleet of Tripoli in the port of Tripoli, dated 10 Feb. 1675, by Narbrough aboard HMS *Harwith* at Malta, now held at National Archives at Kew.
24. This information comes from James Houblon to Sir J Williamson, 10 April 1676, in Calendar of State Papers Domestic, Charles II, vol. 380, no. 157.
25. See Rodger, *Command of the Ocean*, quoting Narbrough.
26. From a letter in the Calendar of State Papers Domestic, Charles II, London, 30 Aug. 1669.
27. From Sir J Williamson to Samuel Pepys, the Calendar of State Papers Domestic, Charles II, London, 4 Oct. 1677.
28. See Calendar of State Papers Domestic, Charles II Entry Book, 40a, fo. 206, 21 June 1677.
29. Narbrough to Pepys, Calendar of State Papers Domestic, Charles II, 2 Sept. 1677.
30. Calendar of State Papers Domestic, Charles II, Portsmouth, 28 Sept. 1677, vol. 398, no. 199.
31. Correspondence between Silas Taylor and Sir John Williamson, Calendar of State Papers Domestic, Charles II, 27 Nov. 1677.

Chapter 2

1. See Earle, *Pirate Wars*.
2. Outlined in a letter, 29 Aug. 1698, from Captain William Burrough to Samuel Herron of Royal African House, part of the Board of Trade, Plantations General, vol. 5, nos. 10, 101., and vol. 35, pp. 34, 35, now held at National Archives at Kew.

Chapter 3
1. See Earle, *Pirate Wars*, p. 146.
2. Ibid. 147.
3. Ibid., p. 154; Earle cites ADM 1/1589/25 18 July 1700 Captains Letters as his source.
4. Earle, *Pirate Wars*.
5. Graham A Thomas, *Pirate Hunter* (Pen & Sword, 2008).
6. This section draws on David Cordingly, *Under the Black Flag* (1996).
7. Ibid.
8. Ibid.

Chapter 4
1. See Richard Sanders, *If a Pirate I Must Be … The True Story of Bartholomew Roberts* (2007).
2. Ibid., p. 17.
3. Ibid., p. 169.
4. Ibid.
5. Ibid.
6. Charles Johnson, *A General History of the Most Notorious Pirates* (1998).
7. Sanders, *If a Pirate I Must Be*.
8. Ibid.
9. Ibid.
10. From Johnson, *General History*: most probably the definitive narrative of Roberts, as it was published only two years after his death and provides most of the detail we know today about the pirate.
11. Sanders, *If a Pirate I Must Be*.
12. Johnson, *General History*.
13. The nformation in this passage comes from Johnson, *General History*, and Sanders, *If a Pirate I Must Be*.
14. Johnson, *General History*.
15. Sanders, *If a Pirate I Must Be*.
16. From Peter Earle's excellent *Pirate Wars*.
17. Sanders, *If a Pirate I Must Be*.
18. From Johnson's detailed account, *General History*.
19. Sanders, *If a Pirate I Must Be*.
20. Taken from Captain Ogle's letters to the Admiralty, ADM 1/2242, 5 April 1722, 26 July 1722 and 8 Sept. 1722, now held in National Archives at Kew.
21. Sanders, *If a Pirate I Must Be*.
22. The facts and following paragraph are drawn from Sanders, *If a Pirate I Must Be*.
23. Ogle's letters to the Admiralty, see n. 21.
24. Johnson, *General History*.
25. Ibid.
26. Sanders, *If a Pirate I Must Be*.
27. Information comes from David Cordingly, *Life among the Pirates* (1995).
28. Johnson, *General History*. Remember that this book was published two years after Roberts's death and so Johnson may have spoken with some of his men who were transported back to England, as well as reading Atkins's notes on the trial.

29. This conversation on the deck of the damaged *Ranger* was taken from Johnson, *General History*.
30. See Earle, *Pirate Wars*.
31. Johnson, *General History*.
32. See Cordingly, *Life among the Pirates*.
33. Again we turn to Johnson, *General History*.
34. See Sanders, *If a Pirate I Must Be*.
35. See Cordingly, *Life among the Pirates*. After the battle the surviving pirates who had been captured complained that their treasure chests had been broken and all their gold stolen. I believe that Cordingly's reference to the *Little Ranger* means the old abandoned *Ranger* that still contained some of the pirates' loot.
36. Ibid.
37. Ibid., which cites a report from the *Swallow*'s officers given during the trial of the pirates: HCA 1/99.3 Public Records Office (now National Archives, Kew).
38. See Johnson, *General History*.
39. Sanders, *If a Pirate I Must Be*, provides a unique insight into the Royal Navy's handling of the Roberts case.
40. Johnson, *General History*.
41. See Sanders, *If a Pirate I Must Be*.
42. Cordingly, *Life among the Pirates*.
43. Sanders, *If a Pirate I Must Be*, p. 230.

Chapter 5
1. Johnson, *General History*, pp. 234–6.
2. See Sanders, *If a Pirate I Must Be*, p. 235.
3. Sanders refers to Atkins's notes, ibid., p. 236.
4. See Johnson, *General History*, pp. 234–6.
5. Ibid., pp. 237–9.
6. Ibid.
7. Sanders, *If a Pirate I Must Be*, p. 232.
8. Johnson, *General History*, p. 239.
9. Ibid., p. 240.
10. Ibid. p. 245.
11. This conversation is taken from Johnson, *General History*.
12. Sanders, *If a Pirate I Must Be*, p. 235.
13. Ibid.
14. Ibid., p. 236.

Chapter 6
1. The account of the Battle of Algiers and the events leading up to it are detailed in Roger Perkins and K J Douglas-Morris, *Gunfire in Barbary* (1982).
2. Ibid., p. 20.
3. Ibid.
4. Ibid., p. 27.
5. Ibid.
6. Ibid., p. 37.
7. Ibid., p. 38.

8. Ibid.
9. Ibid., p. 47.
10. Ibid., p. 66.

Chapter 7
1. See Abraham Salame, *A Narrative of the Expedition to Algiers in the Year 1816* (2005), p. 54.
2. Ibid.
3. Perkins and Douglas-Morris, *Gunfire in Barbary*, p. 92.
4. Salame wrote an extensive account of the battle which is detailed in his *Narrative*.

Chapter 8
1. Salame, *Narrative*.
2. It is interesting to note that Perkins and Douglas-Morris, *Gunfire in Barbary*, state that the *Queen Charlotte* was within 50 yards of the molehead when the first anchor was dropped while Salame, an eyewitness, says it was 100 yards.
3. Salame, *Narrative*.
4. Ibid., p. 42.
5. Ibid., p. 53.
6. The description of this incident and the whole action is from Perkins and Douglas-Morris, *Gunfire in Barbary*, pp. 117–25.
7. Ibid.
8. Ibid.
9. See Salame, *Narrative*, p. 52.

Chapter 9
1. Most of the information about Napier, particularly his letters, come from Elers Napier (ed.), *The Life and Correspondence of Admiral Sir Charles Napier K.C.B.* (2005), vol. 2.
2. Ibid.
3. Ibid., p. 200.
4. Ibid., p. 201.
5. The information in this passage is from Admiral Sir Charles Napier to the Secretary for the Admiralty, 21 Feb. 1849, now held in National Archives at Kew.
6. Ibid.
7. Ibid.
8. The information comes from a letter, 18 Jan. 1852, written by Sir Robert Gardiner of the Foreign Office, stationed at Gibraltar, to Earl Grey, FO 99/69, now held at National Archives at Kew.
9. John Drummond Hay, the British Consul for Tangier, wrote many quite lengthy letters to the Earl of Clarendon, Secretary of State for Foreign Affairs. This information is taken from one of those letters, dated 29 Aug. 1853, now held at National Archives at Kew.
10. From Drummond Hay to Earl of Clarendon, 29 Aug. 1853. He cites a statement made by John Sands, master of the British brig *Vampire*, on 15 Aug. 1853 at the offices of the British Vice Consulate at Oran.
11. The earlier letter referred to is the one by Gardiner cited in n. 8 above.

12. The quotation comes from the Hansard online reference, hansard.millbank systems.com/lords, for HL Deb 1 Aug. 1854, vol. 135, cc. 1062–4: Earl of Hardwicke.
13. Ibid.: Earl of Clarendon.
14. Another letter from Drummond Hay to Earl of Clarendon, 29 June 1854.
15. This is the first mention that we have that all the crew of the *Cuthbert Young* were safe. In all other correspondence and documents there is mention of six of the crew members who were missing and presumed captured by the pirates.
16. Drummond Hay to Earl of Clarendon, 6 July 1854.

Chapter 10
1. From Drummond Hay to Earl of Clarendon, 8 Aug. 1854, FO 99/74.
2. Drummond Hay to Earl of Clarendon, 15 Aug. 1854.
3. Ibid.
4. Letter, 18 Aug. 1854, to the Secretary of the Admiralty from Commander Edward Rice, commanding *Prometheus* out of Gibraltar, FO 99/74.
5. Ibid.
6. The information about the two vessels comes from stories in the *Gibraltar Chronicle*, 18 and 19 May 1855, concerning acts of piracy against the *Lively* and the *Conference*, FO 99/74.
7. Taken from Drummond Hay to Earl of Clarendon, 6 Dec. 1855, FO 99/74.
8. Ibid.
9. On 27 April 1856 Drummond Hay wrote another letter to the Earl of Clarendon.
10. Ibid.
11. This information is from a translation of a letter from John Drummond Hay, British Consul at Tangier, to Seed Mohamed Khateeb, 29 May 1856, FO 99/74.
12. From Drummond Hay to Earl of Clarendon, 30 May 1856. This is the only mention in the available correspondence of the missing sailors from the *Cuthbert Young* being liberated.
13. This passage comes from Drummond Hay to Earl of Clarendon, 8 June 1856.
14. Drummond Hay to Earl of Clarendon, 28 June 1856.
15. See 'Morocco', http://en.wikipedia.org/wiki/Morocco (consulted April 2010).

Chapter 11
1. See Angus Konstam, 'From Cutlass to AK-45', BBC News, 14 Nov. 2007, http://news.bbc.co.uk/go/pr/fr/-/1/hi/magazine/7729256.stm.
2. Ibid.
3. Ibid.
4. Statistics from the International Maritime Bureau for 2008.
5. From Oct. 2009 statistics on the capture of ships by pirates, International Maritime Bureau.
6. BBC News, 'Q&A, Somali Piracy', 2 Nov. 2008, http://news.bbc.co.uk/go/pr/fr/-/1/hi/world/africa.
7. Ibid.
8. Roger Middleton, 'Piracy a Symptom of a Bigger Problem', BBC News, 15 April 2009, http://news.bbc.co.uk/go/pr/fr/-/1/hi//world/africa/8001183.stm
9. Ibid.

10. Ibid.
11. From Simon Cox, 'Who do the Pirates Call to Get their Cash?', BBC News, 29 Jan. 2009, http://news.bbc.co.uk/go/pr/fr/-/1/hi/magazine/7847351.stm.
12. Ibid.
13. Ibid.
14. Ibid.
15. Ibid.
16. BBC News, 'Q&A, Somali Piracy (see n. 6 above).
17. BBC News, 'Italian Cruise Ship Foils Pirates', 26 April 2009, http://news.bbc. co.uk/go/pr/fr/-/1/hi/world/africa/8019084.stm.
18. See BBC News, 'Fighting off the Somali Pirates', 16 April 2009, http://news. bbc.co.uk/go/pr/fr/-/1/hi/world/africa/7999974.stm.
19. Director of Media and Communications (DMC) News Desk, 'HMS *Richmond* Deals a Blow to Human Traffickers', 22 Nov. 2007, http://webarchive. nationalarchives.gov.uk/tna/+/http://www.mod.uk:80/Defenceinternet/Defe nceNews/MilitaryOperations/HmsRichmondDealsABlowToHumanTraffickers .htm.
20. DMC News Desk, 'HMS *Cumberland* Returns from Fighting Piracy', 22 Dec. 2008, http://www.mod.uk/Defenceinternet/DefenceNews/PeopleInDefence/ HmsCumberlandReturnsFromFightingPiracy.htm.
21. DMC News Desk, 'Patrolling for Pirates off Somalia' 26 Feb. 2009. http:// www.mod.uk/Defenceinternet/DefenceNews/MilitaryOperations/PatrollingFo rPiratesOffSomalia.htm.
22. Ibid.
23. Ibid.
24. DMC News Desk, 'RFA *Wave Knight* Disrupts Pirate Attacks', 21 April 2009, http://www.mod.uk/Defenceinternet/DefenceNews/MilitaryOperations/Rfa WaveKnightDisruptsPirateAttacks.htm.
25. DMC News Desk, 'HMS *Portland* Intercepts Pirates', 3 June 2009, http:// www.mod.uk/Defenceinternet/DefenceNews/MilitaryOperations/HmsPortlan dInterceptsPirates.ktm.
26. This account comes from DMC News Desk, 'HMS *Cornwall* Returns from Counter Piracy Operations', 11 Dec. 2009, http://www.mod.uk/Defence internet/DefenceNews/MilitaryOperations/ HmsCornwallReturnsFromCounter PiracyOperations.htm.
27. DMC News Desk, 'HMS *Chatham* Intercepts Pirate Mother Ship', 16 April 2010, http://www.mod.uk/Defenceinternet/DefenceNews/MilitaryOperations/ HMSChathamInterceptsPirateMotherShip.htm.
28. BBC News, 'Navies Struggle with Swarming Pirates', 1 April 2010, http:// news.bbc.co.uk/1/hi/world/africa/8598726.stm.

Further Reading

David Cordingly, *Life among the Pirates*, Little Brown & Co., 1995

David Cordingly, *Under the Black Flag*, Random House, 1996

Peter Earle, *The Pirate Wars*, Methuen, 2004

Charles Johnson, *A General History of the Most Notorious Pirates*, Conway Maritime Press, 1998

Elers Napier, *The Life and Correspondence of Admiral Sir Charles Napier K.C.B.*, Adamant Media Corporation, 2005, vol. 2

Roger Perkins and K J Douglas-Morris, *Gunfire in Barbary Admiral Lord Exmouth's battle with the Corsairs of Algiers in 1816*, Kenneth Mason, 1982

N A M Rodger, *The Command of the Ocean, A Naval History of Britain, 1649–1815*, Penguin Books, 2004

Abraham Salame, *A Narrative of the Expedition to Algiers in the year 1816*, Elibron Classics, 2005; originally published by John Murray, London 1819

Richard Sanders, *If A Pirate I Must Be… The True Story of Bartholomew Roberts*, Aurum Press, 2007

Graham A Thomas, *Pirate Hunter*, Pen & Sword, 2008

Various Calendars of State Papers, letters and correspondence pertaining to pirates in African waters held at the National Archives in Kew

Index